Richard Bangs is the author of fifteen books, including the recent winner of the National Book Award for Outdoor Literature, *The Lost River*. A past president of Outward Bound; founder of Mountain Travel Sobek, the world's leading travel adventure company; and a founding member of Expedia.com, he spent seven years as an executive at Microsoft. Codirector of the IMAX® film *The Mystery of the Nile*, he has appeared on *Today*, *CBS Good Morning*, *Good Morning America*, *Live with Regis and Kelly*, MSNBC, and CNN, among others, and has been a visiting lecturer at the Smithsonian Institution, the National Geographic Society, the Explorers Club, and many other museums and universities. He lives in Redmond, Washington.

Pasquale Scaturro is a renowned geophysicist and adventurer. For the past thirty years, he has led rafting and mountaineering expeditions around the world. In 2001, he led the National Federation of the Blind Mount Everest Expedition, which broke four Himalayan climbing records and became a *Time* magazine cover story. In 2004, he became the first person, with Gordon Brown, to complete the full descent of the Blue Nile and Nile. He lives in Lakewood, Colorado.

MYSTERY
of the
NILE

*The Epic Story of the First Descent
of the World's Deadliest River*

RICHARD BANGS
and
PASQUALE SCATURRO

NEW AMERICAN LIBRARY

New American Library
Published by New American Library, a division of
Penguin Group (USA) Inc., 375 Hudson Street,
New York, New York 10014, USA
Penguin Group (Canada), 90 Eglinton Avenue East, Suite 700, Toronto,
Ontario M4P 2Y3, Canada (a division of Pearson Penguin Canada Inc.)
Penguin Books Ltd., 80 Strand, London WC2R 0RL, England
Penguin Ireland, 25 St. Stephen's Green, Dublin 2,
Ireland (a division of Penguin Books Ltd.)
Penguin Group (Australia), 250 Camberwell Road, Camberwell, Victoria 3124,
Australia (a division of Pearson Australia Group Pty. Ltd.)
Penguin Books India Pvt. Ltd., 11 Community Centre, Panchsheel Park,
New Delhi - 110 017, India
Penguin Group (NZ), cnr Airborne and Rosedale Roads, Albany,
Auckland 1310, New Zealand (a division of Pearson New Zealand Ltd.)
Penguin Books (South Africa) (Pty.) Ltd., 24 Sturdee Avenue,
Rosebank, Johannesburg 2196, South Africa

Penguin Books Ltd., Registered Offices:
80 Strand, London WC2R 0RL, England

Published by New American Library, a division of Penguin Group (USA) Inc.
Previously published in a G. P. Putnam's Sons edition.

First New American Library Printing, February 2006
10 9 8 7 6 5 4 3 2 1

REGISTERED TRADEMARK—MARCA REGISTRADA

Design by Stephanie Huntwork
Maps by James McFarlane

Printed in the United States of America

To Walker Taylor Bangs, from whose tongue the first accents of verity I caught, and from whose glee the first bearings of innocent lands I found—you are a dragon seeker and teacher.

—Richard Bangs

To Adam, whose longest journey is far from over . . .

—Pasquale Scaturro

Blue Nile River

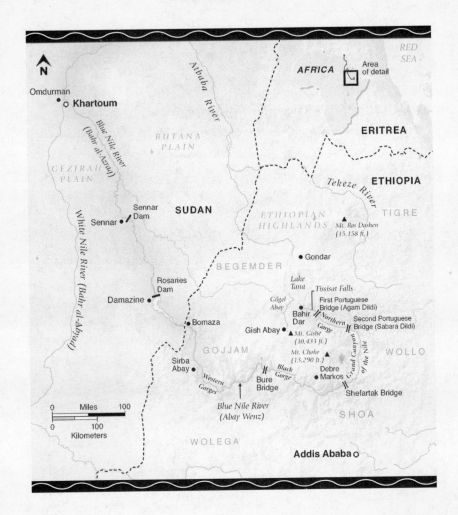

Nile River Basin

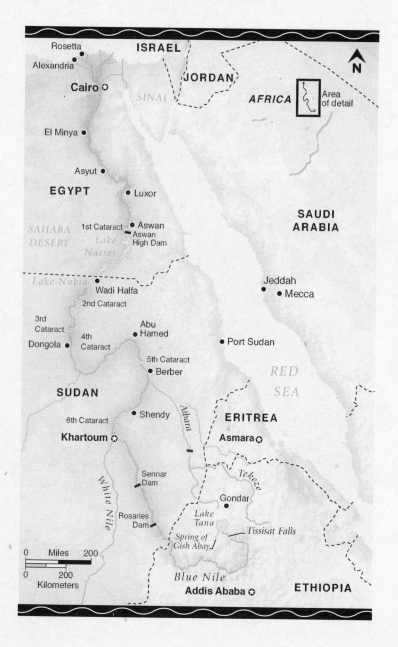

FOREWORD

Exploration of the world seems to have occurred in stages, or waves. The Spanish influx to the New World at the interface of the fifteenth and sixteenth centuries was one such wave; the rapid conquest of the Himalayas' eight-thousand-meter peaks during the 1950s another; the American-Soviet penetrations into space in the 1960s one more. But the fair-haired age of exploration was the middle nineteenth century, when the Royal Geographical Society sent its scientists, soldiers, and missionaries around the world to color the map, and no goal was more coveted than discovering the source of the Nile.

In recent years a new wave has rolled, an attempt to navigate the great wild rivers of the world, sometimes from source to sea. I am guilty of authoring several of these descents, and I made an early career plunging down the headwaters of the Amazon, Zambezi, Yangtze, Indus, and others. But the river that launched a thousand rafts under the banner of Sobek Expeditions was the Blue Nile, and I first pitched down its upper reaches in 1973. I named the adventure company Sobek after the ancient crocodile god worshiped along the Egyptian Nile, thinking the homage might keep the predators at bay. But I was wrong. . . . Over the years, many crocodiles attacked our boats, and the Blue Nile stole the life of my best friend and early partner, Lew Greenwald.

Pasquale Scaturro has been a friend for many years, and we've shared many adventures, many river miles. When the chance came to attempt the first full descent of the Blue Nile, I knew that I would not make the journey myself. But I thought of Pasquale, who is in my estimation the most capable expedition leader of our time, and the only man who could make this mission possible.

What follows is Pasquale's story of this extraordinary journey, as well as glimpses into his colorful and poignant past. I asked Pasquale to keep a record of events and his thoughts as he barreled down the Nile, and during the course of his trip we kept in regular touch through satellite phone calls and e-mail. Afterward, I pored over his journals and conducted hours of interviews, and this book is the result. Though the work is truly binary, Pasquale appears throughout in the third person; his tale as told to me. Occasionally, I make a cameo, as I was in Africa during the initial stages of the expedition and film, before heading home to wait for reports, worrying and hoping that my friend would not find the fate of others before him.

This structure renders the book truly Hapi in execution: Hapi was the god of both the upper and lower Nile. His duality was rendered as twin deities, one wearing the papyrus of the north as a headdress, the other wearing the lotus of the south. Together they were depicted pouring water from a carried vase, or tying the two plants of the northern and southern regions into a knot with the *sema* hieroglyph, symbolizing the union of the two Niles.

Out of the One come Two; out of the two comes this book, and through this book, readers can now journey down the Nile and join this incredible adventure.

—*Richard Bangs*

CHAPTER ONE

Listen! What is life? It is a feather; it is the seed of the grass, blown hither and thither, sometimes multiplying itself and dying in the act, sometimes carried away into the heavens. But if the seed be good and heavy it may perchance travel a little way on the road it will. It is well to try and journey one's road and to fight with the air. Man must die. At the worst he can but die a little sooner.

H. RIDER HAGGARD, *KING SOLOMON'S MINES*, 1886

No boat whatever could be set in here and hope to live.

KUNO STEUBEN, ASSESSING THE NORTHERN GORGE
OF THE BLUE NILE, 1959

Deep within a gash in the skin of the continent, in the middle of a fast, brown river twisting through a dark inner gorge, Pasquale Scaturro was hanging on to his life by a rope, kicking to stay afloat in the cold water, his stout arms stretched to their limits. While a skein of currents blasted about his chest, he gripped with one hand the end of a seventy-five-foot-long yellow safety rope anchored to a basalt boulder upstream. With the other hand he clenched the black neoprene handle of an upside-down sixteen-foot, three-hundred-pound rubber raft, the lifeboat for this ambitious, perhaps imprudent, expedition.

Pasquale needed to make a fast choice. The nylon rope was wrapped around three fingers of his left hand, but it slipped off one finger, then another, leaving the cord tightening around his ring finger. He could feel the feeling drain from his finger; he imagined it being ripped from his hand. But if he let the rope go, he was committing himself to liquid chaos in the rapid called the Gauntlet. Just a few yards downstream was another huge rapid, Class V or worse, and after that another, then another, on for miles. It was here that Lew Greenwald had drowned on an exploratory expedition of the upper Blue Nile in 1976. It had been an eerily similar accident, in which a raft capsized and Lew was swept into a boiling white cauldron.

Pasquale also well knew that the British Army Expedition of 1968 had scouted this section from the air and elected to send rafts down empty, deeming the thirty-mile defile too deadly for human passage. And just an hour earlier, local villagers had told him of two Germans who had steered a big wooden boat into this section the year before. Their craft crashed against the ancient lava rocks and broke into pieces, and one of the Germans and both the Ethiopian guides drowned. The other German barely survived, hiked out, and left the country on the first flight, never telling authorities of the accident, and is still wanted for murder.

As the seconds passed, as his arms stretched toward the popping point, Pasquale considered the options in the last lozenge of daylight. He recognized that the safest thing to do would be to let go of the raft, swing the other hand to the rope, and pull himself back to shore. But if he did that, he would lose the raft to the Blue Nile, likely ending his attempt to be the first to navigate the whole of the river. Worse, he might be sentencing a man younger than his youngest son—who had disappeared around the corner with the raft—to a watery oblivion.

Alemu Mehariw, twenty-three, was a tall, athletic, good-looking Ethiopian, a Special Forces soldier in the Ethiopian People's Revolutionary Defense Front (EPRDF). The EPRDF was the rebel group that had defeated the former military dictator of Ethiopia, Lieutenant Colonel Mengistu Haile Mariam, the so-called "Red Emperor" or "Black

Lenin." Millions had died during his regime, and he was known for chilling acts such as requiring parents of his victims to pay police for the bullets used to kill their own children. Pasquale had recruited Alemu and Baye Gebre Selassie, twenty, another soldier, as guards and muscle for the Ethiopian slice of the three-country expedition. Neither had ever been on a raft, nor in whitewater, and they were not good swimmers, but they had been eager to join the adventure regardless.

So had Gordon Brown, forty-two, a kayaker-cameraman with the physique of a Dragon Volant. He'd locked up his houseboat in Marina del Rey and committed to the endless river, be it a six-month journey or more. Mike Prosser, fifty, owner of Down River Equipment Company in Wheat Ridge, Colorado, had also been seduced by the allure of the Blue Nile. Yibeltal Tsedalu, a trekking guide based in Addis Ababa who couldn't swim and sported a rolling *tella* belly, had liked the three hundred birr a day (about $35 U.S.) Pasquale was offering, enough for him to leave his wife and new baby and join—in a time when not many overseas hikers were seeking out Ethiopia. Even the freelance cook, Yohannes Mekonnen, aka Johnnie Walker, was happy to sign on, though he had a wife and two kids back in the capital and had never been on a boat. He had earned his nickname because Yohannes is Amharic for John, and he was too afraid to run the rapids, so he walked around them. (It was his whiskey of choice as well, but that was incidental to the nickname.)

But while many were attracted to the risk Pasquale proffered, most somehow resisted. His protean buddy Mike Speaks, who had led a variety of extreme river expeditions and who had perhaps spent more time on the Blue Nile than anyone else on earth, had attempted the Northern Gorge in 1996, but a raft flipped, and one of the Ethiopian guides died. Despite Pasquale's constant imploring, Mike declined to join. "My life is too valuable. You couldn't pay me enough to run that gorge again," said the twenty-year career river guide who had run big water on five continents. And he strongly recommended that Pasquale reconsider. "It's a death trap," Speaks warned. And Kurt Hoppe, a longtime partner in

Pasquale's business ventures and companion on Everest and Kilimanjaro signed on, flew from Colorado, and left after five days. At the black entrance to the Northern Gorge, Kurt decided to hike out and head home, after receiving word that his eighty-year-old dad had been diagnosed with a medical condition. In all, Pasquale had personally invited some thirty-five friends to join him, but schedules, costs, obligations, mortgages, divorces, doctor and haircut appointments, restaurant reservations made it impossible.

Nonetheless, Pasquale and his small flotilla of two rafts and a kayak had entered the Northern Gorge, just 182 miles down from the source, in the shank of a hot January afternoon. The rapids to this point had all been easy to run or, if not, to portage, and Pasquale was beginning to think that perhaps the difficulty of the Blue Nile was overrated. But then they came to the Gauntlet, a labyrinthine stretch of liquid lightning. Here, the river, which was more than a half-mile wide just a hundred yards upstream, was pinched to the width of a pickup truck. It blazed like a phosphorus fire as it decanted down a chute; turned sharply for a frothing, foaming run; and then wedged into a crack where it spat droplets into the air. It was so narrow that locals had dropped a three-limbed tree across its canyon as a bridge. Finally it spun through a brief unruffled section before dumping into another dreadful rapid. There was no way that the Gauntlet could be navigated, but they could film an empty raft being tossed down its length.

For the previous six weeks, Pasquale and Gordon had been featured players in an IMAX® Theatre production titled *Mystery of the Nile*. The film was a showcase of the great river, from its Blue Nile source in Ethiopia, to Sudan, where it swings past the black pyramids of Meroe, to Egypt, where it flushes through Cairo and then debouches into the Mediterranean near Alexandria in a plexus of shallow channels.

Pasquale was then to stay on after the crews left to make a try at running the whole of the river, some 3,200 miles from source to sea, an exploration dreamed of for centuries.

To locate the river's source—*quaerere caput Nili*—had been the hope of many great captains and geographers of the classical age: Herodotus, Cyrus and Cambyses of Persia, Alexander the Great, Julius Caesar, even Nero. It was the great nineteenth-century geographical quest that consumed David Livingstone, Richard Burton, John Speke, and many others. Though the White Nile is the longer of the two streams that join in Khartoum to create the Nile proper, it is the Blue Nile that contributes about eighty-five percent of the water that powers Egypt, and most of the precious silt that nourishes its banks. If the Blue Nile dried up, or were dammed or diverted in a significant way, Egypt would wither.

But while successful treks had been made to the headwaters of both the White and Blue Niles, neither had ever been navigated in a linear fashion from the first fountains to the last sighs, as the "Everest of rivers" pours into the brine. Attempts on both had resulted in fatalities and failure. Most happened on the Blue Nile, as it is the bigger, dropping at a steeper gradient, through deeper canyons, and over deadlier rapids—most in the infamous Northern Gorge. Then there was the concatenation of giant Nile crocodiles, hippos, roaming bands of bandits, tropical diseases, the extreme heat, and the incendiary politics along the way. But those would come later.

Pasquale felt he might be qualified to be the first to lead a successful expedition down the entire length of the Blue Nile. He had run major rivers around the world, including the Zambezi, Colorado, Bio-Bio, and Omo, and had made the first descent of the Tekeze in northern Ethiopia. He had been on three Everest expeditions, including leading the 2001 summit bid that put blind climber Erik Weihenmayer on top. And he had spent years in outback Africa searching for crude as an oil and gas geophysicist. Though past fifty, he was strong, fit, and a citizen of "the fourth world," that free-spirited territory where time has no weight, the true religion is exploration, and the inhabitants are rogues, nomads, and pioneers.

When Pasquale and Gordon scouted the Gauntlet, they assumed it would be one of the few completely unnavigable sections of river on the whole journey. But it was so spectacular that they decided to film a "ghost boat," one without human cargo, caroming through. When the thirty or so members of the film crew had returned to their homes in Europe and America for the holidays, they'd left behind a spartan camera package consisting of a forty-two-pound seventy-millimeter large-format camera for Pasquale and Gordon's use—with a forty-pound waterproof housing, a twenty-pound magazine, and six rolls of seventy-millimeter film weighing twelve pounds each. The Gauntlet was obviously worth spending some film on, so they devised a plan.

They emptied the two rafts of all the gear and hired some barefooted farmers to help them carry the gear downriver to the end of the rapids. They then secured the frames and oars of the first raft. Gordon would release it at the top of the three-hundred-yard-long Gauntlet, coordinating with Pasquale via their Icom IC-2 handheld radios, since the bottom and top were not within sight of each other. A waiting Pasquale could jump in at the bottom and row it safely to shore before it pitched into the next cataracts.

They divided up the tasks. Gordon, with help from Baye, set up the camera at a strategic point to capture the wildest action of the empty rafts hurtling through one after the other, and Mike set up a few feet away with a Sony digital video cam. Yibeltal was just upstream and would kick the first raft out into the middle current when he received a hand motion from Gordon. Pasquale, in the meantime, began to make his way to the rapid's terminus. They'd arranged that he would signal Gordon by radio once in position to capture the raft. Yohannes, who wanted nothing to do with this tosh, skittered away like a water bug.

But when Pasquale hiked downstream with Alemu to find a spot where he might catch the raft, he realized that the exercise might be a bad idea. He was on a rock about thirty feet above the river, just below the dark tranche through which the river tore. He could feel the ground vibrating from the river's bass notes as it blew out of the cut and fanned out to a fast but flat section some twenty feet wide and sixty feet long. The opposite bank was a four-story vertical wall, smooth as monument stone, topped with a fine tangled fantasy of branching acacias, a palisade of thorns. If the loose raft barreled down the other side, Pasquale would not be able to catch it in time, and it would bang around the corner, and be gone forever.

He knew he needed another man on the opposite bank in case it came down closer to that side. He spied a small shingle beach on the opposite bank, so he attached two throw lines to a boulder and asked Alemu to take one and swim across the river to be ready to capture the raft from the other side. But with a piercing look of terror, Alemu refused to try to catch the boat from either side—he was not a good swimmer, and he knew even bigger rapids were just downstream.

A row of Talmudic-faced herders, wrapped in dirty coarse cotton cloths and holding long cattle sticks, squatted on their haunches watching the curious activity. Pasquale turned to them and asked if they would help retrieve the forthcoming raft, and offered ten birr each for the effort. They shook their heads no. Pasquale upped the offer to fifty, but again they refused. He peeled out one hundred birr, then one thousand— the equivalent of about $114 U.S., more than a year's earnings—but they were resolute. "The Abay [Blue Nile] destroys," their watery-eyed leader said as flies buzzed about his mouth. "It is not safe."

Realizing that chucking a boat down this fearsome piece of water was not a good idea, Pasquale picked up the radio and squeezed the TALK button. He would tell Gordon to abort the attempt . . . it was a pointless bag of horrors. They would just portage the rafts around. But as he shouted into the walkie-talkie, there was no response. Then the radio emitted Gordon's voice: "Hurry up . . . we're losing light. Give me the signal."

Pasquale knew what was happening. When the batteries were low he couldn't broadcast, but he could receive, so Gordon was hearing nothing from him. And the spare batteries were in a kit up at the start of the Gauntlet.

"If I don't hear from you in ten seconds I'm going to release the first raft," Gordon's faint voice came through the speaker.

"NO! NO!" Pasquale yelled into the handheld. "Don't release the boat!"

"Five seconds." Gordon's words beaded up and rolled down Pasquale's spine.

Pasquale dropped the radio and scrambled up the rocky hill to a vantage where he could wave at Gordon to stop. But as he reached the top, he saw the raft already launched, skidding on a crackling surge of foam. The raft careened around the corner, and in a slow-motion narcotizing moment, it rolled over.

Shit. We're in trouble now, Pasquale thought, and sprinted down to where Alemu was standing, still holding the one rope. The raft started toward their position, its oil-black bottom shimmering with water, the aluminum frame bent and battered. It had no flip lines, nothing rigged for a capsize. Still, they had to try. Knowing he was the stronger—and more able to pull the boat in once a rope had been attached to it—Pasquale shouted, "Alemu . . . take this rope and jump in. Tie it to the raft." Alemu shook his head no, but Pasquale screamed again, so forcefully that it seemed to agitate the air, and Alemu took the plunge, hoping to land just in front of the raft.

But, as a novice in swift water, Alemu miscalculated, landed a few feet downstream of the boat, and vainly dogpaddled against the current. Within seconds the rope he held was stretched taut, and the powerful current started to push him under. Pasquale watched Alemu's shoulders straining with effort, knowing this was exactly how Ian Macleod, a member of the British Army Expedition, had drowned, in this same area, in 1968. Ian had tried to swim across the river to attach a line to the other side. But he erred in his mark, and was pendulumed to the middle of the river, where the shore-anchored rope went rigid and pushed him underwater like bait behind a speedboat. Unlike Ian, though, Alemu was just holding the rope. "Let go!" Pasquale screamed. Alemu stared back, eyes wide with terror.

Finally, he let go of the rope, and was shot like a champagne cork around the corner, out of sight. Pasquale knew from an earlier aerial scout in a Russian MI-17 helicopter that the next rapid, about fifty yards below, began with a recirculating hole that could swallow a raft like a pill. Pasquale had been on previous expeditions where teammates had died in what might have been preventable circumstances, and he desperately did not want that to happen again.

He didn't hesitate. Pasquale took the end of the other throw rope and dove into the cold current. It took precious seconds to reach the raft, where he curled his right hand around the black handle and brought it to a halt. Suddenly it seemed as though the Nile had inhaled and was holding its breath. A silence deep as the river swept in and hovered around Pasquale. It lasted seconds; then the sounds poured in again as into a bowl, and he took a gulp of air.

Now the rope in his left hand was banjo-string tight, slicing through nerve endings. It thrummed against the roar of the rapids. The raft handle was beginning to tear. The canyon was filling with shadows. The current's spray was stinging his face like BBs; his ring finger had gone numb. Like on some medieval torture rack, his muscles screamed for relief. He was out of time. He had to choose. Let go of the raft and insure his own safety. Let go of the rope, and hang onto a turtle-turned runaway raft— hopefully finding Alemu alive, and somehow getting him in the raft and to shore before the next falls.

Pasquale let go of the rope. The raft rocketed around the corner, Pasquale flailing in its wake. There on the other side of a jutting rock, up against a blunt cliff, was Alemu, his raw fingers pried into a chink in the stone, angry water clawing at his chest, face drained of color. As the raft spun toward Alemu, Pasquale, with a surge of adrenaline, reached up to the underside of the raft and bored his index fingers into two of the self-bailing holes, kicked, and pulled himself up onto the eel-slick bottom of the raft. Then he reached over and hauled Alemu on board.

Looking downstream he saw the monster hole just a few yards away—the start of the next rapid. He had no way to steer the upside-down raft as they rode it toward the brink. As Pasquale groped to untie the bowline, he had one thought: *Fuck—now I've done it.*

CHAPTER TWO

A myth was growing up about the Nile, a fantasy embellished with ancient temples and ferocious animals, with harems and slave tribes, with jewels and manuscripts lost in the arid land . . . and the great river, flowing out of nowhere, [which] carried one back and back towards the mysterious origin of things.

ALAN MOOREHEAD, *THE BLUE NILE*

The Ethiopian Plateau, where the Blue Nile begins, is an island amid the currents of history. Pushed up like a vast knot by the same geophysical forces that created the Red Sea, the plateau reaches its peak with Ras Dashen, 15,157 feet above sea level. Its northern flank rises out of the Nubian Desert into the Simien Mountains; at its eastern edges, steep escarpments angle four thousand feet to Somalia. Along the west the plateau drops to the Sahel regions of Sudan, sometimes abruptly, dangerously. South, the mountains descend toward Lake Turkana (formerly Lake Rudolf) on the Kenyan border. This highland massif, with its canyons and cliffs, is a natural fortress, yet here ancient civilizations from the time of Solomon rose and fell, in drama and battle. It is a maze of topography still unfinished, and it is a country as well.

In the midst of these highlands, at just over six thousand feet, is the shallow 1,400-square-mile Lake Tana, surrounded by the tribal lands of the Amhara. South of the lake and higher still, a conical prominence called Mount Gishe (10,433 feet) rises over the Springs of Gish Abay at a small village called Sakala, a holy site of the Ethiopian Orthodox Church since the thirteenth century and quite possibly for centuries before that. Ancient piles of animal bones tell of ritual slaughter, and its waters have long been thought sacred.

From this spring, the Gilgel Abay River—the Little Abay—descends 136 miles to Lake Tana, where twenty-nine monasteries cling to thirty-seven islands at the heart of ancient Abyssinia. From the southeast end of the lake, the Blue Nile starts a 1,070-mile journey over Tissisat Falls, down the treacherous Northern Gorge and Grand Canyon of the Blue Nile, onto the plains of Sudan, and all the way to today's Khartoum. There it joins its sister stream, the White Nile; their combined waters become the longest river in the world, 4,238 miles from source to sea.

The legends of the "fountains of the Nile" have persisted since the time of Herodotus, who wrote of his travels to Egypt in his 440 B.C. *The Histories*. His visit to Egypt took place a full two millennia after its dynasties began, eight centuries after the death of Pharaoh Rameses II, and one hundred years before Alexander the Great. It was Herodotus who documented the peoples and their stories from both Greece and the Persian Empire, and the surrounding circum-Mediterranean kingdoms. His accounts of Egyptian history took him as far south as Gondokoro; he expressed wonder at the Sphinx and sought to unravel the mystery of the Nile's rise and fall and its source. His solution—that snows far upstream in distant mountains flooded the headwaters and led to a rise of waters in the rich delta of Egypt—was not far from the truth. But it was only a supposition; the proof was yet to be found.

At the end of the eighteenth century, Egypt was again being revealed to a larger world, and with it the mysteries of its indecipherable hieroglyphics, its fabulous ruins in the deserts, and the greatness of its ancient civilization. Finding the source of the Nile—answering the question at the heart of the riddle—became not just a mission of intellect and courage, but a metaphor as well. Pilgrims, explorers, and warriors drove ever deeper up the river's course in search of these mystical springs—past the caravanserai of Cairo, the pyramids of Giza, the temples of Memphis, and into Upper Egypt. Then it went farther, into the Nubian kingdoms with their darker splendor, past Luxor and Kom Ombo (the Temple of Sobek, the crocodile god), to a series of cataracts.

Beyond that, there were only rumors. And legends. And there was Ethiopia.

The highlands where the Blue Nile is born comprise the lion's share of Ethiopia's history. No one can underestimate the antiquity of Ethiopia, once called Abyssinia. This is the legendary homeland of the Queen of Sheba, and the resting place of the Ark of the Covenant. The Kingdom of Axum erected the highest towers of African antiquity and invented gold coins. It became the second nation, after Armenia, to embrace Christianity—the Ethiopian Coptic Church dates from A.D. 330, older than Catholicism. And when the waves of Islam broke over Africa's shores, Abyssinia stayed above the flood.

Today, in the streets of Addis Ababa or Gondar, this antiquity is commonplace, rubbing shoulders with the other markers of the past—the palaces of Haile Selassie, the stolid architecture of the Communist era, the bright brand names of advancing consumerism. The Ark Hotel in Axum is not far from the St. Mary of Zion Church, said to house the Ark of the Covenant, which was smuggled from Jerusalem by Menelik I, son of Solomon and the Queen of Sheba. The inestimable Ghion Hotel, named for the river in the Garden of Eden, is where some of the expedition stayed in Bahir Dar, at the southern end of Lake Tana. A rumor persists even still that this valley was Eden—or perhaps Eden was the next valley.

Fables like these are inspired and a bit mad. The same description could apply to many who seek the source of the Nile; it certainly did to James Bruce.

History makes some figures larger than life; James Bruce was larger than life to begin with. "He was six foot four in height and strong in proportion, and he had dark red hair and a very loud voice," describes Alan

Moorehead in his indispensable history, *The Blue Nile*. "He had a reputation as a horseman and a marksman, and wherever he went he seems to have dispensed an air of confident superiority." This superior attitude served him well throughout his career, though even the superior man faces trials and doubt. In Bruce's case, he spent the first forty-four years of his life facing down his trials, and the last twenty years facing the doubts.

A noble-born Scottish "laird," educated at Edinburgh University and torn between his interest in the church and his father's insistence on the law, Bruce took a third option—travel. After a brief marriage to a wine merchant's daughter, who died while pregnant, Bruce studied Arabic and art in Spain and Italy, fought duels, sailed Europe's rivers, and eventually gained a post as a consul in Algiers. Despite the difficulty of the assignment—this was the milieu of the Barbary pirates—Bruce embraced the post, for it was, after all, in Africa, and the avenues of exploration lay open to him.

But his African exploits lay on the far side of still more trials. His retinue to Tripoli was attacked by marauders; he was expelled from Tripoli and shipwrecked en route to Crete; when he reached Crete he was struck down by fever for months at a time, and ill health followed him throughout his subsequent travels to Turkey and the Middle East. By 1769, two forms of exploration beckoned: to take part in a global observation of the transit of Venus across the sun (a phenomenon that seventy-six expeditions worldwide, including that of Captain James Cook in Tahiti, used to determine the size of the planet and the solar system), or to discover the Ethiopian source of the Nile. His astronomical equipment having been lost when he was shipwrecked, he opted for the latter.

It was a grand scheme, suiting a grandiose man. He entered Egypt in Arab dress—though six-foot-four-inch Arabs are rare now, and were rarer then—and secured letters of passage to help facilitate his exploration. During the latter half of 1768, he ventured up the Nile to Aswan, but the lawlessness of the upper reaches of the river frustrated his further advance.

Instead, he joined a caravan to the Red Sea; by September 1769 he was at Massawa, where his progress was again delayed by "a piratical gang that was even more rapacious than those he had left behind so long in Algiers," according to Moorehead. But with diplomacy and bluster in unequal measures he managed to put together a party of twenty to venture into the interior, up the northeastern flanks of the Ethiopian plateau to Axum, ancient capital of Abyssinia. In the first weeks of 1770, James Bruce reached Ethiopia; he was thirty-nine years old, on the verge of a renown befitting his enormous scale and ego.

There was one minor problem in his grand scheme. Bruce was not the first European to reach Ethiopia, and he was not the first to seek, nor to find, the source of the Blue Nile. The Portuguese had been there before, invited by the Abyssinians in about 1540 to fight against the Somali armies of Ahmed Gran. Then, too, they may have been seduced by the legend of Prester John, who some say was an early missionary who became a ruler in the Ethiopian highlands. The truth that the Portuguese found was less religious, but no less fabulous.

Among the Portuguese commanders were two sons of Vasco da Gama, first European to reach the Indian Ocean under Henry the Navigator. At first, things did not go well for the European forces; one of da Gama's sons, Christopher, was wounded, captured, and executed somewhere in the high interior of Abyssinia, and a tradition grew up that a spring appeared on the site, a spring with miraculous healing powers. It may be coincidence, but sixty years later, when the Jesuit priest Pedro Paez came to the Lake Tana region (where the Portuguese armies finally killed the Somali general Ahmed Gran in 1543), the spring he was shown at Sakala and told was the source of the Blue Nile was said to have remarkable healing powers.

Pedro Paez was a Spaniard who had done service in Goa (India) and

Yemen, where he had been held as a slave for several years by the local pasha. Upon his release, he sought to fulfill his religious mission to Abyssinia, and he had some success in infiltrating Jesuit Catholicism in the land of Coptics. So much so, in fact, that he became embroiled in a civil war when he converted an Ethiopian royal, Za-Denghel, who was killed by his followers for this heresy. Paez persisted, however, and in 1618, he finally reached the springs at Sakala with the Emperor Susenyos, whom he had also converted. Paez's account boasts that he "saw, with the greatest delight, what neither Cyrus, the king of the Persians, nor Cambyses, nor Alexander the Great, nor the famous Julius Caesar, could ever discover," and he went on to describe "two round fountains." Herodotus, too, had reported stories of these.

There is some doubt that Bruce knew of all this before he set out, but he certainly knew of it when he wrote his memoir *Travels to Discover the Source of the Nile,* published in 1790, for in it he goes to great lengths to discredit Paez's account. By the time Bruce himself reached the springs of the Little Abay, he had already been to the Blue Nile Falls at Tissisat, another site described by Paez's follower Jeronimo Lobo. Here Bruce's megalomaniacal side made him scoff at Lobo's description, saying that the Falls were "much degraded and vilified by the lies of a groveling fanatic priest."

Bruce's own success in reaching the source of the Blue Nile at Mount Gishe came on November 4, 1770. When his guide pointed out the sacred swamp, the big Briton threw off his shoes, raced down the flower-strewn hill (falling once or twice) and at last stood in the soggy turf he had long sought. "It is easier to guess than to describe the situation of my mind at that moment, standing in the spot which had baffled the genius, industry and inquiry of both ancients and moderns. . . ."

He dutifully measured the modest springs—three in number, not the two that Herodotus presumed—and determined the latitude and longitude of the site to within a remarkable twenty seconds. Almost immediately, however, a bipolar depression set in. Perhaps Bruce intuitively recognized the ceaseless trials he would face, not only on his long journey home but in his own attempts to verify, and justify, his accomplishment. He recorded that on "the very night of my arrival, melancholy reflections upon my present state . . . crowded upon my mind, and forbade all approach of sleep.

"The marsh, and the fountains, upon comparison with the rise of so many of our rivers," he went on, "became now a trifling object in my site. . . . I had seen the rise of the Rhine and Rhone, and the more magnificent sources of the Soane [*sic*]; I began, in my sorrow, to treat the inquiry about the source of the Nile as a violent effort of a distempered fancy. . . . Grief, or despondency, now rolling upon me like a torrent; relaxed, not refreshed, by unquiet and imperfect sleep, I started from my bed in the utmost agony. . . ."

The popular nineteenth-century English poet Felicia Hemans seems to be thinking of Bruce in these verses of her 1826 "The Traveller at the Source of the Nile":

> *The raptures of a conqueror's mood*
> *Rushed burning through his frame;*
> *The depths of that green solitude*
> *Its torrents could not tame,*
> *Though stillness lay, with eve's last smile,*
> *Round those far fountains of the Nile*
>
> *Night came with stars:——across his soul*
> *There swept a sudden change;*
> *E'en at the pilgrim's glorious goal*
> * A shadow dark and strange*
> *Breathed from the thought, so swift to fall*
> *O'er triumph's hour——and is this all?*

Bruce's departure from Abyssinia was delayed for a full year by tribal warfare, and his return through the deserts of Sudan and down two thousand miles of the Nile took more than another year of hardship, sickness, and suffering. He left the highlands via a northern route, far from the long, curving course of the Blue Nile itself; regaining the river only at Sennar, where he had another in a series of implausible experiences that he recorded in his three-volume memoir.

Against his wishes, he was forced to treat the king's favorite wife, who was ailing. Even the usually imperturbable Bruce was taken aback by the size of this woman—"corpulent beyond all proportion. She seemed to me, next to the elephant and rhinoceros, the largest living creature I had met with." He let blood and administered ipecac, and the results were predictably appalling. He also indulged in a bit of white man's magic, predicting a lunar eclipse based on his pocket ephemeris to impress the sheik of Sennar with his power.

Allowed to continue on, he followed the Blue Nile to its confluence with the White at Halfaya, near today's Khartoum. From there, he followed the river northward only to Hassa, where he followed the traditional caravan route across the Nubian Desert to Syene (Aswân). By the time he returned to Cairo in January 1773, after three difficult years in Africa, he was garbed not as a proud Arab but as a beggar.

His graphic descriptions of his exploits immediately raised doubts, if not derision. He was compared, unfavorably, to Marco Polo, the original "man of a million lies," and Baron von Munchausen, the comic charlatan. Bruce's tales of the casual savagery of the Abyssinians—that they cut steaks off live cattle when on caravan and ate them raw, among other anecdotes—evoked skepticism, ridicule, and worse. When *Travels to Discover the Source of the Nile* was finally published in 1790, it did nothing to restore his reputation. It was only long after his death in 1794 that his account came to be accepted as generally true, living steaks and all, and his reputation established as among the first great European explorers of Africa.

Less than a decade after Bruce's book appeared, none other than Napoleon Bonaparte approached the Nile from its end, not its source. Flush with victory in Europe and at the height of his influence and military acumen—at twenty-eight years of age—he deduced that a feint to invade Britain, and an actual invasion of Egypt, would bisect British influence in the Indian trade. He captured first Malta, then Alexandria, and finally Cairo, all within a few months of 1792. In so doing, he broke the stranglehold upon Egypt of the Ottoman Empire and one of the strangest oligarchies in history, that of the Mamlukes (or Mamelukes).

Imagine a warrior class of slaves, captured as children in the Caucasus a thousand miles away, converted to Islam, raised apart from women (and necessarily homosexually inclined), who acted with authority and impunity over Egypt for more than five hundred years. Each generation returned to the Caucasus to "recruit" new boy slaves to train. These were the Mamlukes; that they were powerful warriors is indisputable, but they were no match for the modern tactics of a Napoleon. Their rule was broken, and Egypt entered another phase of its lengthy history.

Napoleon himself left Egypt after less than a year, his fleet destroyed by Admiral Nelson and his attempt to capture Syria unsuccessful; but his army included the first scientific expedition to record the wonders of the pharaohs and the course of the river. The team uncovered the Rosetta Stone, the key to deciphering the hieroglyphs; surveyed the Sphinx (which had already lost its nose, though not to French target practice as the legend holds) and the pyramids of Giza; and sent upriver the artist Vivant Denon, along with a military contingent. Denon made the first graphic catalog of many of the dynastic temples all the way to the First Cataract, and his writings and drawings sparked enormous interest in antiquarian circles. He later became director of the Napoleon Museum, now the Louvre, and one of its wings is named after him.

Another Frenchman followed Denon a generation later, pushing farther still up the river—past the confluence of the Blue and the White Niles, in fact, and like many before him mistaking the larger branch, the

Blue, as the longer. Frederic Cailliaud, a geologist, was in search of gold and heard rumors of the rich mines that lay up the Blue Nile into Sudan and beyond. He convinced Muhammad Ali, by now the Turkish regent of Egypt, to give him passage to look for these treasures, and in a motley party that included an unlikable fellow of Trinity College, George Waddington, and an American named English (George B., a sometime minister, newspaperman, U.S. Marine, and eventual government agent).

In any case, their 1820–21 expedition brought them far upriver to Meroë, the ancient Nubian capital. From there, Cailliaud sailed up the Blue Nile all the way to the Ethiopian border with Muhammad Ali's son Ismail, one of the bloodiest generals in a bloody history. It is estimated that Ismail Ali captured thirty thousand slaves on his campaign; when he was not seizing the natives, he was massacring them. Moorehead writes that they rounded up "without pity every negro they could lay hands on, and when the villagers tried to fight back—shooting off their arrows and rolling boulders down from the heights—they were obliterated."

Finally the marauding band reached the foothills of the mountains at Fazughli, where the Blue Nile "vanished into an enormous gorge which was impassable even to men on foot." And the gold? Cailliaud found only a few grains of the precious metal that came down the river from veins too distant to reach; the villagers stored the gold in feather quills and used it for trade, knowing its value. But the fabled mines were nowhere to be found.

CHAPTER THREE

The White Nile was virtually a cul-de-sac ending at El Ais (about one hundred and eighty miles south of Khartoum) beyond which lay the savage realm of the Nilotic tribes. It led nowhere, was of relatively little importance, and therefore was little spoken of or known; whereas the Blue Nile was a thoroughfare throughout history.

ARCHEOLOGIST O. G. S. CRAWFORD

As the nineteenth century unfolded, exploring the Nile became more common, though no less adventurous. For the most part, the easier route was up the Blue Nile, not its longer counterpart the White—largely because at Khartoum it was clear that the Blue carried far more water, and was thus the more traveled fork. For centuries, there was even a tacit competition between Egypt and Ethiopia, with the Egyptians believing the Ethiopians could somehow turn off the flow of the Nile, and the cannier Ethiopians letting them think so.

But as the lay of the land in Africa became known, it became clear that it was the White Nile that was the longer tributary, and thus—according to widely accepted standards of the day—the "source." Onto this stage stepped Richard Francis Burton.

One of the most intriguing men in British exploration history, Burton was a brilliant and adventurous spirit who made as many enemies in life as he made friends. Expelled from Oxford for studying nonstandard subjects such as Arabic and mysticism, he put his interests to use in the East

India Company and in later travels in Persia and Arabia. He was one of the first (though not the first) non-Muslims to visit Mecca, in 1853 (he disguised himself as an Afghan physician). In 1854, he became the first European to visit the Ethiopian holy city of Harar, and shortly thereafter joined with John Hanning Speke to explore Somalia. Not long after the two started out, natives attacked and Burton took a spear through his face. Both cheeks were deeply scarred for life, adding to his foreboding appearance. In this same ambush, Speke retreated to his tent for firearms; Burton seems to have mistaken this tactical retreat for flight, and tensions between the two men began to fester. (Speke in fact was severely injured and captured in this attack, and he barely managed to escape with his life.)

About this time, the British Royal Geographical Society took a keen interest in the source of the Nile, and in 1857 Burton and Speke set out from Zanzibar to chart the interior, looking for the lakes in the Mountains of the Moon, where Herodotus had believed the source would be found. They made their way to Lake Tanganyika, which Burton initially suspected might be the source of the White Nile. Surveying the lake disproved his assumption—its outflow was to the west, and its waters eventually joined the Congo. On his own, Speke then set out for the north and the rumors of another lake, Nyanza, while Burton was bedridden with malaria.

Here things got gnarly. Speke reached Nyanza on August 3, 1858, almost immediately declared it the source of the Nile, and named it for his queen—Lake Victoria. Burton was appalled at the lack of evidence for Speke's presumption, and perhaps a little jealous of the discovery. In his report to the Royal Geographical Society he therefore qualified all of Speke's assumptions and geography, and focused instead on the territory they had surveyed together. The strain in their relationship over this only grew; by the time they returned to Zanzibar in March 1859, they were barely on speaking terms.

Speke's assumption was "a reckless and astonishing conclusion to jump to," as Alan Moorehead characterized it in *The White Nile*.

Nonetheless, upon returning to England ahead of Burton, Speke immediately made his claim to the Royal Geographical Society and became the toast of the town. Burton was furious, his own luster tarnished by his companion's claims. Subsequent explorations by Speke in company with another traveling companion better suited to his temperament, James A. Grant, only confirmed in Speke's mind his "discovery," but again he failed to provide adequate evidence or measurements. If Speke was right for all the wrong reasons, Burton was wrong for all the right ones—he was more of a scientist, and he clearly had a sharper intellect than his rival; but in the end, Lake Victoria became popularly regarded as the source of the White Nile, though like Lake Tana, it too has tributary streams, the largest and longest of which spills down from the mountains of Burundi, a watershed that neither Burton nor Speke explored.

Their rivalry had a dramatic if poignant conclusion. The conflict between the two grew so intense and public that a debate between them was called at the British Association for the Advancement of Science in September 1864. They had not spoken in years, and tensions were high. The afternoon of September 16, as Burton and the members of the Academy gathered for the much-anticipated meeting, Speke shot himself while hunting and died hours later. An inquest held that it was an accident, but the circumstances remain peculiar to say the least.

Sir Richard Burton continued his career as a philologist, explorer, and writer, but he never again gained center stage as he had in his contest with Speke. His travels and official posts took him from Salt Lake City to Fernando Poo (Equatorial Guinea), Brazil, Paraguay, Argentina, Syria, and finally Trieste. His frank translation of *The Arabian Nights* was scandalous, and he introduced the *Kama Sutra* and *The Perfumed Garden* to the world library of erotica. He was knighted in 1886, and died four years later in Italy. His wife, always uncomfortable with his private interests, burned his papers upon his death.

Other explorers, such as Sir Samuel Baker and Dr. David Livingstone, later set out to confirm or discover the source of the White Nile, which leads to an interesting question: What is it about this obsession with rivers among explorers, anyway? Why did Burton and Speke quarrel so over the origin of the White Nile, or Livingstone pursue the Zambezi, or Mungo Park the Niger—compulsions which as often as not ended in death? It may be that rivers give shape to the world and its borders, defining territories and landscape as no other feature does. The same could be said of mountains, which have likewise magnetized explorers, with similarly mortal results.

Unlike mountains, however, rivers are the great equalizer—they all end at sea level. There was even one early theory, recorded by no less a luminary than Herodotus, that the Nile itself both originated from and flowed into the Ocean, for the Ocean surrounds the world. Maybe we sense a communion with rivers that we don't with other natural features; their courses mimic our own circulation system, their currents our pulse. Then, too, it's no accident that sacred springs are said to be healing, life-giving or -prolonging. Water is cleansing. To find the source, or to follow the flow, is to become in touch with the blood of the landscape, and to communicate with its heart.

Interestingly, up to this point none of these romantic trailblazers ever seemed to think of simply floating down the rivers to see where they went. They opted instead for land-based expeditions with retinues of native support and military escorts. But descents of these rivers were almost unheard of, and possibly unconsidered—at least until the dawn of the twentieth century. At that point, the desire was ignited to attempt to descend the Blue Nile, to penetrate the gorges that hid its secrets.

The first to descend overland the length of the Blue Nile were in fact probably anonymous, peripatetic sons and daughters of highland farmers or artisans driven as much to see what lay downstream as their European counterparts were driven to discover what lay up it. Or perhaps less romantically and more accurately, traders or even thieves who fled by following the river's flow in hopes of escape. A similar scenario characterizes the first to descend the Colorado through the Grand

Canyon. It may not have been John Wesley Powell in 1869, but a prospector and horse thief named James White, who fled down the San Juan River in Utah two years earlier to avoid an Indian attack (or so went his story). He washed up four hundred miles downstream in Nevada, somewhat the worse for wear.

Leaving these speculations aside, the first documented attempt to descend the Blue Nile was made by W. N. McMillan, a wealthy American hunter who hoped to prove that the river could provide an avenue of trade to and from Sudan, and by extension Egypt. McMillan conceived of a two-pronged attack: he hired a Norwegian, Burchard H. Jessen, to travel upriver from Khartoum, while he put in with three steel boats at the confluence of the Muger River (downstream of today's Great Abay or Shefartak Bridge), north of Addis Ababa. His expedition lasted until the first rapids: an S-shaped curve around rocky banks, where one boat sank and one flipped. While the disappointed party camped on the beach that night, a crocodile attacked one of the Somali crew. The group retreated, but McMillan continued to scheme about another assault.

Jessen fared somewhat better. He and his Sudanese assistants managed to get upriver in a forty-foot steam launch as far as Famaka, just a few miles from where Cailliaud had turned back in 1821. Under McMillan's orders, and with his financial support, Jessen returned to the river in 1905 with American H. L. Scott and made an overland journey from Famaka up into the canyons. The plan was to scout the river for its navigability and meet McMillan and his new (and presumably more riverworthy) boats at the Guder tributary for a first descent.

For the first fifty miles or so, the entourage of thirty-two men, twice as many mules and donkeys, and one camel progressed steadily, but when they reached the Black Gorge, things turned challenging. Natives attacked and killed one of Jessen's Sudanese porters at a place the surveyor gloomily named Murder Island. They struggled to follow McMillan's request for a riverside route, but were often forced to climb out of the canyon to follow the rim of the gorge for much of the way. The terrain grew ever more treacherous; "In a single day, Jessen's camel and four donkeys collapsed and died from sheer exhaustion," writes Virginia Morell in her 2001 *Blue Nile: Ethiopia's River of Magic and Mystery.* "Mosquitoes, moths, and stinging insects plagued them by night, while ants and biting flies attacked them by day. Their clothing was in tatters; their boots, in shreds. Scott was half delirious with fever and dysentery, and they barely had enough to eat, although occasionally Jessen shot an antelope or hippo."

When Jessen finally attained a ridge-top view of the Blue Nile for several consecutive miles upstream, the vision was disheartening. "The river itself is continuous cataracts, crooked and full of rocks, while the banks were nothing but piles of jagged sharp boulders, beyond which the hills rose up steep and forbidding looking, with apparently no footing anywhere."

By the time he was snatched away to the local ruler's capital by fourteen armed soldiers to pay tribute, Jessen's patience was wearing thin. When, after returning to the river and continuing upstream, he finally reached the Guder, McMillan was nowhere to be found. Jessen continued upstream for a few more miles, then left the Blue Nile and returned to Addis Ababa, convinced that a boat journey down the canyon was "dangerous for navigation at any time of year."

As it turned out, McMillan had become very ill in the Ethiopian capital, and after hearing Jessen's report had given up on his dream descent. The trade route up and down the river went the way such dreams always had, shattered on the shoals of the rocky cataracts in the deep, black canyon.

The river had still not yet even been completely surveyed, and Major Robert E. Cheesman—like Burton before him a soldier and surveyor, naturalist and linguist—rose to the challenge. After spending extensive time in India and the Middle East, he was appointed British consul to northwest Ethiopia in 1925. He was initially disappointed with the posting, but his curiosity was piqued by his discovery that the maps showed the Blue Nile—one of the most famous waterways in the world—represented by a series of dotted lines. Could it be that it was still uncharted in the twentieth century? This was every explorer's dream: to fill in a blank on the map. "The course of the Blue Nile might be considered as offering the only bit of pioneering exploration left in Africa," he wrote.

Over the next eight years, Cheesman gave exercise to his inspiration. He met with the governor of Gojjam province, Ras Hailu, and obtained the tacit approval of the country's ruler, Ras Tafari Makonnen, the nephew of the late Emperor Menelik II (who had died in 1910), who later became Emperor Haile Selassie. He decided to eschew the river route followed by Jessen—who said that one could see only the sky from the river, and was forever ignorant of the surrounding terrain—and assembled a series of expeditions along the rim of the river canyon to survey the course of the Blue Nile.

Cheesman's route, described in his book *Lake Tana and the Blue Nile,* eventually took him the entire length of the river from Mount Gishe to Sudan over several forays, and he succeeded in mapping all but fifteen miles of the river. He even circumambulated Lake Tana, becoming the first person known to have done so. He descended from the nine-thousand-foot spring at Sakala down to Tissisat Falls at six thousand feet, and then another forty-five hundred feet to the Sudanese border. It was a diligent and invaluable commitment, unequaled until aerial surveys in the 1960s filled in the last remaining blanks on the map.

But not everyone who sought to run the Blue Nile earned government sponsorship or could rely on the support of local consulates or distant institutes. In the 1950s, independent travelers began to become interested in the Blue Nile, and the first of a series of largely unsuccessful, and in some cases life-threatening, adventures were attempted.

Perhaps the first was that of an Austrian man in the 1930s, who launched his canoe at the Second Portuguese Bridge, capsized almost immediately, and was killed by a crocodile while his horrified wife looked on. In 1955, two European couples (nudists, according to most eyewitnesses) put in at the Abay Bridge, almost on a lark in the midst of their "Ethiopian Adventure." They navigated their collapsible kayaks through the rapids adequately for several days, but after twenty miles the crocodile attacks became so intimidating that they fled.

This compulsion to descend the Blue Nile reached its peak in the 1960s, like so many things did, with a litany of things gone wrong: In 1959 and 1960, a young artist named Kuno Steuben, or Schmutnig, depending on which alias you believe, put together a native papyrus reed boat called a *tankwa* and set off from Lake Tana. After the building rapids of the upper gorge that led to Tissisat Falls, just a score of miles downstream, he gave up on the tankwa. The next year, he put together a homemade log raft and descended 160 miles from the Abay Bridge over twenty-some days relatively uneventfully, marveling at the scenery.

He should have marveled at his luck. One morning, four Oromo men walked into his camp, and after making gestures of friendship, attacked and stabbed him. Steuben fought back, wounding three of the four and fleeing downriver on his raft with hastily gathered essentials. In a one-man struggle for survival, he lived on what fish he could catch and tried to fight off fever, until he collapsed. "When he awoke, he was in a native's hut far from the river, on one of the high plateaus," Virginia Morell summarizes in her *Blue Nile*. "The villagers found and rescued him, and in time, they cured him. They offered him one of their daughters as a wife, but Steuben declined. What he really wanted was a mule and a guide, and when these were provided, Steuben started back for the Abay Bridge."

Steuben was not the last independent traveler to be drawn to the Blue Nile. An Italian geologist was said to have started at the Abay Bridge in 1961 and was never heard from again. Three years later, an Austrian sculptor named Gerhard Heinrich, or perhaps Heinrich Gerhard, or maybe just Haas, descended through rapids and crocodiles on a wooden raft using empty petrol drums for flotation. After five days, his boat was destroyed in a ten-foot drop, and he walked back to Addis in his swimming trunks.

Finally, in 1965, someone had some luck. Arne Rubin of Sweden, a forty-seven-year-old former United Nations worker in Sudan, put in at the Shefartak Bridge, descended the length of the Black Gorge, and reached Sudan on an epic solo journey. The next year, he tried to duplicate the feat with a compatriot, Carl Forsmark, beginning higher this time, at the First Portuguese Bridge, just below Tissisat Falls. But after only fifteen miles, Forsmark nearly drowned in a whirlpool, and they gave up and walked back to civilization, leaving their boats behind.

There were several other better-equipped expeditions in this period as well, all bent on making a "first descent" of the Blue Nile. In 1962, a Swiss-French party of six followed the course of the river below the Shefartak Bridge in two three-seater fiberglass canoes. Among the party were world-champion kayaker Henry Hedrnka and Swiss Olympian Dr. Stanley Walter; they were both killed during a native attack just a few days into the expedition. The rest of the party escaped at nightfall, leaving behind all their equipment.

In 1968, the British returned to the Blue Nile, mounting a military-style expedition with seventy combined British and Ethiopian adventurers, complete with military support, airplanes, and wireless radios. Under the command of pith-helmeted Captain John Blashford-Snell, they made a three-pronged assault on the river, ostensibly to catalog its mysteries at the invitation of Haile Selassie, but not without a certain amount of slavering at the opportunity for an epic adventure. They named their effort the Great Abbai Expedition, or the Last Great First.

Blashford-Snell was cut from the same cloth as British military explorers of days gone by. "A youthful love of weapons and explosives led John Blashford-Snell via Sandhurst [the Royal Military Academy] to a Commission in the Royal Engineers," wrote Richard Snailham in *The Blue Nile Revealed*. "He is a big man, broad of shoulder, heavily boned. He wears a military moustache, well-cut suits, and, on frequent festive occasions, hired theatrical costumes representing the great generals as William the Conqueror, Oliver Cromwell or Marcus Vipsanius Agrippa."

He also possessed the military love of tactical planning. His "assault boats" were steel-lined dinghies, over seventeen feet long and weighing four hundred pounds unloaded, powered by forty-horsepower motors; they were captained by Boat Commanders. His camps were called Forward Base I, etc.; nightly Orders Group meetings were held to plan the next day's activities.

The plan of attack was to divide and conquer. The river (called the Great Abbai, among its several Ethiopian aliases) was isolated into three navigable sections, or Phases, each more difficult than the preceding. The first was the stretch from the Abay Bridge at Shefartak downstream to Sirba, essentially the route Arne Rubin had taken in 1965. The second was from Lake Tana to Tissisat Falls, a twenty-mile stretch of sometimes difficult whitewater, but with good rescue access from Bahir Dar. The third and final stretch included the only unknown portion, from the First Portuguese Bridge below Tissisat all the way down to Shefartak. Thus, the same party (with an ever-shifting cast) would run the entire length of the river for the first time.

The assault boats for Phase I were named after notable Englishmen whose interests had touched on Ethiopia, Major Cheesman among them. They launched on August 5; after working out the kinks in their technique, the party made its way down the three sections of the river below Shefartak—the Black Gorge with its rapids and steep canyons, the Broad Valley, where a few settlements were found, and finally the Western Cataracts of whitewater and sheer cliffs. In this pre-GPS era, their on-river navigation was spotty—Snailham recounts that one member "took a series of very good 'star-fixes' at night in every river-bank camp site. These gave him a latitude and longitude accurate to about fifty yards.

The trouble was that when related to any of our maps they revealed that we were actually halfway up some mountain-side.

"Tributaries came in where they should not," Snailham goes on, "and refused to turn up when they should. Mountains were quite unidentifiable and we passed over fords in the full flood of the rainy season without realizing it. . . . The convolutions through which the river went bore no relation to the flattened wiggle on the map."

But the expedition was astonishingly well supplied, for all that. Airplane drops kept them in rations (albeit military rations), fuel, and even whiskey; scientists found plant, animal, and archeological specimens; and though the steel boats were sometimes clumsy and rocks did their damage, all hands made it safely down to the airstrip at Sirba Abay. The biggest loss on the first leg was when one of the steel assault boats dropped from the helicopter as it was being airlifted out, and fell seven hundred feet into the jungle.

The section from Lake Tana to Tissisat had not been in the original battle plans for the expedition, but a flyover of the stretch made it seem runnable as a warm-up to the later section. The crews used twelve-foot Avon Redshanks, a boat that the next generation of river runners found unsuitable for most whitewater rivers—the larger sixteen-foot Avon Pro became the raft of choice for many years. Each Redshank was manned by a crew of three of the nine members of the White Water Team, under the direction of Roger Chapman; one of the members was mountaineer Chris Bonington, acting as a reporter and photographer for the *Daily Telegraph*. In the expedition style, each boat was given a name—*Faith*, *Hope*, and *Charity*.

Almost from the start on September 8, the stretch taxed the skills of the crews. All of the boats eventually flipped, and their crews went swimming; one member almost drowned when he was pinned against a rock in midstream by the current, and it took a daring rescue to save his life. One boat, the *Charity*, was temporarily lost when it went over a falls upside down, with Ian Macleod sitting on top. Macleod made it safely to shore, and the boat turned up relatively undamaged downstream. Though they gave up trying to complete the run above Tissisat, leaving it untouched until 2003, they proclaimed Phase II a guarded "success."

Phase III proved to be almost the undoing of the expedition. From the First Portuguese Bridge down, the decision was made to bypass the heart of the Northern Gorge, a deadly stretch as revealed in the aerial survey. So, they simply pushed two Redshanks into the river and picked them up at the other end. The crew made their plans for recovery and hiked out.

However, in attempting to ford a tributary called the Abaya that came in from the south, luck ran out for Ian Macleod. As he tried to swim across the river with a rope attached to his waist, the current swept him downstream just yards before he reached the far shore. In the scant minutes of panic before the rope could be cut, he lost his strength. His body was never found.

The drama wasn't over.

They relaunched at Sabara Dildi, the Second Portuguese Bridge, with four boats—the two recovered Redshanks with a crew of three, and two motor-powered British Army Recce boats (for "Reconnaissance") with crews of two. John Blashford-Snell went back on the water again, in one of the Recce boats. They made good time that day, over seventeen miles to their first camp. On the second day, however, while exploring an artifact-strewn cave, they were attacked by between twenty-five and thirty armed *shiftas*, roaming bands of bandits, who fired down on the party and hurled rocks. Chris Bonington was struck by a rock, but as Snailham remarks, "Happily their marksmanship was atrocious and their weapons were obviously ancient."

The next day, more than twenty miles farther downriver, they made camp on an island and had an apparently harmless social visit from a half dozen young men who swam out to meet them. Just after midnight, however, Roger Chapman went out to check the boats and found a line of dripping, armed men coming out of the water, bracing for attack.

Guns were fired, flares were set off, and after a fifteen-minute nocturnal battle the assailants fled. Throughout the night, the crew quietly dismantled their camp and kept a keen watch. Before dawn broke, when the attackers appeared, ready to renew their assault, the expedition fled downstream into a large cataract, which they ran in darkness.

By comparison, the rest of the trip was uneventful. On September 24, 1968, the last phase of the Great Abbai Expedition floated into Shefartak and completed their mission. Snailham concludes his account in *The Blue Nile Revealed* by quoting his colleague: "As Chris Bonington rightly concluded, no-one conquers the Blue Nile. The most that can be wrung from this powerful, turgid river is a grudging acceptance that some men and boats have passed over more or less all of it. But they do not do this without a mauling; they come away scarred; some do not come away at all."

There were more attempts in the '70s, '80s and '90s, including several with Sobek Expeditions, but as of 2003, nobody had made the complete passage, by river, of the Blue Nile from its source at Sakala to its confluence with the White Nile at Khartoum, let alone continued to its ultimate effluence into the Mediterranean near Alexandria.

It remained, perhaps, that greatest river expedition yet to be done.

CHAPTER FOUR

God has given us mules but no roads to ride on.
ETHIOPIAN PROVERB

If you love my baby, wait 'til you see her picture.
BRIAN DE PALMA

Twenty-eight years after my best friend drowned on the Blue Nile, I was launching a raft on the same fast waters. It was thirty years to the week since I had attempted a first descent of the nearby Baro River, and there, too, a rider had drowned. Long ago I had sworn not to return, yet here I was pushing the Avon raft with my friend Pasquale Scaturro into the brown current, my stomach roiling like the rapids downstream.

The Blue Nile brought me to Africa in 1973. I had been enthralled by the writings of Alan Moorehead and James Bruce; Moorehead's book *The Blue Nile* swept me into a world beyond the pages of *National Geographic*. I started a correspondence with the author, who lived in Switzerland in the late 1960s, and before he died he sent me a note urging me to travel to Ethiopia to see firsthand the locales of the stories he had told.

My return to the Blue Nile was pulled into motion with a call from MacGillivray Freeman Films, the pioneering IMAX® Theatre film company that has produced many of the giant-format films, from the groundbreaking *To Fly* to the triumphant *Everest*. The company was co-producing a new IMAX® Theatre film titled *Mystery of the Nile,* along with Orbita Max, a Barcelona-based concern run by Spanish filmmaking legend Jordi Llompart.

Jordi had produced and directed a series of reports on the Nile for Spanish television in the mid-1990s, and he conceived the idea of making an IMAX® Theatre film that would celebrate the key stream in the Nile system, the Blue Nile, and look at its effects on Sudan and Egypt, where civilization would not have been possible without the water and rich volcanic soil that spilled from the Ethiopian highlands. It was to be a monumental undertaking in some of the toughest environments in the world, with some forty foreign crew members, seven tons of gear, and a helicopter brought up from Kenya with a high-tech SpaceCam rig.

Greg MacGillivray and Jordi Llompart brought me in as an early consultant for the film, and they offered me a position as director of second unit for the Ethiopian portion of the project, where we would feature some of the legendary whitewater of the upper Blue Nile. I had written and produced a few documentary films, but I'd never directed, and of course everyone wants to direct, so I accepted with alacrity.

But then I began to have doubts. Why was I returning to a place of tragedy I had spent years trying to put behind me? One magnet, I realized, was the 150-foot-high Tissisat (Smoke of Fire) Falls, also known as the Blue Nile Falls. They were, I remembered, the most glorious display of falling water I had ever seen. James Bruce, in his search for the source of the Nile, came upon the falls in 1770 and described them like this:

The river . . . fell in one sheet of water, without any interval, above half an English mile in breadth, with a force and a noise that was truly terrible, and which stunned and made me, for a time, perfectly dizzy. A thick fume, or haze, covered the fall all around, and hung over the course of the stream both above and below, marking its track, though the water was not seen. . . . It was a most magnificent sight, that ages, added to the greatest length of human life, would not deface or eradicate from my memory.

When, in 1973, I first stood before the immense manitou of the Blue Nile Falls, watching the mist shape and move like a time-lapse sequence of clouds, I was struck by how accurate James Bruce had been and how little the sight had changed in more than two hundred years. The other great waterfalls of the world—Niagara, Iguassu, Victoria—are all now surrounded by hotels and tourist boutiques and scenic flights. At Tissisat Falls, however, there was nothing save the raw, deep voice of nature and an architecture supported by the brilliant beams of rainbows. I had no reason to think that they would ever change.

The spray flung up from this gorge created a perpetual soft rain that blew across my face. At my feet, a forest of wet green reeds waved from side to side, like seaweed at the bottom of the ocean. Looking above the falls, I could see a tankwa, a papyrus-reed boat, in which fishermen were propelling themselves with bladeless bamboo poles. I saw flocks of little black birds with pointed pinkish wings flying directly into the spray and landing on the slippery rocks at the very lip where the water made its horrifying plunge. Unconcerned, they flew off again through a rainbow, nearly circular, that hung in the spray like a whirling firework. As the spray washed my face, I felt as vital and alive as I had ever been, baptized into the river of life. The section the 1968 British expedition had deemed too difficult to raft—that missing piece on their map—was what most inspired me. This was a challenge I was ready to take up, and so, after college graduation in 1972, I set about researching the Blue Nile and how to navigate its legendary waters.

The American Grand Canyon, where I had guided raft trips for three seasons, was such a powerful place that it had become the pivot of my identity, around which everything else spun and was measured. As I read the accounts of the British attempt, I became appalled at their inexperience and bungles, their insensitivity to the land. I couldn't help but think that I could do better. I understood whitewater; I knew the Grand Canyon; and for some twisted reason, I loved the notion of running rapids on a river with crocodiles.

But I didn't fare much better. I made a descent of a 140-mile section of the Grand Canyon of the Blue Nile in 1974, coordinating food drops for an American hiker who was making a Colin Fletcher–style walk through the Grand Canyon of Africa. He never made our rendezvous site midcanyon, and he was never seen again. The following year, my business partner and best friend, Lew Greenwald, drowned in the Northern Gorge section of the river below Tissisat Falls. His raft capsized and his life jacket was clipped to the stern line; he was dragged over a series of Class VI rapids. It was then that I vowed never to pull an oar on the damned river again.

Still, the siren call of the river had brought me back, thirty years later. The script for the film called for whitewater action, thrilling runs through big rapids, an oar break, even a capsize. But as I flew over the Northern Gorge in an early October scout with Llompart, I knew I could never orchestrate a film in the abyss that had killed my friend. It was remote, dark, and filled with deadly rapids. I concocted a plan to stage the whitewater scenes on the Zambezi, 2,200 miles to the southwest, on a section of river below Victoria Falls that I had pioneered in the early '80s and that was now a very popular extreme-whitewater run.

There was one problem: the water color didn't match. The Zambezi ran limpid green, and the Blue Nile was churning chocolate. I fretted about this as we flew up the canyon of the Blue Nile's Northern Gorge, but anxiety turned to anticipation as we approached Tissisat Falls. Early October was the best time to see the falls, just after the rains, and I knew I was in for an aerial treat.

But as I gazed downward, something was wrong . . . the falls were but a shadow of how I remembered them . . . instead of a blazing curtain of water half a mile wide, only about a third of the basaltic lip was under the water. The rest of the flow, it seemed, was rolling down a giant canal to the west of the river into a massive concrete spillway. What had happened to the great falls? My nose pressed against the plane's window, I stared, stunned, at the sight.

The Cessna continued upstream over the final twenty miles to Lake Tana, and I shook myself out of shock when I began to register a series of rapids—big, muscle-bound rapids—not far from a road that ran from the lake to the falls. Much of this course weaved through a maze of lush islands and against basaltic cliffs, but the russet-skinned river was scarred with slashes of whitewater every hundred yards or so. As far as I knew, nobody had run this section of river since the British attempt in 1968. On the first day, when they capsized and nearly lost several men to waterfalls and rapids, six of the nine members (including Chris Bonington) quit, saying it was just too dangerous. A smaller reconstituted team returned and ran some, but not all, of the remaining rapids in this stretch, so it remained largely a mystery. Still, it just might offer what we needed for the whitewater sequences in the IMAX® Theatre film.

Too soon we passed over Lake Tana, and I tried to crane my neck and look back at this bravura section of the Blue Nile.

Indeed, this little-known twenty-mile section of the river, from its effluence at Lake Tana to the mighty Tissisat Falls, might be the solution for the wild river scenes I was to direct. But it needed to be surveyed from the river. Jordi and others were scheduled to move on to Sudan and Egypt the next day for more scouting, but I had an idea. With my Iridium sat-phone, I called my friend Pasquale Scaturro. Pasquale was leading a climb on Kilimanjaro when I reached him near the summit. I asked if he could come to Addis Ababa, grab a whitewater raft and gear, and meet me on the shores of Lake Tana in two days' time. He raced down the mountain, flew to Ethiopia, stuffed a raft in a Land

Cruiser, and drove nine hours to Bahir Dar, where he appeared at my hotel at 8:00 P.M.

"Let's make the first descent of the upper Blue Nile," I said. And he high-fived me.

In February of 1992, I had made a multimedia presentation on the great endangered rivers of the world at the Denver Museum of Natural History. After the show a tall, nut-brown, intense-looking man came up to me and extended a right hand missing parts of three fingers. I tried not to notice the gap in his grip, and stared into his eyes. He had a pioneer face—long, lean, and hollow—and a habit of flicking his eyes to the horizon as though searching for a distant mountain. He introduced himself as Pasquale Scaturro. I recognized his name as that of a private mountain and river guide who was active in the fight to save the Bio-Bio River in Chile, a spectacularly beautiful river I had run in the mid-'70s that was about to be drowned by a private dam. Pasquale had donated thousands of dollars to the Bío-Bío Action Committee, and its successor organization, River Conservation International, headed by environmental attorney Steve Gates. In fact, Steve had asked me to join the board as a director, and I had accepted. Pasquale mentioned that he was a founding director, so our six degrees of separation went to one.

We went out for pizza at a local dive, and over a beer Pasquale told me about some of his climbing and rafting expeditions.

"Did you lose your fingers on expedition?" I wondered aloud.

"No, I was in Flagstaff after discharge from the Air Force, and I was building a house since I couldn't afford to buy one."

He also mentioned that it was in Flagstaff that he had met Gary Mercado, who had been with me in Ethiopia in the '70s, and who had told Pasquale wild tales of our adventures there. After that, he'd always wanted to do a river expedition with me.

After a slug of beer and a moment to switch gears, I asked Pasquale what he did when not adventuring. He said that by trade he was a geophysicist, and that he had gone to Ethiopia in 1991 as field manager of a geophysical operation in the Ogaden Desert for Maxus Energy. He also said he was going back to Ethiopia in a few weeks. After his survey work, he was planning to organize a private expedition down the Omo River, another river I had pioneered in the early '70s. Now, with Pasquale telling me he was off to Ethiopia, I told him about the Tekeze, one of the great unrun rivers in Africa, which spilled through the continent's deepest gorge. It was a river I was thinking of attempting. I told him that as far as I could tell, no explorer had ever done more than cross the grand canyons of the Tekeze, and there was no record of any attempt at navigation. I asked him if he might be able to drive up to the Tekeze and take a look. He scrutinized me with a mesmeric gaze.

"I'm in. If I can scout that river, I will. And I want to be there when you run it."

And indeed, Pasquale did the scout, and he joined me on the Tekeze expedition in 1996, and we became good friends in the process. Afterward we began a series of adventures together all over the world, from Namibia to New Guinea to Zambia.

In 2003, when Greg MacGillivray asked for recommendations for an expedition leader to appear in the IMAX® Theatre film, I nominated Pasquale. Greg had heard of Pasquale during the making of *Everest* in 1996, as Pasquale had been on the mountain and assisted Rob Hall in the rescue of a teammate. Greg seemed open to the idea of recruiting Pasquale as expedition leader, but Jordi, the chief financier of the production, had never heard of him. I knew that this ruthlessly ambitious project would require extreme climbing, rafting, and expedition-leadership skills; that it needed somebody world-class to organize and run it. Friendship aside, I felt there was nobody better qualified than Pasquale. He had worked and lived in Ethiopia, spoke Amharic, knew the culture, and had rafted the Omo, Awash, and Tekeze rivers there. Could there be anyone on the planet better suited for the job?

Nonetheless, Jordi wanted to see how Pasquale would do on-camera, and he requested that Pasquale submit an "audition tape." I asked our mutual friend Paul Maritz if he would like to help. So, Paul, a wizard at multimedia, directed, shot, and edited a piece on Pasquale kayaking Seattle's Lake Washington, landing at Paul's lawn, and strutting up to the camera to introduce himself. The video was terrific, but still Jordi did not want to commit.

So, it was fortuitous that Pasquale had been climbing Kilimanjaro during our scout, and that he was available at a moment's notice to hop on a flight and meet me in the middle of Ethiopia. That night, we had dinner with Jordi at the Lake Tana Hotel, and they hit it off. Pasquale regaled Jordi with tales of adventure, and by night's end, Pasquale was officially hired to act as expedition leader for the *Mystery of the Nile* IMAX® Theatre film production.

Early next morning, Jordi left for the airport to continue the scout in Khartoum. Pasquale and I piled into the Land Cruiser and headed ten minutes down the road to where the Blue Nile flows from Lake Tana, the third-largest lake in Africa. We picked up three hitchhikers as well, two non-English-speaking Kalashnikov-wielding local policemen, Andar Gatchew Adungna and Yassab Teffera, dressed in fatigues and black army boots, and a local tour guide, Girma Tsedalu. Local boys helped us rig, and by 9:30 we were in the grips of the turbid Blue Nile. Where the British, the only ones antecedent to us, had had a team of seventy, we were five men in a single boat. Trying to blot out dreadful memories of this river, I pulled the oars downstream, past the papyrus and reeds, swishing into a Jurassic forest.

At first there was nothing special about the descent. We passed Emperor Haile Selassie's now-abandoned summer palace, an aborted birders' hotel, a tannery, and some tin-roofed shanties. At one early point I asked if there were crocs or hippos on this section of the Blue Nile, and our local hosts shook their heads no. But within minutes of their pronouncement, we rounded a bend and purled into a bloat of snorting hippos.

"You know how to keep hippos away from the raft?" Pasquale asked, looking at our hosts while raising his paddle high in the air. He then slapped its blade on the water, making a thunderclap that echoed across the river.

But Yassab smiled and shook his head. He then slapped his Kalashnikov . . . and grinned.

When we were about an hour downstream, the river squeezed around a bend and dropped into a Grand Canyon–sized rapid. We named it Jordi Falls and scouted it for a time. Then I volunteered to row the first rapid on the upper Blue Nile, the first time it had been run since the British attempt. We told the policemen to walk around, as they had little whitewater experience and would be in danger if they rode in the boat.

The rapid was bigger and stronger than I expected, and it spun the raft around, doused us, and bounced us over rocks. But we slid into the eddy at the bottom, high with the success. This could be a rapid to film for the IMAX® Theatre screen.

While still giddy with the moment, we drifted around the corner, and I saw a piece of driftwood slide toward us.

"That wouldn't be a croc?" I asked out loud. Everyone moved to the center of the boat. It was.

And we saw a feast of birds . . . weavers, kingfishers, darters, cranes, herons. And vervet monkeys, anubis baboons. What a treat. My trepidations about a return washed away.

Then we saw a thin line of whitewater stretch across the river. It didn't look big, so we started to row toward it, thinking we might make an easy run. But Pasquale said, "I think I see smoke." Just beyond the ripples was a spindrift wafting like woodsmoke. Only waterfalls and giant rapids provoke enough water to fly so visibly upward. So, we quickly pulled over. We'd reached a twenty-five-foot waterfall that the locals called Arafame; if we had continued, we would have been hurled to oblivion.

This being Ethiopia, which has a population of seventy million in an area about a third larger than Texas, the portage was not a problem. Within minutes, thirty locals had assembled to see the show, and we hired half to help carry our raft and gear around. A few minutes later, we were again caroming down the Blue Nile. The pattern was soon set. There would be a pooled section of quiet water, then a quick tumble over a waterfall or major rapid. We rafted until 5:00 P.M.; as we were just twelve degrees north of the equator, the sun set promptly at 6:00 P.M. We had hoped to make it all the way to the falls, about twenty miles as the crow flies, but when I checked the GPS, I found that we had traveled just eight miles—and what a wild eight miles they'd been.

We pulled over to the western bank and hired a village elder to watch the raft. Our police escorts penned a document on a page of my pocket notebook that described the duties of the guard and the fee we would pay him. The guard could not read or write, so one officer took my ballpoint pen and rubbed its tip over the guard's thumb until it was blue with ink. Then he held the thumb to the document and rolled it back and forth to create a smeared print on the notebook paper. This was the contract.

We hiked a half-mile to the road, flagged down a country bus, and trundled back to the hotel for a hot shower, a cold beer, and a steak. Next morning we hiked back to the raft, pushed off, and once more went rolling down the upper Blue Nile. Again we came to waterfalls and big rapids, and at one huge drop, rather than take the main plunge, I urged that we negotiate a small channel to the far right. This required getting out of the boat and pulling it over a series of shoals. Soon we found ourselves in a jungled canal that pinched the sides of the raft as we proceeded. Vines and thorny branches hung in the way, and finally we could float no farther. With a GPS reading we located our position on the map, and saw we had taken a tiny channel that veered several hundred yards from the main river, with swampland separating us. So we stopped there, having made twelve miles in two days, half the distance to the falls. In this stretch we had found more than enough accessible whitewater to make this look great on the IMAX® Theatre screen. Now I had to check out Tissisat Falls, rightfully a centerpiece of the film.

By the time we made our way down to Tissisat, it was Sunday, and the falls were as I remembered, a plunging diadem of water slinging mist into my face. The scenes envisioned for the film included lowering rafts over the wall of the falls, rappelling down its side, and sending over a "ghost boat," an unmanned, unrigged raft, as the British had done in 1968. The falls were full enough to make this all happen, but I was curious as to why, a few days before, the falls had seemed to be a fraction of this Sunday's volume. Yohannes Assefa, local outfitter for the project and emollient extraordinaire, did some digging around. He discovered that a new, $63 million, 450-megawatt power-generating station, the Tis Abay II Hydroelectric Project, was just gearing up, diverting water on weekdays but not yet on Sundays and holidays, when there was less demand for the power.

More than 90 percent of energy consumed in Ethiopia is derived from biomass fuels, and it is almost entirely used for cooking. The use of these fuels has resulted in massive deforestation and soil erosion. Only 4 percent of the population has access to electricity. Yet Ethiopia, which sits atop a mile-and-a-half-high plateau, has huge rivers and canyons hurtling off all sides, offering vast hydropower potential. So I would ordinarily have greeted the idea of this particular project with enthusiasm, as an environmental boon. But there was no reason to compromise the great Tissisat Falls, one of the great natural wonders of the world, when an hour's flight in any direction would reveal scores of deep-gorge alternatives.

I still didn't quite believe it. When we returned to the U.S. for the break between scouting and shooting, I Googled the Web and searched Factiva to see if there were any further explanations. But I could find nothing . . . just a slew of travel companies offering tours to see the singularly splendid falls in the coming weeks, the traditional high season.

Fearing the worst, though, I scheduled the falls scenes on a Sunday for when we returned a month later.

Not surprisingly, once we dropped into Ethiopia in mid-November, the film was plagued with a panoply of third-world tribulations. Shooting was delayed for several critical days when Ethiopian customs demanded an emperor's ransom in local currency as a deposit (currency that could not be reexchanged for U.S. dollars or any other recognized coinage). There were repeated troubles with the helicopter, including a failed engine that had to be replaced with one that had to be flown in from Paris. Even the SpaceCam, a high-tech aerial camera, broke down, and a part and technician had to be flown in from Los Angeles. Then there were paid permits that were useless, prices that rose exorbitantly at every turn, porter riots, and the usual organizational chaos common in countries on the fringes of the "civilized" world.

For the next few weeks, we shot the principals of the film in various locations near and around Bahir Dar. The feature included Saskia Lange, a Spanish journalist; Mohammed Megahed, an Egyptian hydrologist; Myriam Seco, an archeologist based in Cairo; photographer Michel L'Huillier; kayaker/cameraman Gordon Brown; and Pasquale. Mike Speaks led a team of whitewater experts and raft wranglers who helped with the scenes I was directing.

We spent the time filming the oversized rapids above the falls as planned, and I got a great kick out of my directorial debut, yelling "Roll sound. Roll camera. Action, and . . . Cut!" as each scene played out. I was guided by the great cinematographer Brad Ohlund, who in the last thirty years has probably lensed more IMAX® Theatre films than anyone else.

At one point I watched from the boat behind as Pasquale made a rough run through a Class V rapid and was pitched into a violent hydraulic—a wide, recirculating step of water—and for an instant I feared a repeat of the accident that had taken my friend so many years ago on this river. But Pasquale was pulled back into the raft, and though his leg was punctured and bloodied, he dismissed the accident as just a scrape. At another point, our team was arrested and the boats confiscated as we floated down a four-hundred-yard section of the river just below the lake where the Blue Nile has yet another recent diversion, a low-height weir that allows regulation of the water flow from Lake Tana. A few hours after appealing to the local police commissioner, everyone and everything was released, but again we had stumbled into a little-known scheme that was altering the balance of nature.

We also filmed wildlife, cultural and camp scenes around Lake Tana, and the troglodyte churches of Lalibela, a true ancient wonder of the world.

Lalibela, namesake of an Abyssinian prince, is built on the banks of the Jordan River, a source stream that ultimately flows into the Nile. As legend goes, around A.D. 1200, when Lalibela was born to a royal family, a swarm of bees hung over his cradle, a prophecy of future greatness and wealth. Sometime later in his life, his brother, Harby, became jealous of this augury and attempted fratricide by poisoning. But a deacon in Lalibela's service first sipped the tainted liquid and died immediately. Overcome with grief, Lalibela seized the goblet and swallowed the rest of the brew. But instead of dying, he drifted into a deep three-day sleep filled with celestial visions. When he awoke, he found he was cured of a chronic parasitic disease that had been troubling him. In addition, he remembered that in his slumber, angels had shown him magnificent churches that God commanded to be built. The next twenty-four years were spent creating the churches . . . the heavy lifting done by Lalibela's subjects, the carving—legend has it—done by angels.

Though lore claims angels as architects, history records that a Christian emperor of the Zagwe Dynasty built them. They were not built at all in the conventional sense, but instead were excavated and hewn below ground level out of the solid black volcanic basalt on which they still stand. In consequence, they seemed supernatural—not only in scale, but also in artistry and in innovation. They remain places of living worship eight hundred years after they received their first prayers.

Close examination was required before the full extent of the achievement could be appreciated. This was because considerable effort had been made to cloak their real natures: some lay almost completely concealed within deep trenches, while others hid in the open mouths of huge, quarried caves. Connecting them all was a bewildering labyrinth of tunnels and passageways with offset crypts, grottoes, baptismal fonts, and galleries—a cool, lichen-enshrouded subterranean world, shaded and damp, silent but for the faint echoes of the voices of priests and deacons as they went about their timeless business.

The most striking of the churches was Beta Ghiorghis (Church of Saint George). Standing more than forty feet high in the center of a deep pit, it had been hewn to resemble a cross. It was here, in this well of Christianity, that Jordi shot one of the most spectacular scenes of the IMAX® Theatre film, with priests in full vestments and multihued umbrellas swaying in a pious rhythm, blessing the sacred waters that run past the churches and feed the Nile.

In the third week of shooting, I decided to take a reconnoiter of Tissisat Falls, which I had not seen since the initial scout the month previous. I was shocked beyond shock. It was the Sunday a week before the scheduled shoot when I walked up the familiar path to the palisade overlook of the falls and saw almost nothing there. A thin ribbon of water scraped down the cheek of the dark cliff that once was a breathtaking spectacle, and an icon for Ethiopia. The country's paper currency, the one-birr note, proudly showcases the falls in spate; posters of the falls plaster offices and restaurants around the country. Yet the falls were gone, 90 percent diverted into this new power scheme built by Chinese and Serbian contractors. The river was redeposited a few hundred yards downstream after pouring through penstocks and turbines, but it had left the great falls bald and sallow. This seemed a crime against nature, against aesthetic sensibilities, even against local economies.

The village women and children who sold calabashes, weavings, sodas, trinkets, and walking sticks to tourists complained to me how their livelihood was suffering. Tana fishermen carped that the lake was being drained to keep diversion flows steady, and lower lake levels were exposing fish hatcheries, reducing the fish population. Back at the hotel, I kept running into angry Western tourists who had spent hundreds of dollars and sometimes hours of flying to witness Tissisat Falls at their best and now felt snookered. Tourism, which had dropped to a trickle under the radical socialist regime of Mengistu Haile Mariam in the '80s, had been coming back under the new administration of Meles Zenawi, and Tissisat Falls had been a top draw—but no more.

Before constructing the diversion dam, the Ethiopian government had hired consulting firms from France and the United Kingdom for a feasibility study. The study concluded that, unlike other hydropower projects with big dams, the Tis Abay II Hydroelectric Project would have "negligible impact on the environment, and that it would be economically very attractive for investment." Somehow, though, the project sailed to completion without the cognizance of any international environmental watchdog group, any journalists, or even a blogger. This was the first season in which the diversion project had been put into full effect, and the first season in which tourists were discovering that what they had come to see had vanished, gone with man-made legerdemain.

And it created a dilemma for the filmmakers. The conceit of the film was largely the historical aspects of the water that flowed to and fed Egypt, though it also included the spectacular falls and scenes of modern adventurers re-creating some of what the British expedition had done. The film could change its concept and take an environmental stance, exposing the stealing of the falls by shortsighted, power-hungry bureaucrats. But the falls were just plain ugly in their current state—not a large-screen moment. So, we devised another solution. We called the vice minister of water resources and explained our film and its purpose. And after much negotiating he agreed to close the dam for us for four hours, to enable us to film the falls in full.

At last, on the given day, we gathered at the falls and watched it rise to its previous level. It was as breathtaking as it had ever been. We filmed our scenes of rappelling, roping boats over, and pitching an empty raft down the plunge. It was all fantastic, but somehow tinged with melancholy, for we knew it was not quite real. Some lucky tourists wandered over to the viewpoints and were delighted, though they didn't realize they were beholding a scene that would be not available in a few hours' time.

A few days later, we wrapped the Ethiopian portion of the film, and I boarded an Ethiopian Airlines flight back to Addis Ababa, the capital, where I would connect with an international flight home. As we took off, the pilot circled over the falls, as he had done for years to show off his country's greatest natural asset to the tourists on board. But as he dipped his wings, and I looked straight down to where the Nile makes its greatest plunge, there was nothing there. Just a cold, gloomy, empty cliff.

The second chapter of the Book of Genesis refers to the rivers that flow through the Garden of Eden: "And the name of the second river is Ghion; the same is it that compasseth the whole land of Ethiopia." The Blue Nile, sweeping out from Lake Tana in a wide loop, does indeed encompass the ancient land of Ethiopia. But today, the fountain of this paradise is turned off, and the garden of grasses, reeds, leaves, and lush trees and plants, once showered with a perpetual spray from the falls, are now brown and dry, Edenic no more.

Pasquale and the rest of the crew went on to Egypt, where they would film the quintessential scenes near Abu Simbel, the Valley of the Kings, the Pyramids of Giza, and the Sphinx. But after the first-unit filming was done in late December, Pasquale was determined to return to Ethiopia and make the first full descent of the Blue Nile, from source to sea. It was a crazy idea, and many tried to talk him out of it. I worried for his safety, and desperately did not want to lose yet another close friend to the river. Gordon Brown was the only other crew member who shared Pasquale's vision, and he agreed to join this outlandish endeavor, one that had bitten back explorers for centuries.

Still, if anyone was up to the task, I felt it was Pasquale. He agreed to call me on the sat-phone regularly with his progress, to send e-mail updates, and to keep a journal. This, then, is the story of how the Mystery of the Nile was unlocked by a modest rafting expedition, as told to me by the leader of the affair, my friend Pasquale Scaturro.

CHAPTER FIVE

It was said of Alexander the Great that the first question he asked when he came to Jupiter Ammon was where the Nile had its rise, and we know he sent discoverers throughout Ethiopia without being able to find out this source.
TELLEZ, *THE TRAVELS OF THE JESUITS OF ETHIOPIA*, 1710

It is not given to us mortals to see the Nile feeble and at its Source.
CHARLES-LOUIS DE SECONDAT, BARON DE MONTESQUIEU, 1734

It was well after dark, a couple of days into the expedition, when Pasquale and his small team shambled into the village of Asakwa Bur. Exhausted from a full day's trek, they were also soaked to the bone from the hard afternoon rain. Kurt's head was spinning; Gordon's back hurt. The blisters on Pasquale's feet were bleeding. "Feel like the walking-dead—every bone in my body hurts," Pasquale wrote in his journal. And they were all famished, having only munched on a few small bananas in the morning and some stalks of sugarcane en route. The terrain for the last several hours had been devoid of trees, all slashed and burned long ago for charcoal or cooking fuel. Perhaps, Pasquale thought, they could buy some firewood in the village.

But the village was vacant. It seemed a nonplace, like a scene from *The Twilight Zone*, a stop encountered on the way to somewhere else, better measured in time than in acreage. Pasquale wandered about the *tukuls*—huts made of mud and straw—and saw embers of fires, laundry set out to dry, goats tethered, and straw mats with clay pottery spread about. He called out in the night, but no voices returned. As they had traveled down the stream called the Gilgel Abay they had watched as children and women ran away, while men held their herding sticks in aggressive stances. They had been told they were the first Westerners along this route, and that people were simply frightened of them. Pasquale figured the villagers had been warned of their arrival and gone into hiding.

But then he paused in front of a dung house at the edge of the village. Inside he spied a woman wrapped in white with two small children asleep on her lap. The glow of a single candle lit her face, a countenance with the delicate roundness of a silver bowl. Pasquale was transfixed as she stared in seeming contentment at the ceiling. So different from her counterparts in the West, Pasquale thought. No television, no telephone, no Internet, no radio, no books or newspapers or magazines . . . no external stimulation. And it was just two nights before Christmas Eve, and the whole of the Western world was in a frenzy of flashing lights, bells and carols, besotted celebrations, competitive purchasing, ribbons and wrappings, pretenses of peace, and admissions of anxiety. This woman Pasquale spied seemed embraced in a moment of bliss and tranquillity, in a simple setting with no distractions, no illusions. That, Pasquale thought, was what he sought.

The day after the principal photography work had wrapped in Egypt, everyone had been spent and ready to head home. Tired of the heat, of the food, of people with their hands out—from bureaucrats to police to street waifs—most of the crew boarded flights to the northwest, across the Mediterranean to Europe.

Pasquale's bandaged lower left leg was still festering from the infection he'd gotten upstream after an oarlock gouged him as he was pitched out in Horseshoe Falls. The operations he'd had in Aswan and Cairo had drained the pus, but the wound still leaked, and it throbbed when he walked. The bags under his eyes were big enough for a two-week trip to

Paris. The shoot had already lasted longer than most expeditions, yet Pasquale, Gordon Brown, and Mike Speaks headed southeast on an Air Memphis flight back to Addis Ababa. Now the expedition would begin.

Despite the exhaustion, there was something liberating about leaving the chaos of the film behind, like shedding a heavy skin. Instead of forty or more crew members, and a number of headstrong chiefs, it would now be just Pasquale, Gordon, and a few others making their way down the river, Huck Finns in Africa, hoping to return to a more primitive state of grace.

Pasquale desperately wanted Mike Speaks to join him for the descent, especially the Northern Gorge, the deadliest section, which Speaks had navigated twice before. One of the times, he'd barely survived. But Speaks was adamant . . . he had returned to the Blue Nile against his better judgment to work on the film, and he had no desire to join this part of the expedition. Instead, Speaks offered to help with the logistics of launching the expedition before he flew home for Christmas.

Pasquale needed bodies for the expedition, especially someone to row the second raft. So, in late November, he'd sent out thirty-five e-mails inviting friends and family to join the expedition. Only two responded positively. Kurt Hoppe had little boating experience, but he was an old friend and trusted partner with whom Pasquale had worked on a geophysical project in the former Soviet republics of Azerbaijan and Georgia. He and Pasquale rode the Triple Bypass—a 110-mile road bike ride over three high Colorado passes—each summer. At fifty-four, Kurt had a lean, supple body, though his taste in shirts represented a threat to the ozone layer. Mike Prosser, at fifty, was pale and bulky, with a Hemingwayesque white beard. He owned a rafting-supply business, and Pasquale assumed he was an experienced boater who could pilot an inflatable boat in extreme whitewater.

In Addis Ababa, Pasquale met up with Kurt Hoppe and Mike Prosser at the musty, threadbare Ghion Hotel, named for the river in the Garden of Eden. It was once the grandest hotel on the Horn of Africa, but after a terrorist bomb reduced much of it to rubble in 1996, it never fully recovered. It now served as one of the discount haunts for backpackers, whores, and itinerants.

Pasquale was excited to see Kurt and Mike when he sat down for a beer at the Ghion, and he laid out his plans. He intended to begin at the source at Sakala and then trek and kayak down the Gilgel Abay to Lake Tana over the next week. Then they would launch their rafts at the outflow of Lake Tana at Bahir Dar.

But Kurt and Mike weren't pleased with Pasquale's plan. They'd traveled halfway round the world and had been waiting five days in Addis Ababa. They were antsy to get on the river. "What's the rush?" Pasquale asked. "We're not heading down the Arkansas River . . . we're doing the *Nile!*"

"We're short on time," Mike proffered. "We have thirty-day visas. Let's just start where the river comes out of Lake Tana . . . most people consider that the source of the Blue Nile."

"He's right," Kurt said. "The river from Sakala isn't called the Blue Nile; it's called Gilgel Abay, Little Blue Nile. The river isn't called *the* Blue Nile until it leaves Tana. So Lake Tana is the beginning of the Blue Nile."

Pasquale felt besieged. The director of the film hadn't cared from which source he started. Gordon Brown was ambivalent; either beginning worked for him.

If you go to Google and type in "Source of the Blue Nile," virtually all of the one hundred thousand entries cite Lake Tana as the ultimate effluence. In fact, the sources of great rivers are almost always cited as lakes or bogs with central sections of nonmoving waters, at least by engineers: Lake Victoria for the White Nile; the Benguela Swamps for the Congo; Lake Itasca for the Mississippi—though all have active feeder streams.

Explorers, on the other hand, usually posit the true source of a river as the farthest point of issuing water from the mouth. In this rubric, the Gilgel Abay, which feeds into Lake Tana, would be the bona fide fountain of the Nile.

Pedro Paez, James Bruce, and Major R. E. Cheesman all similarly cited Sakala as the true source.

Pasquale endorsed the explorers' version, and as such his geographical desiderata was to touch the first waters at Sakala. He had set out to be the first to run the whole of the Blue Nile, and he did not want someone to question whether he had started at the true source—or worse, have someone in his wake start farther upstream and steal his thunder. So, he was resolute to start at the indisputable beginnings, and to make a descent that was as linear and pure as possible, all the way to the sea. Nothing—not even a twenty-year friendship now at risk—was going to stop him from tagging the ultimate font of the Blue Nile.

Something in Pasquale's own beginnings, his own source, had shaped him into someone who would go farther than anyone else, who would risk friendship, love, health, and sanity for a mission he believed in. He had complete faith in his own abilities, in the sanctity of his quest. Even though nobody in more than 2,000 years of recorded history had ever negotiated the whole of the Blue Nile, he felt he could do it. He'd grown up knowing he could do what others could not.

Pasquale was born in Hollywood, California, on September 23, 1953, to a German-English mother and a Sicilian father who couldn't speak English. His first home was a tiny affair on Sunset Boulevard, right next to the film studios. For his first eight years, he rarely saw grass or trees, just concrete and pavement and inner-city buildings. He was the second of five brothers, all first-named Vincent, after their father, but with a Sicilian second name; Pasquale's legal name is Vincent Pasquale Scaturro.

His father, Vincent Scaturro, was a chef and owned a small Italian restaurant. His mother, Audrey Carol Bolton Scaturro, was a chanteuse in the style of Jo Stafford, but she retired to raise the sons. Pasquale's father was Catholic, and his mother was Christian Scientist, and they fought like Kilkenny cats all the time. More than once Pasquale watched as the police came to arrest his father for acts of domestic violence. Once his mother tried to run over his father with the car. It was a volatile, passionate household with a high-decibel-level din.

When Pasquale was eight years old, he had a teacher who saw potential and somehow secured funding for him to attend a YMCA summer camp up by Big Bear, California. It was the first time he'd slept outdoors, his first campfire, his first outdoor cooking, and his first time paddling a boat. He loved it. He was, he believed, a son of Nature.

One day, some of the instructors decided to climb San Gorgonio Mountain, the 11,502-foot peak in the San Bernardino National Forest. Pasquale asked if he could join, and they took him, along with five other campers. As they made the ascent, the other kids dropped out early, leaving Pasquale and the instructors. Then one by one the instructors started to turn back, some from fatigue, some suffering from the altitude. Pasquale kept climbing, and toward the end he was crying because he was so tired. But the last instructor urged him to hang in there, and together they summited. As they descended, Pasquale realized he was different from the other boys. He was stronger, and the altitude didn't bother him. And he had a drive to continue when others gave up.

Back at camp, the instructors gave Pasquale a plaque commemorating the climb, which he keeps today on his office wall.

When Pasquale was eleven, his mom started to hear voices and have hallucinations. She would become withdrawn, then start to scream uncontrollably, then plummet into deep depression. She was diagnosed with schizophrenia. Pasquale's dad had moved the boys and their mother to Thousand Oaks, about an hour north of Hollywood, while he stayed in Hollywood attending to the restaurant, visiting perhaps once a fortnight. Their mother became so ill that she was hospitalized, and the boys soon learned to take care of themselves, getting dressed, making their way to school, preparing their own meals. Eventually, she was admitted to Camarillo State Hospital for an indefinite stay, and the brothers were entirely on their own. Pasquale rose to the occasion and became the leader of the pack, helping his siblings in every way he could. While his brothers struggled, Pasquale got into sports and excelled. He ran track and cross-country, and as a freshman in high school he won the two-mile event for Ventura County, breaking the school record.

At fourteen, Pasquale got his first job, as a busboy in a local Italian restaurant, working seven nights a week. Between shifts, though, he found time to read *Bury My Heart at Wounded Knee*. Pasquale related to the Native Americans who were slaughtered; they were the minority, the disadvantaged, the pariahs, and they suffered for it. Ever after, he held a heightened sensitivity for all disenfranchised and third-world peoples; he saw them first as fellow questers who, like himself, were just trying against circumstances to survive and prosper.

At Newbury Park High School, Pasquale fell for Jody Watkins, the homecoming queen. They married at eighteen. His father didn't bother to come to the wedding, but his mother, still on medication, attended. A year later, Jody became pregnant with their first child, Tim.

They moved to Texas, where Pasquale found work managing a string of gas stations. But he was not happy. Texas was too flat; this was not his destiny or desire. One day, as the Vietnam War still raged, he was driving down the highway and saw a billboard: SEE THE WORLD; JOIN THE AIR FORCE. The year before, he had drawn a high lottery number of 305 in the Vietnam draft, so he had not had to enlist. But something about the concept of leaving Texas to see the world resonated.

He drove to the recruitment office, declared that he wanted to be a pilot, and took the exams. He received perfect scores on two of the four written tests. The recruiters were excited, until one more test result came back. A uniformed man somberly told Pasquale, "We got a problem . . . you're color-blind. You're not going to fly." Instead, Pasquale ended up a squadron leader, where he learned how to manage people. He was shipped to England, leaving behind Jody, who was then in her third trimester. Jody would join her husband after the birth of their son. He was slotted into a weapons program, learning about napalm, machine guns, and explosives. His superiors, impressed with Pasquale's aptitude and abilities, let him take college courses at the University of Ipswich. He signed up for a geology course and was smitten.

When Pasquale finished his tour, he enrolled at the University of Arizona in Flagstaff, took more geology courses, and graduated with a dual degree in geology and geophysics. He and Jody had two more children, Sarah and Adam, and Pasquale was working two day jobs building houses and also cooking at an Italian restaurant at night. On weekends he coached his son's basketball team. One night, at about 11:00 P.M., he was tired and trying to finish up some work. He slid a board into his carbide-tipped table saw, and his hand slipped. The saw's whine dropped to a lower timbre, and suddenly blood and flesh were flying. He looked down and saw that three fingers on his right hand were gone. He picked up his fingers and was driven by a neighbor madly to the hospital. But the doctor said they were too mangled to save. Two days later he was back up on the roof pounding in shingles. And now, when strangers ask about his missing digits, he tells them about the crocodile that got away. "You think I suffered. You ought to see the crocodile."

In 1980, Pasquale landed a job as an exploration geophysicist at the Denver office of Amoco Oil and moved the brood to Lakewood, a Denver suburb. But in the coming years, he and Jody drifted apart, and a few years later they decided to divorce.

In 1985, Pasquale cofounded a geophysical company, Seismic Specialists, and as the president and chief geophysicist, he began to lead oil and gas expeditions to remote corners of the world, including Ethiopia. At the same time, he got involved in adventure as an avocation. His formative years had taught him independence, self-reliance, leadership, and a profound love of the outdoors. He had never worked as a professional guide for a commercial company, but he began to organize and run his own private climbs and river trips, and before long he was scaling the Himalayas and plummeting down the great wild rivers of the world.

Everything in his life was leading up to the Blue Nile; he was gradually accumulating the skills, knowledge, and desire to actually pull it off.

CHAPTER SIX

I stood in rapture. . . . It is easier to guess than to describe the situation on my mind at the moment, standing in that spot which had baffled the genius, industry and inquiry of both ancients and moderns, for the course of near three thousand years. Though a mere private Briton, I triumphed here in my own mind, over kings and their armies.

JAMES BRUCE OF KINNAIRD

On Sunday, December 21, Pasquale and the gang drove the long, bumpy route up to the high plateau that cradles Sakala. The road was a dirt affair created by Haile Selassie in the '60s to reach the sacred springs, and it was outstanding in the number and depth of its ruts. For someone who has spent much of his life embracing discomfort for extended periods of time—such as waiting weeks in cramped tents at various high-altitude base camps for weather to clear—Pasquale has a fuse that often burns fast and hot. The hired driver for the Land Cruiser was slow and sloppy, so at the first bio-break Pasquale wrested the wheel away and from there on they sped down the road, flying over the furrows and potholes.

At the village of Tillili they stopped to buy beer and supplies. Tillili was a typical dirt-poor Ethiopian road village of tin-roofed shops, dismembered vehicles, and children who had grown up learning to beg from passersby, mostly truck drivers. As Pasquale and his team stopped, a score of dirty urchins bore in, hawking peanuts and baked maize, hair combs and bananas, truck-tire sandals, cooking pots, and packets of seed. Others were just pleading for handouts. They pressed so hard that it was difficult to move, or to speak above the clatter.

Late in the day they arrived at the area known as Ghion. To the east were the jade flanks of the Amadamit range, rising to 11,000 feet, and beyond that, the massif of 13,290-foot Mount Choke. To the north were a fantastic set of bare lava cores of extinct volcanoes that stepped off into the distance. To the west, just a mile away, was a blunt peak called Gishe. It was from here that the first waters seeped out to become the Blue Nile. To the south, the Blue Nile crashed in a curling forelock through an undulating landscape.

Arriving just after dusk, the four men—Pasquale, Gordon, Mike, and Kurt—staked out a campsite in a fold above the sacred birthplace of the river, a flat spot in a meadow of short grass. Pasquale's altimeter read 9,899 feet. Not many *ferengis* (foreigners) had ever made it to this outpost, and thus the hospitality was warmer and more subdued than it had been en route. Several families, including a couple dozen children, gathered wood in the leaden evening light and quietly went about building a big fire for Pasquale and his band, asking nothing in return.

It had been a long day, so everyone turned in early. But in the middle of the night Pasquale awoke, and he witnessed a sight he recorded in his spidery scrawl:

JOURNAL DAY 1

There are two very small girls sleeping on the ground next to the campfire. Apparently they were told to stay with us and keep the fire burning all night so we wouldn't get cold. Can you imagine leaving two of your young daughters to stay with strangers to keep a fire burning? What innocence and politeness.

The next day, Monday, December 22, Pasquale and his team were eager to get going, so they each grabbed a banana and quaffed some coffee for a quick breakfast—except Mike, whose stomach had been acting up a bit. He hadn't eaten in three days.

They walked a half-mile to the village to hire some porters for the trek from the source to Lake Tana. While there, they also visited the seventeenth-century Christian churches of St. Michael and Abuna Zera Baruk and met the hoary high priest of the churches, Mergeta (Holy Instructor) Berhane Tsegaye. He demanded a payment of one thousand birr to visit the springs, which were, he asserted, under the auspices of the church. Pasquale countered with an offer of one hundred birr. But Mergeta, spreading his vestments, shook his head no. Pasquale offered two hundred birr, but Mergeta shook his head again and said, "You know, the Trinity was three." Pasquale understood the "prophet" motive, and he offered three hundred birr, which the priest accepted. "I am in charge here, and you will have no problem now with entering the springs."

Confident that they now had full permissions, they set off through the sedges, up a thin line of water grass and rushes toward the fountainhead. The springs emerged from a reedy marsh bound by a rock-and-wood fence and funneled through a rusted half-inch-in-diameter metal pipe into a little stone house. From there, it trickled into a baptismal pool. White-and-green-robed pilgrims—here to find healings or blessings or prosperity—milled about waiting for the midday ablutions.

As Pasquale ducked to enter through the low wooden door, he could hear the water spanking about in the pool inside. But then he heard another sound, a low, gravelly sound: *"Yellum! Yellum!"* (No! No!) A man in a ragged uniform, wielding a Bible as a weapon, was yelling as he ran toward the Americans. He pushed Pasquale aside and demanded a payment to let them enter.

"But we already paid the high priest," Pasquale protested.

"Do you have proof?"

Pasquale was tired of arguing, so he peeled off another two hundred birr, and this time he asked for a receipt. But then, before he stooped to enter again, the guard grabbed his arm and asked if he was pure.

"Sure, I'm pure," was Pasquale's rejoinder. "What exactly does pure mean?"

"Have you eaten anything today?"

"Well, a banana for breakfast."

"Then you are not pure. You may not enter."

"Gimme a break!"

"If you touch the *tabal,* the sacred water, and you are not pure, you will die."

"I didn't eat this morning," Mike Prosser piped up. "I haven't eaten in days."

The caretaker let Mike pass. Pasquale handed Mike a yellow Nalgene bottle and asked him to fill it with the tabal. Mike stooped to enter, bottled the bright water like a genie, splashed some droplets on his head, returned to the daylight, and handed Pasquale the full bottle. Pasquale wrapped it shut with duct tape to make certain it wouldn't spill, and to ensure that nobody drank it by mistake. With a pen, he wrote on the silver tape, "Holy water from the springs of Gish Abay," and tucked it into his backpack. He hoped to carry the sacred source water the length of the Nile to Egypt and the Mediterranean.

As Pasquale shouldered his pack, he straddled the stream that seemed impatient to be gone, restless for the journey. "Let's go!" he called. But Mike Prosser announced that he would not be joining the trek down the river. "What do you mean?" Pasquale asked, visibly disappointed.

"I can't walk that far," Mike said, and climbed into the Land Cruiser. He told them he'd meet them at the south end of Lake Tana, where the raft portion of the trip could begin.

Meanwhile, Gordon was grappling with his own pack, which was stuffed with a camera, personal effects, hammock, water filter, a pot set, books, and more. It weighed eighty pounds. Pasquale suggested that Gordon use porters to carry such a heavy load, but Gordon huffed,

"Nobody carries my shit but me," and buckled his chest straps while leaning so far forward he almost tipped over. Pasquale paused and wondered for a moment about Gordon's judgment. It just didn't make sense to try to carry that much weight so soon, and so far, on a major expedition. Pasquale couldn't do it, and he was in great shape, though years older. But perhaps Gordon was even stronger than he appeared.

At 10:23 A.M., Pasquale, Gordon, and Kurt took their trek-commencing steps along the first shallow cut into the earth, which cradled a brook that bled green about its edges. After months of planning, preparing, and production, this was officially Day One of their expedition. It was hard to fathom that the water from this chipper rivulet had carved one of the deepest canyons in the world not far downstream, and that it was responsible for life and civilization in Egypt, so far away. They first hiked in a northeasterly direction, then west, along the course of the snaking stream, leaping over the cressed headwaters every few yards. They traversed a valley of yellow daisies that was hemmed by verdant mountains and swept with willows and hardwoods. Dusky lyre-horned cattle lingered by the water; women in white dresses washed clothing. Nothing, it seemed, had changed since the late eighteenth century, when James Bruce had walked this vale.

About a mile downstream, Gordon dropped his pack with a thud. It was too heavy, even for someone with the back of a bull. They hired two more porters, divvied up his gear, and continued the trek.

Late in the day a heavy rain began to fall, and they poked their heads into a circular wattle-and-daub hut with a high, beehive-shaped roof. Inside were four massive wooden pillars supporting the dark thatch above. Across the back was stretched a partition of sackcloth, over which, from time to time, a shy child peeped. Wooden stools, gourds, and large clay dishes lay scattered about. A woman squatted by a stone hearth, making *buna* (coffee) over a flat-cake dung fire. They were waved in, and they sat on the hard mud floor.

They rinsed their hands ceremonially as the woman poured water over them into a bowl. It was impossible not to notice her forehead and cheeks, upon which were tattoos of Coptic crosses. She reached into a crude cupboard and produced several tiny cups, flower-patterned and handleless, which she then filled with fresh coffee. Pasquale raised his to his blistered lips. They were all thirsty. Kurt took a sip and spit it out immediately. The coffee was heavily salted, which, to Ethiopian palates, enhances the coffee flavor.

The head of the household was an enthusiastic soul named Taruna Falade, with a long oval face. Pasquale liked the man, and asked if Taruna might be their guide for the next few days. Taruna balked at the idea, calling it too dangerous and saying he would not accompany them for any price.

So, after the coffee break, and hearty thank-yous, they once again hit the trail. Their way was increasingly bare of vegetation, now just a few eucalyptus trees scattered about, the Australian gums imported in the 1920s as cheap fuel and construction material. But just a few minutes later, Taruna showed up with his leather overnight basket of *injera* (a fermented flatbread that is an Ethiopian staple), saying he had changed his mind and would help guide. He didn't want the hyenas to get his newfound friends.

They trekked until twilight, when the river ran phosphorescent. They began to comb the banks for firewood to build a bonfire that would keep the wildlife at bay, but they found none. They'd now passed into an almost completely deforested area. A century ago, about 40 percent of Ethiopia had been covered with trees; today it is 4 percent.

The plan was to hike a few more miles to find a campsite along the river. Pasquale asked Taruna how much farther, because it was rapidly becoming dark.

"About fifteen minutes," Taruna said.

Forty-five minutes later it was completely dark, a heavy night with no moon. The group had one headlamp among them. Soon they came upon a ten-foot-high rickety bridge, made from tree branches, crossing a stream that fed into the Gilgel Abay. It was dark, and the bridge was covered in mud and slippery. Kurt took a slip and almost fell into the raging river.

"This is crazy, Pasquale," he said. "The expedition hasn't even started yet. If one of us falls in, it's over."

Just beyond the village of Asakwa Bur, Pasquale called camp. It was still pouring rain. Kurt's hip was hurting, and everyone was beat. They'd made fourteen miles down the Nile. They hadn't found firewood, but damn the hyenas. Pasquale wrapped himself up in a tarp and fell into a deep sleep.

The next day, December 23, dawned, the light blurred and milky. They found enough kindling to boil tea, then continued downstream. The watercourse, six inches wide at its beginnings, was now twenty feet wide, and meandered so much that they tried to intersect the goosenecks by walking a straight path. At one point, Taruna started to lead them toward the southeast. After a few hours' walking, during which they hadn't seen the river, Pasquale pulled out his Garmin Etrex Vista GPS and checked the coordinates. It appeared they were going the wrong way. Pasquale asked Taruna what was going on. He replied that he was taking them on the shortest route to Bahir Dar, the city at the south end of Lake Tana.

Pasquale exploded. He wanted to follow the river, not go to Bahir Dar, he yelled to the dismayed guide. So, around they turned and retraced their steps. By the time they saw the river again, Pasquale's foot sores were again bleeding. Kurt was in pain, suffering in the heat, and barely lurching along. Taruna gave his umbrella to Kurt to ward off the sun.

At a small wooden bridge, the local militia stopped them and demanded papers of authorization to continue. Pasquale pulled out an old, creased red Ethiopian ID card he'd gotten thirteen years earlier, when he'd been working on an oil and gas project in-country. He flashed it to the guards along with fifty birr, flashed his nuclear grin, and they were waved past.

They were out of food, so at lunch, they plucked sugarcane and stumbled on down. Their goal was the Piccolo (Italian for "little") Abay Bridge, the first road bridge across the Blue Nile. There, Mike Speaks was supposed to rendezvous with two kayaks: Gordon's butter-colored eight-foot Eskimo Salto kayak, and an Aire inflatable kayak.

They trundled along, keeping the river on their left, but by dark they were still five miles short of the bridge, as the crow flies. Then they lost the river. An old cattle herder offered to guide them to the bridge for a fee, and Pasquale grudgingly paid the man—it seemed everyone was on the dole. By 10:00 P.M. they had reached the Jamma River, a major tributary coming in from the right. It ran pitch-black, and as they waded across, they stopped at what sounded like the wails of ghosts. They stood shivering on rocks in the middle of the river and watched as a herd of donkeys carrying burlap sacks of coffee crossed in front of them, braying through the darkness.

Near midnight, they reached the Piccolo Abay Bridge, and old reliable Speaks was waiting with a bonfire, cold beer, a pasta dinner, and the kayaks. They chowed down, and then Speaks headed to the Land Cruiser to return to Bahir Dar, and from there home. Since they had only two single kayaks, Kurt gladly hobbled over to the vehicle to hitch a ride to Bahir Dar as well, where they'd launch the rafts.

CHAPTER SEVEN

On Christmas Eve morning, Pasquale and Gordon pushed downstream in their thin boats. They ran some small rapids, dragging over shoals, etching the bottom of their crafts with the sharp, scoriaceous lava rocks. About two miles down, Gordon pulled over and announced, "We're not going any farther. I'm not going to wear out this kayak pushing it over rocks . . . it won't last the whole way."

"We can't separate," Pasquale answered from the river. "Get back in . . . The river will get bigger; lots of tributaries coming in." Reluctantly, Gordon slid back in, and sure enough, a few bends later the volume increased so that they were floating down something that approximated a real river, replete with significant rapids. In fact, they knew that in the first thirty-five miles the Gilgel Abay dropped 2,735 feet, or 78 feet per mile. By comparison, the Colorado through the Grand Canyon drops just twelve feet per mile.

One of their first significant challenges came that afternoon, when they came to a rapid that stepped down toward a funnel, disappearing between two boulders in a cloud of white spray. Pasquale scouted it and pronounced that only a madman would attempt such a drop, and Gordon promptly paddled in, making a clean run. After Gordon negotiated the Class V rapid, which they baptized Gordito Falls, he scrambled back upstream and helped Pasquale portage his inflatable. They were certain that nobody had ever boated this section of the Nile; it was too steep, sharp, and technical for any except the utterly fearless; for anyone except Gordon Brown.

That evening, they camped on a beautiful small island, while Pasquale attended to his blisters. Gordon prepared a Christmas Eve dinner from supplies Mike Speaks had brought them. They dined on Skippy Super Chunk peanut butter spread on dried biscuits; sardines; Mars bars; and bananas. After dinner, Gordon prepared tea and brought a steaming cup to Pasquale. As they sipped in silence, Pasquale pulled out his journal and began to scribble his thoughts.

JOURNAL DAY 3

On the river at last. Good to be with Gordo. Good teammate. Easy to get along with. Considerate.

Then as they were cleaning up, some children swam over to the island. Pasquale shooed them away: He wanted some peace for Christmas Eve. But then a young man swam over with a small axe on his shoulder. He had bandy legs and bare feet wide as dinner plates, crispy with calluses. Pasquale asked if he would chop some firewood, and the young man gathered a few pieces of driftwood and split them for the Americans. Pasquale handed the man a couple birr, and away he swam.

A short time later, the young man swam back to the island, this time carrying three eggs and a gourd of milk. Pasquale was incensed. It was Christmas Eve. He was sick, so sick, of being hustled all the time. All through Ethiopia, all through Egypt—for the past two months— everywhere he turned, someone was trying to sell him something, or beg, or somehow extract money from him. He was pissed, and he chased the young man away.

Then as Pasquale tucked into his bag, looked to the stars, and listened to the frogs chirping, he could not force sleep, but rather found himself wandering through the rooms of his conscience. Here they were far from townships and villages, far from roads, in a region so remote that they had been told nobody along this stretch had even seen white-skinned beings. So, perhaps the man had not been hustling, but offering a gift. Suddenly Pasquale felt really, really bad. For the first time on the trip he felt he had screwed up, had done the wrong thing. He was letting exhaustion and frustration color his relations with other people, and he had always prided himself on being someone who treated everyone with dignity and respect. It was, he thought, one of his worst Christmas Eves ever.

Before the dawn was whole, Pasquale rekindled the fire that had been built courtesy of the visitor the night before, and began to brew some coffee. Then, out of the mist, the young man reappeared. He stood hesitantly on the perimeter of the camp, but this time Pasquale waved him over with a smile. The young man again presented the three eggs and the cow milk, which Pasquale drank with delight . . . it was good, creamy, fresh milk. He cooked up the eggs and offered a cup of coffee to the caller. They exchanged pleasantries in Amharic, and then the young man got up to go. Pasquale gave him a hug and a handshake, and handed him one hundred birr, which he refused with a slight bow. Then the visitor vanished, never to be seen again.

It was, Pasquale thought, a very fine Christmas morning indeed.

It was a quiet Christmas morning as well. Without fanfare, they loaded their boats and started paddling. About two miles downstream, Pasquale heard the sound of a mosquito in his ear. Odd, he thought. The elevation here was too high for mosquitoes. Pasquale turned to swat, but the sound got closer. Then the vervet monkeys on the banks began to squawk and scatter, and around the bend appeared a single-engine helicopter. It hovered above them. Pasquale pulled his radio out of the dry bag and turned it on. "Pull over. Pull over," said a voice. "I've been sent to pick you guys up." Pasquale recognized Jack Tankard, the buoyant, unkempt aerial cinematographer from the main shoot.

"We don't want to be picked up," Pasquale yelled into the radio.

"You gotta be picked up. We gotta film pickup shots. Pull over."

Jack was a kindred spirit. He'd traveled the world shooting films, and at fifty-six his merry milk-blue eyes still lit up when discovering new places and shooting new sights. Pasquale respected him. So, he turned his boat to shore, and Gordon followed.

In a whirlwind of red dust, the helicopter landed, and Pasquale recognized the bird, a French-made A-Star with Kenyan registry. It disgorged Simon Everett, brother to actor Rupert Everett, and the pilot for the shoot. Pasquale bristled, knowing this meant bad news. In the first days of production, the turbine in Simon's helicopter had seized at start-up, and a new engine had had to be flown in from France via Nairobi and installed in Bahir Dar. The problem had set back the critical aerials schedule so much that they never got all the shots that had been storyboarded.

Simon yelled to Pasquale over the rotor noise, "I've been sent to pick you guys up. You need to abandon your gear and come with me. Give the boats to the natives."

"As I said, we don't want to be picked up," Pasquale barked back. "Second, we ain't abandoning shit. This gear is getting us down the Nile. We're not here to make a movie; the movie's done. And it's Christmas, for God's sake."

Simon's face clenched. But Jack intervened and suggested that the gear could be brought by helicopter to Bahir Dar and then airlifted back to this spot after a couple days of pickup shots.

Pasquale at last agreed. They deflated and rolled up his kayak and tied Gordon's hard-shell beneath the chopper. They lifted off, and first flew back upstream to rerun and film Gordito Falls and some other dramatic pieces. From the air, Pasquale thought, the zigzags of the Gilgel Abay seemed to bind the whole plateau together, like stitches along a gypsy's cheek.

Then all was reloaded into the chopper and flown back to Bahir Dar. There they transferred to a hotel van and drove down to Leaping Lizard rapid, where they inflated the expedition rafts and floated through a luxuriant adagio of islands as Brad Ohlund tried unsuccessfully to grab a crocodile shot.

That night, Christmas dinner was bad spaghetti within the cracked and discolored walls of the Lake Tana Hotel. On the shores of Lake Tana, a bastion of early Christianity, there were no twinkling lights, no Christmas trees or wreaths, no carols. Pasquale sat with Kurt and Mike, and they toasted the holiday with Ethiopian Gouder wine, thick as Robitussin and almost as tasty. Simon sat at the nearby bar, drinking the last of the milk of human kindness, a scotch on the rocks.

Sometime before midnight, Pasquale wandered to the expedition-gear storage room and collapsed on the hard single bed. It was humid and hot, and mosquitoes seemed to be singing carols around his head as he drifted off to sleep.

The next day Pasquale awoke with a sore throat and a cold. He desperately wanted to stay in bed, to take a much-needed rest day. But even more, he wanted to get the film obligations out of the way so he could return to the expedition.

The main of the day was spent at Jordi Falls, which Pasquale and Gordon ran five times as the helicopter flitted overhead and captured the all-important aerials for the IMAX® Theatre screen. While they portaged the raft back upstream, a local militia guard approached. Pasquale feared the worst . . . that the guard would demand payment or papers. But instead the syrupy-eyed man, Demaka Ashegri, handed Pasquale a throw bag containing a seventy-five-foot safety rope. It was one that had gone missing back in November, when the full crew had been filming the rapid. Pasquale was so impressed that he hired Demaka and his brother as guards for the day and overpaid them by half.

That night they returned to find that Simon had landed his helicopter, without warnings or permissions, on the roof of the creaky old Lake Tana Hotel, as the airport didn't open until 8:00 A.M. and he wanted to get an early start. Simon tried to refuel the chopper on the roof by carrying large plastic jugs of jet fuel up an old ladder, spilling the fragrant contents with the effort. "He's a cowboy," was Pasquale's philippic to Gordon.

The next day was to be the final of the helicopter shots. At breakfast, Simon assured Pasquale that if they finished shooting by 4:00 P.M., he'd fly them back to where he had plucked them from the Gilgel Abay. They shook hands on the deal.

Pasquale and Gordon hied through the filming, setting up portage scenes, walking along a facsimile of the source stream, passing under the first Portuguese bridge again. By 2:30 they were out of film, and Brad called a "wrap." Though still feeling a bit whacked, Pasquale was nonetheless relieved, and he looked forward to getting back on the river and the real mission. He and Gordon began to run up out of the canyon to meet Simon at the landing field as agreed, and Pasquale radioed to report their imminent arrival. But Simon got on the radio and in a louche voice said, "Sorry, boys. Gotta go." And away he flew, like a migratory bird.

Pasquale howled in anger. He clicked the radio button repeatedly, but it was like tossing rose petals into the Grand Canyon and waiting for echoes. Simon was gone.

He and Gordon humped back to the hotel and furiously repacked for the drive back to where they had left off. They trundled two hours over the same pocked road the next day, back to the Piccolo Abay Bridge, where they then retraced the progress made three days before.

On Monday the 29th, Pasquale saw an inland ocean in retreat through a palimpsest of reeds and weeds. At last they rowed into the paludal, buggy estuary at the southern end of Lake Tana. Eight hours later, beneath a bouquet of flies, they arrived at the end of the lake, at the Lake Tana Hotel.

Finally, on December 30, Kurt Hoppe and Mike Prosser got what they came for: They were rafting down the Blue Nile. The team launched at the concrete bridge just below where the Great Abay, as it was locally called, spills from Lake Tana. Mike Prosser captained one raft, Pasquale the other, with Gordon spinning the double blades of his kayak paddle like windmills. Their Ethiopian support—Alemu, Baye, and Yibeltal— were also on board, along with an AIDS-orphaned teenager, Thomas, whom Mike had befriended in Bahir Dar. They ran the upper section, past the hippo pool and down through Jordi Falls for the twelfth time.

That night, they pulled in at Arafami Falls. At last, they were rafting on a real expedition, and spirits all around were high. "I don't know why, but I love this river," Pasquale proclaimed. Anatomizing the appeal of the Blue Nile, like translating a poem, risks leaving behind the unanalyzable spirit of the river, its beautiful and hazardous play upon freedom. All Pasquale knew for sure was that the appeal of the Nile was overpowering, and he was being irretrievably pulled into its dazzling currents.

On New Year's Eve, they continued rafting down the upper Blue Nile, through the big rapids, one of which almost pitched Mike out of the boat. Pasquale saw that Mike was not as experienced a rafter as he'd expected. But he was all Pasquale had: If just for safety, he needed two rafts on the expedition. And nobody else in the whole of Ethiopia was qualified to man the sticks.

That night, they rowed to a campsite just above Tissisat Falls, near the village of Tis Abay, where Yohannes, who had hiked in, barbecued a freshly slaughtered goat for New Year's Eve dinner. They made a bonfire and popped champagne at midnight.

Pasquale called me on the Iridium sat-phone that night and wished me a happy new year. I sensed a satori in his voice that resonated from more than ten thousand miles away. Pasquale had cast off a muddled year, one that had brought him to his half-century mark and had begun with little focus or bearing. He had thought about sailing around the world, or moving to Namibia to manage an ecolodge he co-owned, or becoming a photographer, or getting back into oil and gas. But in this trip he'd found purpose. He was looking forward to the task ahead, a hurtle through a pathless wilderness unbounded by geography or history, utterly unconstrained by social bonds. Running the length of the Blue Nile was an overwhelming proposition—overabundant in its challenges and perils—but his one New Year's resolution was that he would do it.

CHAPTER EIGHT

If the primary aim of a captain were to preserve his ship, he would keep it in port forever.

THOMAS AQUINAS

Fortune brings in some boats that are not steered.

WILLIAM SHAKESPEARE

Unlike most of the world, Pasquale didn't sleep late on New Year's Day, nor did he ponder the future, or the meaning of passing time and life. At the break of dawn he unfolded his bruised body like a deck chair and promptly went to work. This was Day One of a New Year, and Day One entering the most dangerous part of the Nile basin. They were about to enter the Super Bowl of rafting.

They began by portaging the rafts to below Agam Dildi, the first Portuguese Bridge, just a few hundred yards beyond Tissisat Falls. Gordon, however, didn't participate in the portage. Instead, he carried his little boat to below the massive falls and launched just below the wide crashing curtain of water. He paddled just a few yards, then got out and rappelled himself and his boat over a twenty-five-foot lower falls. From there, he went on to run the Class V rapids between the falls and the bridge, a section of sheer white madness that no sane boater would ever consider. Yet Gordon liked Pasquale's notion of a "pure" descent, and he had earlier kayaked to the lip of the 120-foot drop of the main falls and lowered himself over. All he needed now was to stitch in this last piece. And he did. Without cameras rolling or crowds cheering, he ran one of the most impressive sections of wild water in the world, where in the course of a couple of hundred yards the half-mile-wide Blue Nile squeezed down to a slot the width of a truck.

Once through, the reunited flotilla negotiated down past the reentry pipe of a hydro-diversion project. They set up camp for the night on a grassy, parklike meadow. As the skin of day was cast away, Solomon appeared, pushing a goat into camp, wheelbarrow fashion, on its forelegs. He promptly slit its throat and cut it into manageable sections, and Yohannes began to barbecue it up. As the woodsmoke curled through camp, hollers came echoing down the canyon. Across the river they saw a gaggle of ragged kids, thin as whippets, looking like the Lost Boys. Pasquale hopped into his raft, rowed to the other side, and peeled out fifty birr, which he handed about. Then he challenged them: If they could bring back beer by 7:00, he'd buy the brews at a premium. Pasquale knew this was a tough task, as the closest village was Tis Abay, about five miles back upstream. But off they scattered.

Come 7:00, there was no sign of the kids. By 7:30, Pasquale had given up on them. At 8:00, the men were picking the last bones of the goat when the Lost Boys came running down the opposite bank, picking their way barefooted from stone to stone. Pasquale rowed across again, picked them up, and brought them to camp, where they proudly pulled from gunnysacks twelve bottles of beer and two bottles of Gouder wine. Pasquale was so impressed that he hired them on the spot as porters, and they stayed with the expedition for the next two days.

Now the soulless canyon walls got darker and narrower; the river rushed like an arrow. It all seemed preternaturally forbidding.

They were in the dreaded Northern Gorge. Because the walls were so black, they absorbed the heat and turned the canyon into an oven. At lunch they found a single large shade tree, a thick ficus with a mass of trunks tangled in a Gordian knot, its whole surface marred with axe cuts.

They huddled in the shade and munched on crackers spread with canned tuna and sardines, and more crackers with Nutella. Just then, a large herd of cattle and donkeys showed up, surrounding them, pushing for water like urchins for money. It was too much—the odor, the pressing cowhide—so they cut short the repast and headed downstream.

At Catfish Falls, the first major rapid on Mike Speaks' map, the river arched like a cat's back, snarled over a waterfall on the left, mewed through a maze in the middle, and poured like milk down a Class III chute on the right. Gordon chose the right, running it with flair. Then Mike Prosser did the same. Pasquale went last, but he missed the mark on the chute and shot through like a bullet, smacking into a rock that dispatched him into the back bilge of the boat. The local children, who had likely not seen white-skinned rafters before, had skittered away like klipspringers, but they couldn't resist peeking out from behind bushes to see Pasquale's run. He could hear their laughter as he crawled back onto his seat.

Kurt also emerged from the rapid wet from head to toe. He'd been thoroughly soaked in several rapids to this point, and he didn't like it. He privately worried about contracting schistosomiasis, or bilharzia, the fatal snail-borne disease found in slow-moving tropical waters. He was concerned, though he had only been sprayed with quick water.

That night they killed another goat for dinner. "Don't know how many more goats we can eat," Pasquale logged in his journal. Sleep was not easy, as the stringy goat meat sat all night in his belly like a stone.

The next day, Kurt announced that he was leaving the expedition. He was going to hike back to Bahir Dar with the support donkeys and catch a flight to Addis Ababa, then on to the States. He said he was concerned about his dad, and his developing medical condition, which might require sudden surgery. He had tried to reach his dad with the Iridium phone and couldn't. Pasquale was disappointed, and even a little concerned for Kurt's safe passage to Bahir Dar. For some reason, he was reminded of the story behind Separation Rapid on the Grand Canyon, named on John Wesley Powell's 1869 first expedition down the Colorado. After several close calls, three members of the team had decided to hike out the north side rather than risk continuing down the dangerous river. "How surely we will all die if we continue on this journey," one of the men said to Major Powell. Each party had thought it was taking the more judicious route. But while Powell's expedition reached civilization safely, the three hikers were never seen again. It was later presumed that they were killed by Shivwits Indians who mistook them for miners who had killed a Hualapai woman a few weeks before.

Kurt gave Pasquale a long, hard bear hug and then wished him luck. He later confessed that he was thinking this could be the last time he would see his friend. Then Kurt turned his back on the river and started to coil back up the canyon.

A few hours later, Pasquale wondered if Kurt had indeed made the wiser decision. For it was here that he reached the Gauntlet. As he plunged, with his body splayed over the upside-down raft, through the bottom of Gauntlet Falls, he was suddenly slapped with a vision of déjà vu. He remembered hanging on to an upside-down raft in cold water, his fingers forced into the self-bailing holes, knowing a waterfall was just ahead.

I can't believe this is happening again, he thought. The difference was he was now fifteen years older and fifteen pounds heavier, and the Blue Nile was fifteen times harder.

Hell, I'm gonna die. This is just like the Selway.

It was the summer of 1987.

Cited by cognoscenti as the wildest river in the lower forty-eight states, the Selway, in Idaho, is also considered one of the toughest. It boasts forty-five named rapids in the forty-seven-mile run from the Paradise Guard Station to Selway Falls, and it has a reputation for swallowing rafters whole. Some claim Lord Grizzly still roams here; nobody disputes that the corridor hosts rattlesnakes, wolves, black bears, mountain lions, bighorns, cutthroat trout, black flies, and mosquitoes. Its weather is notorious, with snow and freezing rain possible anytime through June. Even Lewis and Clark were daunted here. When they crossed what is now the Montana-Idaho border in 1805 and considered the cruel country surrounding the Selway, they turned north for Lolo Pass instead.

The summer of 1987 was a big water year on the Selway. The Lowell gauge at the put-in read 7.5 feet, which meant very high water, dangerous water. But Pasquale had waited several years to win a permit in the annual lottery, and he wasn't going to turn back. So, with a group of friends and three rafts, he set out. His friend Kimball Gardner, a jack-Mormon from Wyoming, captained the second raft, and Gary Hall piloted the third. They launched into the champagne-clear water. For two days they ran sprightly rapids and bathed in the beauty of the granite-and-pine canyon.

Then they came to Ladle Falls, considered the toughest rapid on the river. They made a long scout. There was no logic to Ladle—the river took sudden tours around rocks, split off in two or three erratic directions at once, then convened again, as though in a square dance of the mad. Only through close study could Pasquale see if a route would play, or veer off into an illusion or a rock—or worse, into the craterlike fissure of a souse hole. Pasquale was tempted to plot his course on paper, analyzing the hydraulics, factoring the weight distribution on his boat. But he finally just walked back upstream, tugged his life jacket tight, and headed into the maelstrom.

At the first ledge drop, Pasquale's whole boat dove under the water, and two of his friends, Brenda Gallagher and Riley Skeen, were sucked out of the boat. Pasquale dumped the oars, grabbed Brenda, pulled her into the bow of the boat, and then grabbed Riley, and pulled him into the stern of the boat. Then he grabbed the oars and started to make a pull to the right side of the river, hoping to make shore before the next big drop.

He couldn't make it; the current's grip was too overwhelming. So he spun the boat, pointing the bow downstream, and prepared to take the holes head-on.

But suddenly the raft jerked to a violent halt just above a hole. It held and vibrated like a water-skier's tow rope. Pasquale jerked his head around and saw the cause. Riley had hurled the safety-line throw bag to the other raft, where Kimball had grabbed it and tied it to his frame as Riley tied his end to Pasquale's frame. The seventy-five-foot rope had played out, and the result now was a pendulum effect, swinging Pasquale's raft toward a wall.

The raft smacked the wall, and the contact oar pivoted handle-end-up and was pinned against the rock. Pasquale jumped onto the wall-side tube of the raft to try to prevent it from riding up the wall from the pressure of the river. That and the taut rope seemed to be doing the trick. But then he saw Kimball wielding a knife, and he yelled back, "Don't cut the rope!"

Kimball cut the rope.

The boat crawled up the wall like a monkey. Riley washed out first. Then Brenda. Pasquale balanced on the tube, hoping that if the raft continued its roll, he might actually be able to maneuver over with it and stay on it even as it turned upside down.

Then the pinned oar sprung loose and smacked Pasquale across the head. His first sensation was hot liquid flowing down his face. And then the boat went over, and the black lights flipped on.

Pasquale hung on to the perimeter rope of the raft as it pitched through a monster souse hole. For a long moment, the raft recirculated like a cork in a whirlpool, then shot out with Pasquale still hanging on. With a kick and a pull he hauled himself on top of the flipped raft. He poked his fingers into the bailing holes and hung on for the next three miles. The ride was so violent at times that he felt as though his arms were about to be ripped from their sockets. It was freezing cold. It started to rain. Finally the raft swung into an eddy, and Pasquale leapt to shore with a line and arrested the runaway raft.

Pasquale collapsed on the ground. About a half hour later, the other rafters showed up. Riley was white; he had been floating facedown, close to drowning, when the others pulled him out of the current.

"You look like shit, Pasquale," Kimball said. The skin above Pasquale's eye was hanging down from a gash. Pasquale could barely see. Riley poured tequila on the wound, then gave Pasquale a slug as Gary Hall and Kimball stitched him up. Eight stitches, with ten-pound-test monofilament fishing line. It left a scar, but today Pasquale says he's better-looking for it.

CHAPTER NINE

It was only a few seconds before they reached the next rapid, like the last a stretch of ugly rocks and boiling eddies and green, inclined slopes of hurtling water, where the eye had to be quick and the brain quicker still, where the hand had to be steady and strong and subtle and the will resolute.

C. S. FORESTER, *THE AFRICAN QUEEN*

N ow, on the Blue Nile, Pasquale was again about to be pitched into a monster souse hole. Having just ridden the overturned boat through the Gauntlet and rescued Alemu from a rock, he now feared the worst. But suddenly the squirrelly current skidded the raft toward the eastern bank. Pasquale jumped into the water, gripping the bowline, and threw the rope around the nearest boulder. The rope went taut just as the raft was on the brink, and the whole boat began to vibrate like air in a bottle when you blow across the top. Alemu still hung on its back, trembling in fear. Pasquale tried to pull the raft in, but couldn't. The water pounded the side of the boat. Something was about to give. The D-ring to which the bowline was tied would snap; the raft would puncture with the pressure; the rope would break . . .

Then, out of the woods, an archangel suddenly appeared in the form of Baye. He gripped the rope with Pasquale, and together they began to slowly draw it in. Baye was a farmer's son, the only Ethiopian on the trip from a rural background, and as such was stronger and more comfortable in wilderness than the others. With his added strength they were able to get the raft to shore, where they flipped it right side up and tied it off.

Only afterward did Pasquale realize how close he had come to disaster. It was one of the most foolish things he'd *ever* done, allowing someone to jump into the river after a boat, not knowing how well he could swim, assuming he could . . . and then going in after him. He should have just let the boat go.

But he also knew that we learn from mistakes. Nothing is learned from good experiences. Everything is trial and error. People who've never made mistakes don't make good leaders.

He asked himself why he had allowed this to happen; what had led to these decisions? For one thing, the radio was bad. He should never have relied solely on the radio without first making sure it worked perfectly. He should have developed a plan for equipment failure, and perhaps thus avoided a near disaster.

The experience was flooding Pasquale with memories, not just of the Selway. There was a worse one: that of the Alsek River in Alaska. It still haunted him.

It was the summer of 1993. Pasquale organized a private expedition down the Alsek River, one of the biggest and wildest rivers in western Canada and Alaska, running through the Wrangell–St. Elias Wilderness. He invited his future wife, Kim, and his eldest son, Tim, who was nineteen at the time. He also included several friends, among them Mike Rhodes, a geophysical client and longtime pal, and Mike's fiancée, Harriet Nicholson, a vivacious redhead thrilled at the chance to raft among the grizzly bears. Pasquale had run the supernaturally beautiful Tatshenshini, a tributary to the Alsek, four times—but never the Alsek, which he had heard was even more spectacular.

Pasquale and friends flew into Haines, Alaska, where Sobek, the guiding company that pioneered many of Alaska's wild rivers, is based. There Pasquale met with a Sobek senior guide, who hand-drew a detailed map to supplement Pasquale's series of topographical charts, replete with aperçus. The guide advised that the only rapid to warrant concern was called Lava North, a Class IV-V with fast water and big holes. He marked it clearly on both sets of maps. The guide assured Pasquale that he would see it coming—the rapids blazed into the air like fire—and when he did, he had to pull over to the right-hand side of the river to scout. It was runnable, but a route needed to be plotted from shore.

Riding in Pasquale's raft were Kim, Mike, and Harriet, who was inexperienced in whitewater but game for the adventure. Pasquale was rowing the lead raft, and his son, who had rafted a number of Colorado rivers, was behind. A third raft was piloted by his old buddy Kimball Gardner, the man who had helped stitch him up on the Selway.

Kimball, concerned about bear, had smuggled in a brand-new handgun. It was a .488 Magnum, custom-built, something that made Dirty Harry's .357 Magnum look like a popgun.

Unregistered handguns are not allowed in Canada. It's against the law to bring guns or booze across the border. But the Alsek is prime bear country, with a higher concentration of grizzlies in its watershed than anywhere in the world. So, when driving to the Alsek put-in in Kluane National Park in the Yukon Territory, Pasquale and his crew hid two rifles and the Magnum, as well as bottles of Yukon Jack, under the dry boxes when they crossed the border.

When they got to the put-in, they hired some locals to shuttle their trucks back to Haines. Kimball couldn't help showing off his new .488 Magnum. Then, unbeknownst to Pasquale, after they launched, the Canadian shuttle driver immediately drove to a pay phone and called the Mounties.

It was a beautiful float. They were purling through the world's largest nonpolar glacier system: There is more ice in this region of southeastern Alaska than throughout the Brooks Range above the Arctic Circle. They passed Mount Kennedy and Mount Fairweather, then drifted into an inland bay dotted with icebergs. They wove and glissaded through a maze of shimmering ice flotsam, mammoth pointed polygons turning slowly in the current, sparking like windowcase jewels.

Suddenly, a helicopter appeared from over the glacier and buzzed the rafts. A booming voice through a bullhorn ordered Pasquale and his group to pull over.

The helicopter landed, and three Royal Canadian Police jumped out, pistols drawn and shotguns leveled. The leader strutted over and said, "We need to check your rafts."

They read the rafters their rights, saying they had a sworn statement that unregistered firearms were on the boats; they presented a search warrant. Kimball was still on his raft during the confrontation, and he quietly dropped his handgun into a foot of water off the back of the boat.

On Pasquale's raft, Kim was holding the maps for the trip, and when she was summoned to speak with the police, she set them down on the seat.

The Mounties searched the boats and found the two rifles, and wanted to know where the handgun was. Kimball declared, "There are no handguns."

"We know there is a handgun. We have a witness. If you conceal it and we find it, you're going to jail. Stand aside, eh?"

They scoured the boats once again, bilge to bow, searching through every kit, checking every seam. Finally, they gave up, wrote a summons for the group to appear in court, and stepped back into the helicopter, confiscating the rifles and a couple bottles of booze. As the rotors sped up, a wind stirred, and it blew the maps off Pasquale's boat and into the river, where they floated away.

When the chopper was out of sight, Kimball retrieved his Magnum from the water. Pasquale was seething to have lost the expedition's Weatherby rifle. But what really upset him was the discovery that the maps were gone. They marked everything for the trip, from campsites, to hikes, to a portage, to the risky rapid called Lava North.

They took off down the river without maps. Pasquale racked his brain trying to remember the places marked on them. He told the other two rafts' pilots to stay behind him for safety, as they were now on an exploratory.

The next day, the water began to pick up speed, started to agitate almost imperceptibly; delicate swirls appeared on the surface as if traced by a feather. Then they multiplied and cut deeper. And then, around the next bend, Pasquale saw the licks of rapids on the horizon line. *This is it*, he thought. He yelled back to the other rafts to pull over to the right.

But as he pulled hard against the strong current, he looked upstream and saw that his son Tim was out in the middle of the river, heading for the rapids. "Get over!" Pasquale yelled. And Tim yelled back, "I can't . . . the river's too fast!"

The words beaded up and rolled down Pasquale's brow. He desperately didn't want his teenage son swept into a major rapid on an ice-cold river with no rescue raft within reach, so he spun his own raft around and headed toward Tim midriver. Sucked into the rapid in the worst place, Pasquale dropped into the biggest hole he had ever seen. "Hang on!" he screamed to Kim, Mike, and Harriet as the boat submerged, twisted around, and rode up the far side of the hole, where it flipped.

Immediately they were enveloped in a cocoon of ice-cold water. The air was sucked from Pasquale's lungs; his body felt pierced by a thousand ice picks. It took about fifty yards before Pasquale was able to climb up on the bottom of the raft, and from there he grabbed Mike and yanked him on board. He scanned the river and saw Kim crawling up the right bank, but he didn't see Harriet.

"Where's Harriet?" His yell pierced the cold.

"I think I saw her behind us. I think she got into an eddy," Mike coughed back.

Thinking Harriet safe—she had a life jacket on and was probably in an eddy—Pasquale pulled the oars off the locks and used them as paddles to get to shore. He beached and started to unload the overturned raft when Tim rowed over. He had made a clean run.

"Did you see Harriet?" Pasquale asked.

"No, I thought she was with you, Dad."

Still, Pasquale assumed that things were okay. And Kimball's raft was still upstream, where he had pulled over to scout. So, Pasquale went about righting the raft, and started a fire for his shivering raft mates, and for Harriet when she showed.

Then Kimball's raft finally appeared. An oddly shaped tarp was strapped to the bow.

Inside was Harriet's body.

When the raft flipped, she had hit her head on the oarlock and been knocked unconscious. Kimball had found her floating facedown in the eddy.

In the emotional aftermath, Pasquale replayed the sequence of events over and over in his mind. It wasn't a single large error, but a whole string of little slips, each building on the other, that led to disaster. In 1963, the meteorologist Edward Lorenz presented a paper to the New York Academy of Science in which he suggested that a single flap of a seagull's wings could alter the weather forever through a gradual accretion of energy. On expedition, the details, and their cascading aftermaths, were the Devil or God.

For two years after Harriet died, Pasquale couldn't get into a raft.

CHAPTER TEN

Death to the young is more than that undiscovered country.
MAYA ANGELOU

Pasquale thought about the incident on the Alsek as he worked his way back up the bank of the Blue Nile to where Gordon and the others were waiting. He knew that small, careless mistakes had again brought him to the brink of disaster. He vowed it would not happen again.

Gordon had no idea that anything had gone wrong, and he had been blithely awaiting word to send the next raft down. Now, though, they all portaged the second raft, the IMAX® camera, film canisters, and other gear to the bottom of the Gauntlet. They were bone-tired; the air crackled with tension. They found a spot on a high ledge above the river on the western bank and wordlessly made camp. The Ethiopians on the trip were in a somber, quiet mood, and Pasquale felt they were upset because he had put them at such risk and were apprehensive about what lay ahead.

Pasquale was nervous as well. There had been a number of deaths in this section of the river, and no expedition to date had made it through without incident. Was this just a sampling of the ordeals they would face for the next three days? They were at the bottom of a mile-deep canyon, a hundred miles from nowhere, in the midst of one of the wildest sections of whitewater in the world, with an inexperienced crew, most of whom could not swim.

Maybe Mike Speaks had been right when he said people did not belong in the Northern Gorge. Maybe Kurt had been right to walk out. These were his thoughts as he tried to force sleep.

The morning light stirred Pasquale awake. His body ached; his finger was still numb from the rope the day before. Slowly, they prepared to begin their day on the river.

With caution, they worked their way downstream to the next nightmare. The gorge pinched even more as they eased toward the chambered roar of the next major rapid, named the Crux. As they approached, they could see the spray from an exploding wave marking the entrance to the falls; not far beyond the horizon line, a sheer wall interrupted the river's progress, sending the rapid into a screaming right-hand turn around a blind corner.

It was a manifestation of the dread that had haunted Pasquale in the weeks before, a potentially untenable situation. There was absolutely no way to row back upstream—the current was too strong. There was absolutely no way to hike out—the canyon walls were far too sheer. If there was no way to negotiate the rapid, they were stuck. No exit.

As they pulled over at the brink, they saw the entire river pouring over the edge into a huge fissure and exploding out the other side. It then slammed into a black cliff on the west bank, through an S-turn, and into the east bank, where it disappeared into a thirty-foot-long undercut, then bounced back out, creating a giant white pillow of water. Then the river spat downstream and vanished around the corner, heading to the next rapid.

Worse, the rapid was not portagable. The walls on both sides sliced into the river like meat cleavers.

That left three choices: First, attempt to navigate this horrific stretch. Second, ghost-boat the rafts through, as they had done in near-disaster with one raft at the Gauntlet. But this time the rafts would be fully loaded with all the gear, weighing perhaps one thousand pounds each, making them that much harder to pull in. And third, with ropes strategically attached and paid out, try to line the rafts down the maelstrom while standing on sharp side boulders and hanging on to tiny outcroppings in the cliff walls.

Quickly and unanimously they decided to rope the boats through the upper part of the Crux, then jump in and attempt to row the second part into the undercut. Pasquale would go first, and if successful, then a nervous Mike Prosser would follow. Pasquale had four hundred feet of ten-millimeter fixed line, some of the strongest climbing rope made, and several pulleys and carabiners. So, with Gordon's help, he set about rigging an elaborate belay system, anchoring around a house-sized boulder. Gordon was positioned at the boulder with the long rope rolling through two pulleys and carabiners. Pasquale had Mike and the Ethiopians hold on to three other lines as backup. But as they lowered the raft, it fell into the first hole, submerged, and surfaced full of water, adding thousands of pounds to the weight. Then they discovered that they had miscalculated the distance and run out of rope. Pasquale jumped into the raft and tied another two ropes onto the frame, bringing the total of fixed ropes to six.

Then Gordon started to shout. His pulleys and carabiners had started to bend, then pulled apart. Two snapped. The raft started to scream down the river. Gordon tried to hold on, but the rope quickly burned through his leather gloves. There was the smell of burning flesh as the others tried to hold on as well. The raft swung out to the middle of the river with Pasquale on board, but there it held tight. For the next two hours, the crew slowly wrested the raft back to shore. It was now halfway through the Crux.

They decided to lower the second raft next, but to secure it with even more ropes, keeping it closer to shore in the process. They wrestled it over shore rocks and let it down a few inches at a time, then rested, then continued. It took about an hour to reach the anchorage of the first raft. Then Gordon made his way back upstream, wormed into his kayak, and rotored through an uncharted crevice of water. He capsized midway, knocked his helmet against a rock, and then fired through upside down. Pasquale, nervous as hell, jumped into the first raft, ran into the under-cut, piled into the pillow, and spun safely into the eddy below.

Now it was Mike's turn. He pulled hard against the current, but he lost control and was swept into the underhang, spun around, and then spat out sideways. He emerged shaking his head, eyes wide with terror. Pasquale was worried. *Two huge rapids; two near-disasters,* he thought.

But it got worse. Just downstream, the river took a sharp left-hand turn and tumbled through another set of steep rapids. They pulled over to scout, and Pasquale traced the route for Mike, who was so nervous he was shaking.

Gordon went first in his kayak, and fashioned a run as smooth and gleaming as a needle, pinning down the rapid by its corners. Once through, he held his paddle vertically, the blade to the sky, the sign that it was okay to proceed. Pasquale pushed out into the current and yelled back to Mike, "Follow me!"

Pasquale dropped into the rapid—and was stopped cold. The raft was swamped with tons of pounding water, but he kept it straight and after a pause it shot through. "Wow. Bigger than I thought," he mouthed, as he looked back upstream to watch Mike's entry. Mike missed his mark, throwing the raft sideways into a hydraulic. Pasquale watched as the raft rode up on its side, a tubestand, and for a long second seemed to consider whether to fall back or go over.

The raft flopped back right-side up, and was immediately submerged in the hole. It completely disappeared. When it popped back up, only Alemu and Solomon were on board, frantically waving their hands back and forth and screaming.

Mike was gone.

More bad memories crept from the black corners of Pasquale's mind.

In October 1993, the same year as the Alsek drowning, Pasquale had joined a twelve-man expedition up Pumori, the pyramidal peak just to the west of Mount Everest. At 23,494 feet in elevation, it was to be Pasquale's personal best for altitude. It is also considered one of the most beautiful mountains in the world, the first high peak that trekkers see when approaching the Khumbu region of Nepal. And it's the most deadly mountain in the Himalayas. There have been more deaths on Pumori than on any other mountain in Asia.

The expedition was led by a Tim Brill, and the expedition doctor was Greg Gordon from Santa Fe, a climber in his early forties. At the time, Pasquale had thought a person in his forties was too old to be on expedition.

The climb was disorganized. There was little intrateam communication; loads weren't assigned; individuals took off by themselves. Nonetheless, after days of climbing, from Camp Three, Pasquale managed to make an early-morning summit, with Greg Gordon right behind, in extremely cold and windy weather. They then struggled back down to Camp Three on the Eastern Col, a saddle connecting Everest and Pumori in Tibet, and spent the night there.

The next morning, Pasquale suited up and prepared for the descent. But Greg just lay in his bag. When Pasquale stirred him, he looked up and said, "Pasquale, you have to stay with me."

Pasquale didn't want to linger. He was dead tired and cold, and he knew that to remain too long at this elevation in these conditions would mean death. But he couldn't abandon Greg either, so he set his kit down and helped him get up and ready.

Together they slowly made their way down the mountain, and after a few hours they reached Camp Two, which had been abandoned by other team members who had given up without summiting and gone down.

They rested there, Greg so tired he could barely move. He was completely out of water and food, so Pasquale melted some water, got him hydrated, and gave him his last few cookies.

Finally Greg had enough strength to stand up. The conditions were getting worse, and the snow swirled, creating a near-whiteout. Greg pleaded with Pasquale not to leave him, and said, "Don't get ahead of me; you'll lose me." Pasquale promised to stay with him, and to be only a few steps behind.

Slowly they unwound the mountain, until they got to a vertical rock-and-ice section. A rope had been fixed with a piton every fifty feet or so down the five-hundred-foot cliff. They both clipped in to the rope with carabiners attached to their harnesses, and started the vertical descent.

Pasquale rappelled a few feet above Greg, but he was worried because Greg was hunched over, as though about to fall asleep.

"Be careful," Pasquale yelled down. "Be very careful."

They made it down the first pitch and stopped to rest before clipping in to the second rope, which was fixed to a sheer wall of ice. Again, Greg took the lead. As he began to move again, Pasquale checked his waist to make sure his carabiner was locked. Suddenly, he heard a yelp. *"Ugghhh!"* Greg was falling. He dropped down the ice face to a steep snow section and rolled downhill, picking up speed, doing somersaults. Then he disappeared.

Greg had forgotten to clip himself back to the rope.

Pasquale freaked. He ripped off his backpack, tied it to the fixed line, and climbed down with both ice axes, descending three hundred feet past a trail of bloodstains. There, in a pile of granite rocks, he found Greg. Dead.

His head was smashed; his arms were twisted and broken behind his back. He looked like a heap of bones.

Pasquale was devastated, but he knew what he had to do. He climbed back up, got his pack, and worked down to base camp and reported that Greg had died. Another climbing team, led by well-known mountaineer Henry Todd, climbed up and found Greg's body, and then buried it in a bivysack under a mound of rock and ice.

As Pasquale considered what had happened, he swore he would never share an expedition with inexperienced team members again. He swore he would not let himself or others get too tired to make good judgment calls.

And then he reconsidered adventure itself. He'd witnessed two deaths in less than a year. Perhaps he should give up expeditions altogether.

CHAPTER ELEVEN

O Lord, methought what pain it was to drown,
What dreadful noise of waters in mine ears,
What sights of ugly death within mine eyes!
WILLIAM SHAKESPEARE, *RICHARD III*, ACT I, SCENE 4

Now, on the Blue Nile, with a questionable partner, with inexperienced team members utterly exhausted, Pasquale pivoted his boat toward Mike's pilotless raft and wondered if disaster was again at his door. He pumped his oars as hard as he could, but he couldn't reach the other boat. He watched as Alemu and Solomon, scared shitless, caromed down the river toward the next sharp curve.

Then, after perhaps a minute, Mike popped up, twenty yards behind the boat, his face a rictus of terror. He'd been sucked to the bottom of the river, spun around like laundry, then tossed back up just as his lungs were about to burst. He started waving his arms at Alemu and Solomon, but they had no idea what to do.

Pasquale yelled at the top of his lungs for Alemu and Solomon to get Mike back in the boat, but they were helpless until Mike took a few frantic strokes and got within an arm's length. They both grabbed Mike by his life jacket and tried to pull him in. But Mike weighed 225 pounds, about as much as both of them, and they couldn't manage it. Alemu gave up and scrambled for the oars, but Pasquale yelled, "Forget the oars!

Get Mike!" So Alemu dropped back, and pulled again, and this time they hauled him over the stern into the bilge. Pasquale did a double-take—Mike had no pants on. He was totally bare-ass naked. The river had taken its own sacrificial offering; Mike's river shorts had been sucked right off in the hydraulic.

Mike was tossed around in the bilge as the raft, without pilot, plummeted into the next rapid sideways. It rode the far wave to its crest, see-sawed at the flipping point, and then slewed back right side up as it whipped around the corner.

Gordon took off after the runaway raft, with Pasquale close behind. They chased it about a half-mile downstream through several more rapids, through an attenuated gorge. Narrow trees hung over the top, a canopy that blocked the sunlight.

Finally, Mike's raft spun into an eddy, and Gordon and Pasquale grabbed it. Mike was in the bilge, hands on knees, head between his hands, shaking his head.

The Ethiopians, staring at Mike shivering naked in the bilge, began to laugh . . . a nervous laugh. Pasquale barked, "Cut it out," then asked Mike if he was okay. With his head still between his hands, Mike replied, "I can't believe it. . . . That was the closest I've ever come to dying."

"Do you want to go on, or rest?"

"Rest."

"Do you want to get a new pair of pants on?"

"No. I just need to rest. Need to rest." Mike lifted his head, his eyes closed. His face shuddered like the hide of a horse disturbed by flies. For the next twenty minutes he remained huddled in the bilge. Finally, he crawled onto the shore. Pulling another pair of shorts from his kit, he put them on and slouched back to his raft. "We gotta keep going," Pasquale said. "We need to find a camp."

So, they pushed back into the current and cautiously rowed downstream in the late-afternoon light. The gorge was narrow here, with cliffs on both sides cutting into the river, and no beaches or level spots for a campsite. Mike started to protest, saying they needed to find a camp soon—he couldn't handle going much farther. He was dead tired. Everyone was scared.

At the first notch in the canyon wall Pasquale pulled over, and there was a nice level gravel bar, so he called camp. But when Gordon pulled in, he protested, "No trees here. I need two trees to sling my hammock. We gotta keep going. We'll find a better campsite."

Against his better judgment, Pasquale acquiesced. As they got deeper into the canyon, it started to get darker. Mike was at the end of his rope, and started to insist that he needed to pull over and rest. But there was no place to stop. The canyon began to narrow further, and at the next turn they could hear a thunderous roar rolling up from below.

"Damn!" Pasquale cried.

He knew there were more Class V rapids ahead, but he hadn't expected them so soon. As he pulled back on the oars, he noticed a slot in the canyon. He sent Gordon down to check it out, and Gordon returned reporting that they could park there for the night, but they were not going to like it. The twenty-five-foot notch in the canyon wall was full of shit.

In this inner gorge, a small version of the Grand Canyon of Africa, there were very few places to get cattle down to the river. But this was one, and it had probably been a watering spot for two thousand years. It was six inches thick with cow shit, and electric with flies.

But there were no other choices. They were on the soft verge of darkness. To seal it, Mike said, "Pasquale, I'm not going any farther."

So they spread out several blue plastic tarps over the shit and made camp. Pasquale rolled his sleeping bag out on the end of his raft, and pushed the tied-up raft as far out into the river as he could to get away from the smell.

Mike passed out right away on his bed pad on a blue tarp. He woke up about two hours later. Pasquale heard him stirring, so he went over to speak with him.

"Pasquale," he said, "I can't go any farther. I'm gonna walk around the rest of the Northern Gorge."

Pasquale looked around in the moonlight as he considered Mike's words. Just downstream he saw a chill, bending flame that funneled into a wide eddy and crashed against a cliff. Then it occurred to him, as he reviewed the design of the rapid, that this was likely the exact place where Greenwald had drowned in 1975.

On January 16, 1975, Sobek Expeditions launched the first attempt to raft through the Northern Gorge of the Blue Nile. The six guides dropped two Avon rafts into the river just below the First Portuguese Bridge, Agam Dildi, and soon found themselves in a series of tight, twisting black basalt gorges, packed with Class V and VI rapids. They spent much of the trip portaging or lining the boats through. The second day, January 17, Jim Slade, Sobek's senior guide, awoke and wrote in his diary: "Dreamed my brother had died, and that Lew was my brother. Hope it was not an ill-omen or presentiment of things to come on this trip." It was the first time Jim had ever dreamed about death.

Downstream, later that day, they came to a rapid that seemed less difficult than what they had already battled. The river split, then reunited. They took the right channel. Then it split again, and the boat got caught in a small recirculating eddy on the right side where the water piled up against a wall black and smooth as oil. It didn't seem too dangerous, and they were tired of portaging. The water was fairly low, and they felt the current was forgiving enough that they could actually push the boat down the side of the wall and back into the main current.

Nobody was rowing; the oars were shipped. John Yost, Conrad Hirsh, Lew Greenwald, and Jim Slade were all standing on the tube and pushing the boat, working it along the wall. They made good progress, until they reached a section of the wall that stuck out a few inches, where the boat got lodged at the strongest intersection of the main river current and the back current of the eddy. With the powerful main current pushing against the outer tube, the boat slowly started to rise up the wall. The four tried to push the raft back down, but the current was far too strong, and it continued to rise. It became clear that the boat was going to capsize. John was closest to shore, and he made a flying leap and landed on solid ground. The boat continued to rise to a near-tubestand. Conrad was next, and he jumped as far as he could and landed waist-deep in water. The raft was now starting its rollover, and Lew jumped next into water over his head, right where the stern line was trailing. He went under, surfaced with a frightened look, and then screamed that his life jacket had gotten clipped to the stern line.

Jim jumped, but by then the raft was over. He and the boat sailed out into the main current and over a steep drop-off rapid. Jim was out front, and a couple hundred yards downstream, he managed to make his way to the left shore. He then saw the raft charging toward him, swam back out, grabbed a D-ring, and with all his remaining strength, dragged it to a gravel bar.

John was on the opposite shore, and as Jim was catching his breath he watched John jump into the raging current and swim the entire width of the Blue Nile. He splashed to the boat, and between gulps told Jim that Lew was missing and before disappearing had yelled that he was caught on the stern line. They immediately checked the stern and bowlines, and found a nick in the former where it looked like something had snagged. They checked under the boat, where people often get caught in a capsize. And then they searched the banks, howling Lew's name, sweeping the river, fearing the worst. At nightfall they collapsed in exhaustion.

With daybreak they could think of nothing to do but head downstream. A few turns downriver they found Lew, floating in an eddy, his orange Mae West life jacket pulled halfway up his head. They could only assume that Lew's jacket had accidentally clipped to the stern line, which dragged him over the next falls, and downstream until he drowned. It had then somehow come loose.

ving crew pulled Lew's body to shore and weighed their
y had an unknown distance yet to run, and in all likeli-
angerous rapids yet to face before reaching the Second
__guese Bridge. And from there it was a full day's hike to the village
of Mota, where they could catch the once-a-week plane to Addis Ababa.
So they decided to lay Lew to rest by the Blue Nile. The ground was too
hard to bury him, so they found a hollow, laid him in, and covered him
with stones. Then they built a small fire, a funeral pyre, on top, and performed a simple ceremony.

They had no idea they were being watched. But a year later Karen
Greenwald, Lew's wife, hiked into the gorge, and she met villagers who
said they had witnessed the funeral. They took her to the spot. She re-
moved Lew's remains and took them to a Jewish cemetery in Addis
Ababa, where he was laid to rest in consecrated ground.

CHAPTER TWELVE

I will be conquered; I will not capitulate.
SAMUEL JOHNSON

As the moon lit up the black canyon walls of the Blue Nile, Pasquale turned to Mike: "Mike, it creates a big problem if you leave. There are two boats and only one of me. We have another eight to ten miles to the bridge."

But Mike refused to raft any further in the Northern Gorge. He suggested that Pasquale take his boat all the way to the Second Portuguese Bridge, then hike back and row the second raft down.

Pasquale had no idea how long that would take, piloting one raft down the river, trekking back up, and taking the second raft through. But Mike was adamant; he insisted he wouldn't go on. Pasquale cast about for alternatives. He considered having one of the Ethiopians row, at least between rapids. They could hopscotch down the canyon, Pasquale taking one raft through each rapid, then the next. But the Ethiopians had no experience rowing, and even in calm water this section was dangerous. One missed stroke and a raft could plunge to oblivion.

Then it dawned on Pasquale that perhaps they could hire local cattlemen to carry the second raft and its gear all the way down to the bridge. That way, he could continue to row his raft, and Gordon could kayak. He liked that idea, and decided to sleep on it.

But he couldn't. That night, out on the end of Pasquale's raft, sleep wouldn't come, even as the waterbed rocked gently in the current. He had a terrible side-ache. He rolled up in a ball, and his mind pulsed with worries. "Could my spleen be rupturing because of malaria?" he wondered in his journal. He'd had several bouts of malaria over the years, and knew that a ruptured spleen was often an aftereffect.

Then the pain moved to his stomach, and he thought perhaps it was a kidney stone trying to pass. He was the right age and gender, it was hot, and he was tired. He was in such pain that he couldn't stand up to fetch medication. So he rolled to his medical kit and popped ten aspirin and a few Percocet to ease the pain. And Pasquale began to wonder for the first time if he was physically able to finish this expedition. The odds of success seemed insuperable.

The sky lightened from lapis to sapphire. Pasquale's throbbing had subsided a bit, but the pain still coursed, so he popped more painkillers. He got to his feet, walked up the trail, and found some cattle herders. He offered them a handsome fee for the chore of carrying the rafts and gear. But they refused. Money was not an inducement in this outpost. It was not a money economy, and the task did not sound appealing.

Pasquale slouched back to camp and shared the dilemma with the Ethiopians. Baye spoke up: "I'll take care of it," he said, slinging his AK-47 over his shoulder. He walked up the path. A few minutes later, the herders stepped down the path to Pasquale's raft, followed closely by Baye, who was holding his firearm in a ready position. The herders bowed and volunteered their services.

Pasquale deflated Mike's raft, rolled it up, and prepared the gear for the portage. But when he presented the loads to the herders, they balked. Baye again pointed his rifle and started to yell at the locals, but they yelled back in protest. Finally Gordon cried, "Fuck you guys!" He grabbed the two-hundred-pound rolled-up raft, slung it over his shoulder, and started to climb out of the canyon. Pasquale shook his head. Gordon's rage, he recognized, had been lurking undetected for a while. Pasquale knew he was infamous for his own hot-blooded temper, but he didn't think it appropriate when it was flashed at the expense of the dis-enfranchised. He hoped Gordon's outburst was just an aberration.

Gordon made it to the top of the ridge before he mulishly dropped the bulk on the rocks. He then started to yell back to the Ethiopian herders, and Baye and Yibeltal started to swing their weapons threateningly. At last the locals started to pile the gear, including the raft, on donkeys. They slung the IMAX® camera on a pole and carried it safari-style. Mike took off as well, saying he would rendezvous with them at the bridge that evening. "I'll be there hours before you." Mike grinned. "I'll fix the G-and-T's."

Pasquale had Alemu and Baye, the two strongest Ethiopians, accompany him to help with loading the raft onto the donkeys, while the others set off to hike with Mike. Then they returned to the boat, and they all pushed downstream into a sinuous canyon full of ferns and waterfalls. "One of the most beautiful canyons I've ever run," Pasquale recorded. But it was also packed with huge rapids. One, dubbed Cave, had carved an undercut, similar to Red Wall Cavern on the Colorado River in the Grand Canyon. It was pocked with monstrous cysts of swirling water. Pasquale figured a one-in-five chance of making it through without capsizing, so he and his tiny crew made a four-hour carry around.

They continued to race down the river, running the loosed-lightning rapids with such names as Zig-Zag, Blind Corner, and Box Car. They were all more difficult than Mike Speaks had described, likely because he had passed through in higher water. Then, late in the day, they heard thunder pealing through the burled gorge. It was deep-throated and tetchy. It was the sound of a very big rapid, a Venti-sized cup of foam.

Pasquale pulled over and checked his map, one of two sets he carried. Ever since the incident on the Alsek River, he always carried at least two full sets on expeditions. On the Blue Nile he kept one stowed in each raft.

As he matched the map to the topography, he concluded that this had to be Bad Seeds Rapid, the last really difficult rapid in the Northern

Gorge. Pasquale crawled up to an overlook to view the hydrotechnics. Even from fifty feet above the river he could see the grotesque mushroom boils, the sharp falls, the holes that led down to the gates of hell. The river seemed to go insane, liquid chaos frothing, twisting, skibbling around and doubling back on itself like rogue fireworks.

He also saw the big tributary, the Abaya, that spilled into the Blue Nile through a slot canyon at this juncture, and he knew of its unpleasant history. In 1968, when the British Army was in the midst of its epic Blue Nile expedition, they made an aerial recce of the Northern Gorge and deemed it unnavigable, even in whitewater rafts. So they decided to trek around. When they came to the Abaya, it was too deep to wade, so they decided to swim a rope across, and it was here that Ian Macleod drowned.

It was too late to portage Bad Seeds Rapid. It had to be run. Pasquale was seized with a feeling of horror. "I was nervous, probably the most nervous I've ever been in my life," he recalled.

There was a cheat run down the left, a chute that stepped down a series of smaller waterfalls, but it was only as wide as the aisle of a jetliner in places, barely broad enough for a kayak. So Gordon took off and stitched the current like a Needleman.

Pasquale swallowed and started to row in, hoping to edge down the opposite bank. But at the first wave he pulled so hard that he ran into the wall, ricocheted off, spun around, and fell into a hole, where he and the crew were buried in a trench of water. Then he suddenly slammed into a rock that was radiating water like a fan. He hit it square, and the boat buckled in half, yanking his right oar from his grip and rearing as if intent on catapulting him into the roiling soup. The buzz of the river's prop sliced through him ear to ear. Against the river's will, he managed to hang on. He snatched the flying oar from the air, pushed its throat back into its lock as the boat skidded, out of control, through the last part of the rapid.

For the next three miles, they ran a continuing millrace of wild water.

"It was the longest stretch of whitewater I've ever run in my life," Pasquale said later. Then, as they rounded a corner, the water still flowing fast and dark, he looked up and saw, some three hundred yards downstream, Sabara Dildi—the Second Portuguese Bridge.

He felt as though someone had taken a sack of lead off his shoulders. He couldn't quite believe that he and his crew had made it through the Northern Gorge. Alemu and Baye, in the bow, turned and screamed in survivors' delight and hugged each other. Pasquale started to cry.

Sabara Dildi was an unlikely structure. Originally built by the Portuguese in the seventeenth century, in the court of King Fasiladas, it consisted of two stone arches over the river and three increasingly smaller ones on each side. There were two quite impressive approach ramps, with low walls. But the setting of the bridge was bizarre, for both banks rose up almost sheer above the bridge. There was nowhere for the approach ramps to go; they ended abruptly at the foot of a daunting rock scramble some three hundred feet to the cliff's top.

The bridge had collapsed at some earlier stage, and in 1908 Emperor Menelik II ordered its reconstruction. Menelik added an imposing gateway on the Gojjam (western) side, on which there was a cement panel commemorative of this work. At low water, as it was when Pasquale arrived, the bridge loomed high over a deep cleft like some Victorian railway viaduct. But he could see the high-water marks where the river had swirled at the tops of the ancient legs.

More recently, it had suffered another grave blow. In the late 1930s, the Ethiopian resistance was trying to stop Italians in Begemdir (the eastern side) from joining up with those in Gojjam. A local squireen with a band of forty men dug up the central arch. Unfortunately, it collapsed into the river while they were still digging, and all forty drowned. The Italians shot a further six men in Mota as a reprisal.

Since then, the bridge has never been permanently repaired. An ugly steel affair spans the gap, across which herdsmen now unconcernedly drive their tan-and-white goats.

As they approached the bridge, Pasquale saw Michel L'Huillier, the Chilean photographer from the earlier shoot. He was jumping up and down on the stone ramparts, waving wildly. Jordi, the director, had proposed that Michel join Pasquale's expedition from Sabara Dildi down to Khartoum, a stretch that avoided the worst of the rapids but passed through some dramatic gorges during which Michel could take photos to help promote the film. Michel had done a bit of rafting on the Bío-Bío River in Chile, so Pasquale was thrilled that Michel was joining to help out.

Just above the bridge Pasquale pulled over, jumped out, and gave Michel an emotional bear hug. Then he looked around. He saw two other Western faces, and several Ethiopians, but no Mike Prosser.

"Where's Mike?" he asked Michel.

"I don't know. I haven't seen him. He's not with you?" Michel replied.

Pasquale explained what had happened. "We left Mike less than ten miles upstream. It doesn't take all day to hike that."

Pasquale said he would go looking for Mike after they set up camp, and he started to unload the raft. A white woman walked down and offered to help. She introduced herself as Zoë Keone, along with her partner Chris Rollins, an engineer. She explained she worked for an organization called Bridges to Prosperity. The founder had read about Sabara Dildi, the broken bridge, in a *National Geographic* article about the 1999 Sobek expedition that started rafting at the bridge. In the piece was a photo of the broken bridge with a boy trying to cross above the boiling waters using a crude and risky rope system. The founder of Bridges to Prosperity, Ken Frantz, had put up $250,000 to place water-resistant steel beams, topped with concrete, across the gap. It looked terrible, grossly out of place in the natural grandeur of the Northern Gorge, and though the intention was noble, for a fraction of the cost the locals could have finished the job with natural materials. Zoë explained that she was assigned to trek in and inspect the bridge once a year, and by sheer coincidence her visit this year had coincided with Pasquale's arrival.

As they were talking, a very old man walked across the bridge, made a syrupy cough, and handed Pasquale a crumpled piece of paper. It read in a ragged scrawl: "Help Pasquale. Unable to make it. Have to sleep out tonight. Send water. Send food."

It was from Mike.

Pasquale sent Baye back up the trail with food and water, then collapsed into sleep.

CHAPTER THIRTEEN

He who has not seen the Blue Nile will praise a stream.

ANCIENT ETHIOPIAN PROVERB

The great object is sensation—to feel that we exist. It is this craving void which drives us to travel to intemperate but keenly felt pursuits of every description whose principal attraction is the agitation inseparable from their accomplishment.

GEORGE GORDON, LORD BYRON

It had now been two weeks on the Blue Nile Expedition, and it seemed a lifetime. Pasquale slept in until 7:00 A.M. About 9:00 A.M. two local villagers appeared, carrying a small tree trunk over their shoulders. Strung between them with some old rope was the IMAX® camera, swinging back and forth like a dead body. Soon afterward Mike Prosser showed up, so exhausted that he staggered like a drunk. He collapsed and fell asleep on a rock.

As his teammate slept, Pasquale wondered if Mike might leave at this point, as here there was a good path out of the canyon to the village of Mota. But after Mike rested for the better part of the day he got up and said, "Count me in," for the next stretch. There were no rapids of consequence in the 140-mile slice to the Shefartak Bridge, the next resupply.

The following day, Wednesday, January 7, they spent the morning re-rigging the rafts. Zoë, who had developed an instant crush on Michel, hung around, and volunteered to help with an IMAX® Theatre scene that Gordon decided to shoot.

Then, with little flourish, they pushed off and headed down into the stretch known as the Grand Canyon of Africa. It is one of several places called that, including the Fish River Canyon in Namibia, which has the colorful sedimentary rocks of Arizona's Grand Canyon but is not even half its depth; and the Tekeze Canyon, the next watershed north of the Blue Nile, and which at seven thousand feet deep is really the deepest gorge on the continent. The 1968 British Army expedition had coined this particular moniker for a canyon about as deep as America's Grand Canyon, just under a vertical mile.

After an uneventful day, in the still gloaming, they pulled over to a wide beach with a sparkling tributary. Out came the Gouder red and the Johnnie Walker. It was *Ganna*, Ethiopian Christmas, in accordance with the Julian calendar of the Coptic Church, a time to celebrate the Feast of the Epiphany—as well as surviving the horrors of the Northern Gorge. More than half of all Ethiopians are Orthodox Christian, and this crew was fairly pious, so while the *ferengis* took a bath in a gin-clear pool, the Ethiopians went off to pray. But afterward they all partied. The Ethiopians ate too much, drank too much, and then prayed again as they slouched into sleep.

The next day the team poured through a slice of natural grandeur. Across the line of the river from the Gojjam bank, a fifty-foot vertical slab of basalt reared up. Here and there, trees were adorned with the spherical nests of busy, black-headed, yellow-bodied weaverbirds.

The cliff went on for miles, increasing in height as they passed along it, first to sixty feet, then eighty, and finally after some miles to a cathedral-like scale of about 120 feet. The rim was lined with a restless nation of black vervet monkeys. At water level, the wet basaltic lava shone like a black sculpture.

Then, around one long corner, they encountered two huge, ithyphallic basalt pillars, slices of cliff cut off by the river. They soared like twin towers, narrow and sheer, to about 120 feet, beautifully shaped and crowned with mossy trees and shrubs. It's been suggested that J.R.R. Tolkien found much of his inspiration in Ethiopia, with his descriptions of Middle Earth matching much of the phantasmagoric outcroppings of the Abyssinian plateau, and with identical place names, such as Gondor. And yet, these towers were unreachable except by specially designed boats, nonexistent in Tolkien's time.

In all this wildness, it was a shock to suddenly see in the cliff face a man-made wall and doorways—one triangular, the other semicircular. There were no signs of steps from the river to the grottoes, twenty-five feet up, or from the top of the cliff downward. How did people get there? The only human modification had been a platform of dressed stone at the mouth. There was no sign of any permanent or even temporary arrangements for getting into and out of the cave. Pasquale named them the Shifta Caves, as he assumed this would be the ideal place for bandits to hide out.

The next day, they drifted down through a section previously christened "the Gorgeous Gorge," an inner canyon with 150-foot-high sheer walls. Sandstone outcroppings and tamarisk trees lined the banks, along with a fairy-tale waterfall that leapt over the edge and spilled diamonds in the sunlight as it splashed into the Nile. It was eerily similar to Cataract Canyon in Utah, one of Pasquale's favorite rivers, though the sand was a darker gray due to the volcanic soil.

It all reminded Pasquale of his first trip down the Colorado in 1981. He had been an oilman in the midst of the oil boom, and the owner of a helicopter exploration company had invited him on a boondoggle. Pasquale had been flown from Denver on a private jet to Grand Canyon Village, where he spent the night in a suite, feasting. The next morning, he was helicoptered to the confluence of the Colorado and the Little Colorado, and from there he rafted as a client for the next five days, all expenses paid. While at Northern Arizona University in Flagstaff,

Pasquale studied the Coconino Sandstone region of the Grand Canyon, though he had never been into its layered belly, and it was a special thrill for him to be floating on the river that had carved the book of the earth. So, while the others on the trip saw the experience as just another in an endless collection of trophy experiences, Pasquale found it life-changing. He loved the wildness of the river, its unruliness and quietude. It was at the moment of takeout that he first decided to buy his own raft and master the art of river running. Three years later he was running Chile's Bío-Bío River and planning a series of global descents, including in Ethiopia.

Pasquale's reverie was interrupted when, from the top of the cliffs, they heard a number of whooping cries, the sort often heard exchanged between travelers in the quiet of the Ethiopian countryside. But here, they were excited and in concert. The team was slow to appreciate the significance of the whoops echoing back and forth across the gorge until the river was pocked with little eruptions made by a fusillade of rocks. They looked up: About seventy-five yards away, along the rim of the cliff, among the fringe of gnarled trees and scrub, appeared a motley crowd of about a dozen men carrying rifles, shouting angrily and gesticulating. As the ragtag warlord of the group gave a signal, more rocks were fired down. Spurts of water danced up in the stream around them.

The team was dumbfounded. Pasquale knew the British Army had been attacked by shifta gunfire in this section of the Blue Nile, but up to this point all his encounters with Ethiopians had been friendly. It had almost seemed the shifta terror was a myth, although one exchange before the trip suggested otherwise. Pasquale had corresponded with a Steve Hammat from Mount Vernon, Washington, who had lost his brother in this section of the Blue Nile in 1974. Inspired by Colin Fletcher's book, *The Man Who Walked Through Time,* an account of the author's traverse by foot of the entire Grand Canyon, Bill Hammat decided he wanted to make a similar traverse through the Grand Canyon of Africa and write a book about the trek. The e-mail Pasquale had received was as follows:

Bill and Peter (sorry, I don't recall his last name right now) were trying to walk the river from the source to where it became part of the Nile. There was a German team also on the river at the time, but they were in boats, Bill and Pete were walking the gorge. Apparently they were attacked by bandits and were never found. Some of their gear was apparently found later, but no evidence of exactly what happened ever surfaced.

The embassy personnel that were in contact with Bill and Pete were suddenly transferred back home, the money source for the entire journey was a bit mysterious, and the Mission Fellowship pilot that was supporting the mission with supply drops was returned to the US, somewhere near Langley, VA. Just a bunch of weird things happened that by themselves mean little, but maybe when taken together and from a perspective of time, could have meant more.

Steve

Now, under attack, it didn't take long to react. Pasquale and Mike leaned into their oars and started rowing as hard as they could. Angry men continued to fling jagged pieces of basalt at them. At the next bend they were pulled into the magnetic field of a rapid and whipped out of sight of the shiftas. For whatever reasons, the shiftas didn't use their rifles—perhaps because the bullets are expensive and hard to replace—and Pasquale's team suffered no scars from the attack.

Thinking they were out of range, and hugging the opposite side of the two-hundred-yard-wide river, they drooped over their oars to catch a breath. Then another salvo of rocks hit them broadside from the nearer cliff rim. They looked up and saw a troop of gelada baboons taking aim. Their low, mastifflike barks hung in the air, echoing between the canyon walls. "Those little shits," Pasquale cursed. "The baboons have been taught to throw rocks at people."

Again, they pulled out to the middle current and escaped around the corner. This time, as they drifted, they all eyed the horizon for rock throwers of any stripe. But when Michel heard a loud splash, he looked down and saw a beast with skin like radial tires charging toward him, now just three feet away. His heart, already shaking in the cage of his chest, nearly exploded. He uncorked a scream and pitched back, almost falling into the river off the other side of the raft. The crocodile slowly slipped underwater and disappeared.

This was their closest crocodile encounter to date.

The ancient Greeks called it *kroko-drilo,* "pebble-worm"—a scaly thing that shuffled and lurked in low places. The most deadly existing reptile, the man-eating Nile crocodile has always been on the "man's worst enemies" list. It evolved 170 million years ago from the primordial soup as an efficient killing machine. More people are killed and eaten by crocodiles each year in Africa than by all other animals combined. Their instinct is predation—to kill any meat that floats their way, be it fish, hippo, antelope, or human. To crocs, Pasquale and his team were just one dish in the food chain.

The rest of the afternoon was anxiety-filled. In the awful heat, team members constantly watched the cliffs and the river surface for foes.

Despite the distractions, by late afternoon they had made thirty miles, a good distance. At about 5:00 P.M. Pasquale saw a broad beach camp on the right, and he urged the group to pull over. But this time Gordon and Michel and Mike all protested and insisted on going farther, confident of greener pastures. They were wrong. The gorge narrowed, and the few sand spits that spilled from side canyons were coated in dung. A man usually capable of swift, certain decisions, Pasquale now kicked himself for letting the group make a bad decision. "Need to make future decisions myself," he wrote in his journal. He was far and away the most experienced, and the leader, but something within him sometimes allowed Pasquale to let his better judgment be overridden.

As light the color of cognac painted the walls, they finally found a spot up a steep slope among some trees. Yellow-eyed local herders drifted down and begged for *wova medani,* antimalaria medicine, the two-hundred-milligram prophylaxis tablets that keep the sporozoan parasites from the bites of anopheline mosquitoes inactive. Most of those accustomed to the bright horizons of the plateau fear to go down to the place they regard with superstitious awe, and malaria is the chief reason. With no prophylactics or cures, the villagers risk malaria and other riverborne diseases whenever they leave the cool highlands, but Pasquale's presence was just too unusual to resist. Even though his own supply was diminishing, Pasquale unscrewed a bottle of Lariam and handed out the tablets, patiently explaining how to use them.

The herders bowed low three times in gratitude and then headed back up the hill. Pasquale's enormous charity and concern for the well-being of those who crossed his path were legendary in expedition circles. In every city, one-story town, and village through which he had passed, there was someone whom Pasquale had helped by buying a bicycle, setting up a business or school, or sending money or anodynes. A sort of beneficial virus, he infected everyone he met.

It was too hot for a sleeping bag, so Pasquale spread a sheet along his pad and lay down. His skin was burning, so he had to find a position on his side. The weather, increasingly hot and dry, was taking its toll. He made his final journal entry for the day: "Sunburned and browned. Cracked skin on feet. Cracked fingers very sore. Sore muscles from rafting 30 miles in a single day."

CHAPTER FOURTEEN

What am I doing here?

ARTHUR RIMBAUD, WRITING HOME FROM ETHIOPIA

The next day found them deep inside the Grand Canyon of Africa. As they traveled, they were slicing through history. When they began the journey, the river walls had been basalt: the volcanic layer from the Tertiary and Quaternary periods perhaps sixty million years old that covers much of the highland regions of East Africa and forms the upper crust of the Great Rift Valley. For days they'd wound down through 1,500 vertical feet of Vulcan's rock until they reached a band of fluted limestone left from some long-ago sea. Then they spilled through a vertical half-mile of Mesozoic Era sandstone, a strata formed perhaps two hundred million years ago that seemed to emanate soft light. When Pasquale closed his eyes and reopened them, he was certain he was on a river in the American Southwest.

Today the walls at river level turned dark and hard, exposing another page in this living textbook. They rode into metamorphic shales, Precambrian stone six hundred million years old. This had been a violent place back then, and evidence was everywhere. The landscape was bent, fractured, and torn; it had folds and faults, monoclines and synclines, dikes, sills, schist.

They saw several crocs sunbathing with their mouths agape, prehistoric creatures to match the prehistoric scenery. A few more cruised the shallow waters near shore, looking for easy prey. The team also sighted a fifteen-foot rock python, big enough to capsize a canoe or a kayak and swallow a man whole. Alemu fired three rounds at the python, but it was either too content or too tired to move, and just lay coiled around the rock.

Most of the side canyons were dry now, and the few thorn trees looked blackened and dead, as though a fire had swept through. At one point they passed a convocation of warthogs. They seemed to be sniffing something on the north shore, but when they saw the yellow flotilla, they shot their fly-swatter tails straight into the air and scrabbled away in a line, with neat, small steps.

The team made camp that night even deeper in time. The gorge here was steep and narrow; the rock was granitic, the core of the earth. It seemed they couldn't cut much deeper without coming out the other side.

Pasquale awoke in the morning to the sounds of Yohannes making coffee—something he and most other Ethiopians were adept at, since coffee originated in Ethiopia. As Pasquale sipped the brew, he felt a renewed pain in his lower left abdomen, but he tried to ignore it and began to prepare the rafts. They were about as far away from a doctor as one can be on earth, so he and everyone else had to make do.

As they went about their chores, Pasquale noticed Yibeltal level a look at Gordon, the cold, unblinking eye of a lizard. Not long after, Gordon pulled Pasquale aside and said they needed to talk. Pasquale had noticed that increasingly, Gordon's cool, affable demeanor had been more of a pointed sneer, and he'd watched disapprovingly as Gordon made snide quips to the Ethiopians. "I can't stand Yibeltal," Gordon confided. "He stares at me all the time. I confront him, and he still stares at me. He's arrogant! I want him off the expedition."

"No, Gordon," answered Pasquale. "We can't do it. We need him. And you're reading him wrong. . . . It's an Ethiopian trait to stare. Let it go."

Despite his assurance, the encounter bothered Pasquale. There was a kind of willed remoteness about Gordon, a desire to keep his own interior as inviolate and inaccessible as this canyon. Pasquale wrote in his journal, "I'm trying to keep the peace between Gordon and Yibeltal, although it's getting difficult. I need to keep discipline, to hang on, to keep going." All were principles of expedition leadership that he had learned on Everest.

Pasquale first attempted Everest in 1995 on an environmental cleanup expedition, the goal of which was to retrieve hundreds of discarded oxygen bottles that littered its slopes. He climbed alongside Rob Hall, the New Zealander who died a year later in the disaster chronicled in Jon Krakauer's *Into Thin Air*. Pasquale made it to the south summit, but the weather was turning, and it was getting late, and Rob Hall had a rigid turnaround rule—if the summit was not reached by a certain time, no matter how close they were, they must turn around. It was this rule that he violated with fatal consequences in 1996.

But this time they played it safe, and without reaching the top, they went back down to Camp Three at 24,500 feet. When the weather cleared a couple of days later, several teammates went back up and made the summit. But Pasquale had broken out in alternating chills and fever, and he headed down. Four years earlier, Pasquale had contracted malaria in Ethiopia, and now he was having a relapse, poleaxed on Everest.

He was shivering violently, and it was very difficult to negotiate downward, really hard to get through the treacherous Khumbu icefall, where most deaths on Everest occur amidst the shifting ice. He was so sick that he had to lie down on the ice and rest, hoping he wouldn't be killed by a collapsing serac (ice tower). Still, he managed to drag several discarded bottles of oxygen off the mountain as part of the cleanup effort. He brought one back to me, from an early Russian expedition, and it sits in my office today.

But the failure did not daunt Pasquale. He returned to Everest in 1998. The weather was bad, but Pasquale fought hard. When a storm hit on May 19, the party in front of Pasquale turned around at the South Summit. But Pasquale persisted, and the following day he kicked the first trail of the season up the Hillary Step and to the summit itself.

It was a wonderful experience. Pasquale later said about that moment: "I remember vividly crossing Bishop Rock [named for Barry Bishop, first American to climb Everest, in 1963], the last piece of exposed granite before the summit. I walked a few feet forward, looked up, and I could see, fifteen yards ahead, the little triangle that the Chinese had left a few years earlier. I made the final steps, and fell on my knees, clenching my fists, and yelling, 'Yeah, didn't die. Did it!' "

As Pasquale drifted farther downstream through the Grand Canyon of Africa, he noticed that for the first time, no matter how far he gazed—even through binoculars—he could see no sign of Man or Man's works. No huts, no cattle, no goats, no farms, no fields . . . just raw wilderness. Pasquale pulled out his notebook and wrote,

JOURNAL DAY 19

In reality, man can only do so much to the earth. If everyone in the highlands died tomorrow, all of Ethiopia would probably revert back to wilderness quickly. In the scheme of things, man is pretty small and insignificant.

Then suddenly Pasquale heard a splatter, and he spun around to see a twelve-foot croc closing in on Gordon's eight-foot kayak from behind. "Croc!" Pasquale yelled. Behind him, he heard a distinctive *chick-chick*, as Alemu chambered a round in his AK-47 and aimed. But the other raft was just beyond the croc, and all the boats were bouncing down the current. A bad shot might have disastrous consequences. "Don't shoot,"

Pasquale ordered, and they watched as Gordon spun his paddle in trochal form to outrun the charging croc. The croc had come within two feet when Gordon smacked the water with the flat side of his paddle, making a sound like a rifle shot. Like a ghost, the crocodile vanished below the surface. All was silent, and the soldiers scanned the water, rifles cocked and ready to fire. A fish eagle lazily rode a thermal, adjusting his wing tips mutely as he wheeled. They watched a wind-pipple on the water, and the croc rose like a submarine, sprouting up just under Pasquale's oar. Pasquale grabbed the grip and hit the croc on its head with the blade, then pushed off from its back. It dropped down and didn't return.

They pulled over to eat some lunch, and to reassess the situation. "We gotta keep the boats close," Pasquale said. "It's getting too dangerous. We need to be in range if one of us gets in trouble." Gordon looked nonplussed, but he agreed. Out of nowhere, a totally naked Ethiopian showed up—lean and black—and stood over them as they ate. Mike pulled out a can of Spam, peeled back the lid, and offered the treat to the visitor. He studied it for a bit, then plunged his finger in and pulled out a wad on his index crook. He put it on his tongue, and then swallowed. His face cinched and contorted, and he tossed the can in the river and stomped away.

But then Pasquale noticed a swirl of smoke where the man had disappeared up the canyon. "Let's go look," he said.

When Pasquale and crew crested a small ridge, they faced a charred, ravaged wasteland, acres and acres of smoldering devastation. There on the edge they found a group of charcoal makers—subsistence farmers who, against government interdiction, clear-cut and scorch trees to create charcoal. It takes about ten trees to create a four-foot-high sack of charcoal, which sells for about a dollar a bag along the roadside. "Forest in a Sack," environmentalists call it. While Ethiopia is one of the richest nations in the world in terms of nature and biodiversity, it is one of the poorest economically, with an average annual per-capita income of less than $100. The typical rural family has eight or nine children, and the country posts a 3.5 percent annual population growth. To feed these folds, parents cook with the cheapest fuel: charcoal.

For most in Ethiopia, environmentalism is a long-sighted luxury that clashes with current crying needs; the next meal is the priority. Yet, if alternatives to existing practices aren't adopted soon, the present will be a burnt sacrifice to the future. Burning down one's own environment ultimately becomes self-immolation.

Alemu and Baye, Pasquale's personal EPRDF soldiers, had carried their Kalashnikovs up the hill, and now they gathered the charcoalers and asked to see their burning permit. When the men shrugged, Alemu made them promise to cease and desist, saying he would check back in a week and throw any who violated the law in jail. They promised to stop burning and turned to walk toward the plateau. It was all a farce, of course—everyone knew that as soon as the rafts turned the corner the burning would begin again.

In the crepuscular light they found a camp at the edge of a wide eddy, the sort of spot that is a favorite among crocs. Pasquale carried a Q-Beam spot floodlight, which emits one million candlepower, and he swept it along the banks as dinner was being prepared. As the beam traveled, it caught the bright red eyes of half a dozen crocs hovering a few feet from shore, waiting for potential prey to visit the river for a final nighttime drink. Gordon went down to retrieve his kayak, so the devil-eyed monsters wouldn't steal it.

For the next two days, the river slowed, the wind ceased, and the sun took on the weight of molten lead. The team found themselves repeatedly stuck on gravel bars, dragging the rafts across in the one-hundred-degree heat. The river took on more personalities. They watched as black-and-white colobus monkeys sailed between treetops, issuing scratched-washboard cries. They passed vervet monkeys and more baboons, rock hyraxes, defassa waterbuck, dik-diks, hyenas, and bounding klipspringers. January was a good time for game viewing: Drought in the highlands forced animals to seek the water of the river. There are about 830 different species of birds in Ethiopia, a couple dozen of them unique to the country, and the team spotted a good number: sacred and hadada ibises (with mocking cries), snowy egrets, yellow-billed storks, herons, bee-eaters as vivid blue as sapphires, bateleur eagles, malachite and giant kingfishers, a covey of plump blue-and-gray guinea fowl, masked weavers, and the African fish eagles with their regal white breasts, tails, and heads. Egyptian geese were everywhere, and at every alarm, imagined or real, they would take flight, hissing and honking about the rafts with a proprietary air.

And there were crocs . . . lots of them. Several times the group was charged. One clamped onto Mike's oar blade, leaving deep teeth marks on both sides. It gave Pasquale pause, and he worried for Gordon in his tiny kayak. "Why don't you just give up on the kayak and ride the rafts with us?" Pasquale asked. Gordon would have none of it. He was going to paddle the entire length of the Blue Nile, or die trying.

The nights were getting humid now, air like wet velvet, and clouds of bugs appeared whenever headlamps were turned on—a festival of irritation. While Michel took to sleeping in the saunalike tent, Pasquale sprawled in the relative cool of the outside, preferring buggy to muggy. The next morning, Pasquale awoke with a swollen left eye, courtesy of some creature of the night.

At 10:50 on Tuesday, January 13, exactly three weeks after the start of the expedition, they passed beneath the great central arch of the steel Shefartak Bridge, or Great Abay Bridge, one of the only two modern spans in Ethiopia that arch over the width of the Blue Nile. When the Italians invaded Ethiopia and temporarily occupied much of the country in the 1930s, they found it necessary to build a bridge across the Blue Nile to consolidate their grip on the country. The rims of the canyon at this point are fully eighteen miles apart, allowing a long, gently graded switchback road that connects the north and south, Addis Ababa to Bahir Dar and the source of the Blue Nile.

There, waiting on the abutment, were several soldiers, friends of Alemu and Baye, and Zelalem with the resupply from Addis Ababa. Passing under the bridge was another very emotional moment for Pasquale, who realized he was that much closer to the end of the trip and would most likely never pass this way again. He wondered how many people had crossed this bridge and looked upstream and down, wondering where the river began and where it ended. For them, that was the mystery of the Nile.

As they pulled over and parked just below the high bridge, they found that due to some miscommunication, the resupply truck had been waiting for two days, and some of the bread, vegetables, and eggs had gone bad in the 110-degree heat. Yohannes, the cook, hightailed it up the road to the nearby village of Dejon, ostensibly to buy some fresh foodstuffs. While there, he checked into the local brothel for a three-hour respite. Pasquale was pissed by the delay, but then he forgave Yohannes. "He's a horny little Amhara, but he's a great cook," Pasquale wrote.

Mike Prosser packed up and left the expedition here. His visa was about to expire, he missed his family, and he had done enough, had more of an adventure than he had bargained for. Still, everyone was sad to see him go, and all held back tears as deeply felt hugs were exchanged. That left Michel to row the second raft, which gave Pasquale concern, as they were about to enter the Black Gorge.

It was more than the color of its rocks that had earned it that name.

CHAPTER FIFTEEN

From my youth I had been inured to the hardships and endurance in wild sports in tropical climates, and when I gazed upon a map of Africa I had a wild hope, mingled with humility, that, even as the insignificant worm bores through the hardest oak, I might with perseverance reach the heart of Africa.

SAMUEL BAKER, MAY 1861

There may always be an element of indeterminacy in river mechanics that is simply beyond rational comprehension.

LEOPOLD AND LANGBEIN, 1963

As they entered the Black Gorge, the weather began to change . . . midday temperatures now were consistently at 110 degrees or higher, and hot winds blew fine, stinging sand into every wrinkle and orifice. A bisque haze hung over the canyon. On the first evening there was even a light rain, the first in four months. One of the mysteries of the Nile, Pasquale conjectured aloud, was how the Blue Nile, which runs chiefly through barren landscapes, maintains such a robust flow year-round. There are no melting glaciers, no snowfields, no big mountains draining into the basin, no big jungle catchments as in the Amazon or the Congo. Like the Ethiopian travelers who stand on the Shefartak Bridge, Pasquale wondered where the water came from.

With the loss of Mike Prosser, Pasquale went about teaching Michel and the Ethiopians how to rig and manage the second raft. He gave them rowing lessons, but when they didn't pick it up readily, his patience was tried. Pasquale kept pushing for a fast pace down the sluggish, meandering river, but the second raft, which veered back and forth across the river like an infant learning first steps, had trouble keeping up. The tension mounted as Pasquale yelled to keep up and the others yelled back. At one point Pasquale discovered that Yalew had been collecting rocks, weighing down the second raft, and when Yalew wasn't looking, Pasquale tossed them into the river.

Pasquale called Kim, his wife, on the sat-phone—and it only made things worse. He'd been away for almost three months, and she was missing him. Even though she'd well known she was marrying an expedition leader when they wed in 1998, Kim didn't expect such long absences. "What's this marriage about? About you being gone all the time?" she asked when he called. But the louder news on the home front was that she was fighting with his youngest son, Adam, who was in the midst of a divorce. He was trying to maneuver more money from a trust set up from an accident, and Kim thought it inappropriate. He spoke with both of them until past midnight, trying to mediate, but it just couldn't be done from half a world away. He went to bed aggravated and angry. Off in the distance, high above the canyon walls, he could see little licks of flames burning holes in the night—the charcoal makers at work.

Whenever Pasquale was home in Colorado for more than a few weeks, he became "far-sick" and needed to take flight to some foreign place. But now, in his sleeping bag, he thought of home. He remembered the scents and colors, the reliquary of his garage, the oak tree in the front yard that he and Kim had planted when they married. Sometimes when they argued he threatened to take a chainsaw to the trunk, but he knew he never would.

Now he felt impoverished in this faraway place. Whatever self-sufficiency he could claim, his distance from things, the consolation of being in control—all were shaken. For the moment before sleep he missed gnawing on the old bone of his amicable common life in Colorado.

The British named the Black Gorge for the tall walls of brimstonelike Precambrian gneisses and schists that encase the river. One consequence of the dark rock is that it turns the river corridor into an oven, and tempers flared with the temperature. There were arguments about food preparation, sanitation, rigging, how to pack boxes, camp routines, just about everything. The team stopped squabbling briefly after two shiftas wandered into camp at 3:00 in the morning carrying automatic weapons. Alemu and Baye produced their superior firepower and chased the shiftas away. But next lunchtime the bickering recommenced, this time over the yellow mustard. Pasquale wanted to know where it was; Yohannes said it had gone missing, and Pasquale went rifling through all the kitchen boxes. When he found the bottle, Pasquale picked it up and threw it at Yohannes. It turned out that Yohannes had misunderstood him, as happened not infrequently between the *ferengis* and the Ethiopians. When the dust cleared, Pasquale apologized.

And Gordon seemed more and more to dance to his own drum. When a crocodile followed Gordon through a rapid, Gordon raced through and ahead, and then turned his little boat around and paddled aggressively straight toward the reptile. Gordon proffered that crocs are predators, and just like bears or lions, they go after the weak or injured. His theory was that if he turned and counterattacked a charging croc, it would back right off.

Pasquale shook his head. "Gordon, what are you talking about? Your theory is insane. If a croc attacks from behind, and you don't see him, you're dead. Your arms are only six inches off the water. A croc can grab one of your arms, and once he has it, he'll start spinning, spin you right out of the kayak; then you're gone."

But Gordon was convinced otherwise, and he began to practice his technique in the eddies. Pasquale watched as Gordon pretended a log was a croc. He would whirl around to face it, and make waves while rushing at the make-believe croc, slapping the flat side of his paddle on the river's surface and making pirouettes, scaring the log to death.

The river began to attenuate like a funnel, from a half-mile wide to less than twenty yards bank to bank. The walls were decorated with pegmatites of quartz, like wands tracing magic dust in the dark. It was beautiful packaging for the ugliness that was brewing.

Camp that night was on a sandy islet in the river's middle. It was here that the Franco-Swiss Expedition of 1962 had met grim disaster. The six expedition members were sound asleep on the island at about 1:30 A.M., under a full moon, when shiftas suddenly opened fire. Two men were killed instantly; another was wounded as he and the survivors took to their boats and launched downstream in the darkness. Another hail of bullets and the boat was holed and a paddle smashed. Only the remaining four survived.

After dinner, Yohannes announced that he was going to leave the expedition at the Bure Bridge. He didn't like all the yelling. Pasquale yelled back that Yohannes could walk out right there without pay. Yohannes reconsidered, and agreed to stay until the Sudanese border. Again Pasquale apologized.

Late in the day on the 15th, they reached Castanio's Folly, which looked more like an old fort than a bridge, with the fat roots of fig trees twisting about the stone in knots. In 1896, an Ethiopian engineer of Italian descent named Castanio had received a commission from the reigning Emperor Menelik to build the first modern bridge across the Nile, to connect the capital to the rich provinces to the north. While Castanio waited for steel to arrive from Milan, he went to the river to oversee the construction of the huge granite stone abutments on either side. He chose a site that allowed for a relatively narrow span of 279 feet. Though the steel arrived safely in the French port city of Djibouti, it mysteriously disappeared while in transit to Addis Ababa. Castanio reordered, only to have the steel go missing again. How do tons and tons of steel disappear? Another mystery of the Nile. Unfortunately, by this time the Emperor had lost patience, and he cut off further funding.

Undaunted, Castanio returned to the crossing in 1933 and built a flying pontoon ferry—a barge held against the current by an overhead cable. He connected the cable to the stone abutments he'd built more than thirty years earlier. The frayed ends of those cables still protrude from the abutments today.

About five hundred yards downstream of Castanio's original attempt, the occupying Italians had built a flying pontoon ferry connecting Gojjam and Wolega. It continued to operate from the 1930s until 1974, when the socialist-inspired Military Coordinating Committee, known as the Dergue ("committee" in Amharic), violently overthrew the government of Emperor Haile Selassie and cast the country into chaos. A casualty was the Second Castanio crossing, which fell into disrepair, and today is just a rusty cable spanning the river.

Zoë Keone, of Bridges to Prosperity, scouted the site in March 2002 and met with village elders and Kebele leaders on both sides of the Nile. She estimated the population of villagers living directly on either side at more than a quarter-million, and many had family members on opposite sides whom they hadn't seen in thirty years. Trade is virtually nonexistent between the two sides—the crossing is too dangerous, what with crocodiles and mad currents. The round trip to the other side by trail or road takes more than three days by bus and another two by foot. So Zoë had told Pasquale that Bridges to Prosperity was currently in the process of engineering another flying pontoon ferry, one that would turn the Folly into better fortunes.

Castanio's seemed a good spot for a rest, so Pasquale called a layover day. He took the time to catch up on his journal:

JOURNAL DAY 24

Very tired. I need to calm down and explain myself more fully. Perhaps too much stress. Over two months away from home. I hate to be an asshole but occasionally it works, especially in a country like Ethiopia where discipline is in short supply. Hot, long days. Relationship between Gordo and Yibeltal is not good—very tense. Two do not like each other—all this takes a toll on me.

That day they washed clothes, patched small holes in the rafts, recharged batteries with Pasquale's homemade solar charger, explored the faux bridge, and went for a bath in a deep swimming hole up the Guder Shet tributary, which was where the British made their first airdrop of food and supplies in 1968. Here it was, thirty-six years later, and Pasquale and crew had no such outside support. They carried what they needed between the few bridges, and made do.

The crew had hoped to sleep in a bit the next morning, but the sandflies were out at first light and leaping over every inch of exposed skin. They were about the only sign of life so far in the Black Gorge. The team hadn't seen people in two days, nor wildlife along the banks, and even the grass and trees were burned black and dead.

Moving through the Black Gorge was like passing through a grand black marble hallway with finely sculpted walls. The metamorphic cliffs were five hundred feet high, scoured clean of any vegetation, and polished to a sensual sheen by the high water in the rainy season. When the British Army motored through here it had been during the monsoons, and the water level had been fifty feet higher.

The rapids marked on Mike Speaks' maps just didn't seem to exist at this water level. Entire falls were now leveled out in the low flow. *Perhaps the Black Gorge would be easier than Speaks described*, Pasquale thought. At least there were no shortages of gorgeous beaches for campsites.

At lunch they pulled over at the confluence with the Fincha Shet. They'd hoped to fill their containers with freshwater, but the tributary was running molasses-brown with eruptions of dark foam and giving off an awful stench. A couple of incense collectors appeared at lunch, foraging for the oaklike *hagenia,* whose seeds are burned in the Ethiopian coffee ceremony. They explained that up the Fincha Shet was a hydro-station and a sugar factory, and the pollution was its effluence. It seemed an environmental atrocity in the midst of such a pristine wilderness, but Pasquale found a small offset when he offered the incense collectors his used bottles and cans, which they accepted with alacrity. At least he had found a way to recycle.

In the afternoon they began to see wildlife again—two herds of kudu, a klipspringer, more baboons—which made Pasquale think the canyon was again stretching out and becoming accessible. It also meant that perhaps whatever rapids remained on the map might be washed out. But then they came upon a Class III configuration. Pasquale went through first and had Michel watch the run. Then Michel took the oars and followed the vector exactly, executing a perfect path. Maybe he had been worrying too much about Michel and his lack of whitewater experience. *Might be a nonissue*, he thought.

That evening a burly old desert wind began to blow up the canyon from Sudan. The fading sun was turning the canyon walls a menacing blue-black. They weren't far from the border, where the dangers would be of an entirely different order.

Monday, January 19—the twenty-seventh day of the expedition— began like many others, with banter around the campfire in the pale morning light. The canyon looked the same as it had in the pitch of night: angular, distant, coolly impersonal. As the sun approached the horizon, a thick line of neon crimson bled along the edge of the earth. It hung there a long time—it seemed like an hour—before one spot bloomed and the sun rose. In the meantime, distant layers appeared in the rest of the sky, as if glass plates separated the pink morning air from the indigo shadows of night.

After coffee, Pasquale decided to hike a nearby five-thousand-foot mountain for the view and some photos. Pasquale sped up the peak in his Teva sandals, stepping through sharp, burned elephant grass. On top, he sat down to soak in the panorama. The views were unencumbered: all clean lines and empty spaces. Pasquale could see for leagues. And in his eyesight there were no fields or farms or villages, just the residue of the burning. The Black Gorge of the Blue Nile was a natural barrier, one that separated the highland Amhara peoples from the Nilotic Gumuz and Oromiya to the south. But it had also helped keep Ethiopia itself independent through the centuries. In fact, Ethiopia is the only country in Africa never to have been colonized, if you regard Liberia as a colonial construct. Its fierce topography and equally fierce people kept all invaders at bay, except for the brief interregnum of the Italian occupation in the '30s.

The Italian army crossed from Eritrea in October 1935. The Ethiopian army engaged them, in the Tigre region in January 1936, just as Haile Selassie appeared as *Time* magazine's Man of the Year. After a couple of minor Ethiopian victories, Italy's superior airpower, and its use of mustard gas—prohibited by international rules of war—proved decisive. Haile Selassie went into exile, and the streets erupted into anarchy and violence.

Throughout the Italian occupation, the Ethiopian nobility combined time-buying diplomacy and well-organized guerrilla warfare to undermine the foreign regime. The Fascists' response was characteristically brutal, and included tactics that Haile Selassie would later incorporate as his own. When, in 1937, an unsuccessful attempt was made on the life of the Italian viceroy, the Italian Blackshirts ran riot in the capital, burning down houses and decapitating and disemboweling Ethiopians, mostly at random, though the intelligentsia was particularly targeted. The Ethiopian resistance won few battles of note, but its role in demoralizing the occupiers laid the foundation for the easy British victory over the Italian troops in the Allied liberation campaign of January 1941.

British Lieutenant-Colonel Orde Wingate led the emperor back from exile at the head of "Gideon Force," which marched from Khartoum with fifteen thousand camels. (Sadly, only fifty camels reached Addis Ababa—an officer reported that "a compass was not needed; one could orient the column by the stink of dead camels.") Haile Selassie was returned to his throne immediately after the Allied troops drove Italy back into Eritrea, and once there, he asked the United Nations for Eritrea to be folded into his imperial government to allow access to the Red Sea. Both Britain and the United States had vested interests in keeping a Red Sea territory in friendly hands, and they lobbied other member states to grant Haile Selassie's request. After no meaningful consultation with Eritreans, the United Nations forced Eritrea into a highly ambiguous federation with Ethiopia.

As the oil-rich Middle East, just across the Red Sea from Eritrea, came to play an increasingly important role in international affairs, so did Ethiopia and its Red Sea harbors in United States foreign policy. In 1962, Ethiopia formally annexed Eritrea with hardly a squeak from the international community, but Eritrea launched a war for self-determination that lasted almost thirty years and cost the lives of more than one hundred thousand Eritreans, though it never once figured on the United Nations's agenda. The United States did more than look the other way. In exchange for use of the country as a spy communications center and a military base, the United States developed a military training program for Ethiopia that by 1970 absorbed more than half of the American budget for military aid to Africa.

Few modern leaders have became so deeply associated with a country's image as Haile Selassie. He ruled almost unchallenged, except for the brief Italian interlude, between 1930 and 1974. But for all the mystique surrounding him, Haile Selassie did very little to develop his country, and there were endless rumors of vast wealth siphoned into Swiss bank accounts while thousands in remote villages starved. In essence, the Ethiopia of the early 1970s—just before the coup that toppled the Hidden Empire—was no less feudal than the Ethiopia of 1930.

Over the years, Haile Selassie had suppressed coup attempts, resistance movements, and any challenges to his absolute authority with the same brutal techniques that had been employed by the occupying Italians. Few lived to incur his wrath a second time. Cries for land reform (most peasants were still subject to the whims of local landlords) came to a head over the 1973 famine in Wollo in Tigre, during which an estimated two hundred thousand people died.

But it was the oil crisis that kicked Selassie in the gut. He had declared that taxi drivers in Addis Ababa could charge only a fixed price of twenty-five cents wherever they took passengers in the city. This worked fine when oil prices were low, but when the embargo of 1974 sent oil prices rocketing, the drivers found themselves losing money with every fare. Attempted strikes in the past had met with quick and repressive measures by the government, but the cabbies felt they had little choice, so en masse they went on strike again, and braced for the worst. To everyone's surprise, Haile Selassie acquiesced and agreed to a subsidy for gas prices.

This was such a huge victory that within a few days the bus drivers went on strike. A creeping revolution had begun. Again, the emperor capitulated to the strikers' demands. Next came students, trade unions, and air traffic controllers. Even two hundred thousand Coptic Christian priests threatened to go on strike for more pay. The emperor began to go along with reforms that dismantled centuries of feudalism.

This didn't go unnoticed by the military, whose members also felt underpaid. They too went on strike for better pay conditions. And they got it. All the while there were demonstrations, local peasant revolts, rebel groups fighting in the north and south, food and fuel riots, and mutinies within the military.

Finally, the royal regime, one of the most oppressive in modern-day

Africa, melted like a wax witch. But in its stead came the so-called "Red Emperor," or "Black Lenin," Lieutenant Colonel Mengistu Haile Mariam, trained by the United States military. On August 25, 1975, Mariam smothered to death with an ether-soaked pillow his prisoner of almost a year, the two-hundred-twenty-fifth consecutive monarch in a royal line tracing to Solomon the First, the son of David: Emperor Haile Selassie. The remains would be secretly buried under a latrine.

CHAPTER SIXTEEN

I heard a fly buzz—when I died.
With Blue—uncertain Stumbling Buzz
Between the light—and me
And then the windows failed—and then
I could not see to see.

EMILY DICKINSON

Back on the river, the expedition encountered some small rapids, and Michel was piloting well. Then they came to what Pasquale would name BG06 (Black Gorge #6), a monster drop that apparently didn't exist in high water, for it was not noted on the map.

They pulled over to the north bank, a sheer cliff, and tried to scout from the rafts. Pasquale looked into the maw of several huge holes, and then looked at Michel. Pasquale could see in Michel's eyes that he was petrified, and counseled him to be careful, to keep the raft straight and in the middle. For the last several days everyone on Michel's raft had taken to not wearing life jackets, as the river had been benign and the temperature hot, but now Pasquale told everyone to put them on and cinch them tight. Yohannes, Baye, and Solomon, who were riding with Michel, resisted, saying they no longer needed the flotation devices. "Get your life jackets on. This is not a game, this is real. You want to die in these rapids?" Pasquale bellowed, and they snapped them on.

Gordon made the initial run and seemed to navigate without problems. Toward the bottom of the run, he held his paddle high and vertical, signaling it was safe to come down the middle. But just as Pasquale pulled the raft out from the cliff, he saw Gordon begin to point his paddle to the right shore.

In almost a month of running big rapids—perhaps more than one hundred to date—they had never crossed visual river signals. As Pasquale entered the dark-green tongue of the rapid he pulled to the right, following, he thought, Gordon's instructions. Instead of a clean run he dropped over a twelve-foot waterfall, into first one enormous recirculating hole, then another. He was buried in an avalanche of whitewater, tossed and thrown about in a rolling squall. He dropped the oars and high-sided the raft. Then his raft washed out the other side, all intact. He hollered back up to Michel, who was following his line: "Get back to the middle! Don't follow me . . . *get back*! Don't go sideways . . . you'll flip!" But it was too late.

Michel dropped into the first hole, and he was spun sideways and shot out. He then plunged into the second hole perpendicular to the flow, disappeared into a shaking cave of froth, and then rode up the far side of the wave and stalled. His boat hung at the crest for a long few seconds, and Pasquale's stomach churned at the sight. The boat continued to hang at the ridge of the wave, and everyone washed out. Then the raft flipped.

It looked like a garage sale in the river. Michel and his crew had neglected to tie their gear on, so the Nile was filled with hats, shoes, clothing, water bottles, a scattered box of bobbing oranges—and Michel's confidence.

Pasquale scrambled for a rescue throw line, and then heard the cry *"Azo!"* which means "crocodile" in Amharic. Immediately the hair went up on the back of his neck. There must be a crocodile in the eddy going after one of the swimmers.

Pasquale jumped on the oars and rowed madly toward the bobbing heads in the fast current. Michel suddenly appeared, climbing to the top of the upside-down boat, and pulled Solomon in, who continued to yell "Azo!"

"Where?" Pasquale yelled as he spun his head around looking for the croc. They were in the corridor most heavily populated with crocodiles, and the carnivorous creatures often positioned themselves at the bottom of rapids, a good place to catch fish and other live meat disoriented after being spun through whitewater.

Then Solomon pulled a coughing Yohannes in, whose wrist he had been gripping through much of the ordeal. "Where's the croc?" Pasquale inquired as he got to the flipped raft. "No azo," Solomon said. "I was yelling '*izo*' to Yohannes, which means 'I have you!' "

As they wrestled the turned raft to shore, Gordon stroked over to Pasquale, red-faced, an overwrought teakettle at the edge of its scream. "Why the hell didn't you follow my signals?"

"I did, dude. . . . You signaled to go right."

"I did not. You misread my signal!"

And on they went, exchanging bastinadoes. Gordon accused Pasquale of being an inept leader. "I think you should be more careful or people will get killed," Gordon shouted in front of the crew. "You put us at risk. You're dangerous. I'm the one out front; only I can decide whether and how to run the rapids."

"Gordon, you're totally out of line. I hate to tell you this, but it's not that way. If you want to help me guide this thing, great, but if not, you get out of here. I make the decisions whether to run something or not."

To Pasquale, Gordon's actions were mutinous. The Ethiopians stepped forward and said they hadn't signed up to be maimed or to drown. They were concerned about insurance for their families, and without such they said they were abandoning the expedition, hiking out immediately.

"Fine," Pasquale said, and pulled out the sat-phone. He called the offices of MacGillivray Freeman Films in Laguna Beach. He spoke with Mark Krenzien, the line producer for the IMAX® Theatre film, and began by saying, "I don't think Gordon is in control. Gordon cannot stand any sort of stress whatsoever. I don't know how far we can go. I don't know if I can continue with Gordon." Mark, being the good diplomat, calmed Pasquale down by suggesting that the heat, remoteness, and challenges would take a toll on anyone, and that it was best to make peace and keep things going. Pasquale sighed and agreed, and then explained that the Ethiopians needed to be insured immediately. Mark said he would get right on it.

Gordon continued to simmer and stew, though. After all Pasquale had done to make this expedition happen, he expected to have arrived at a point of privilege. But instead he tried to deconstruct the semiotics at work. He then sat down with each expedition member individually. He cupped his hands prayerfully, pressed his fingertips to his lips, and listened to their concerns and grievances. He apologized, and responded to each point. He promised that nobody would die; that nobody had to ride any more rapids. He pledged they would be paid and have adequate insurance. And he assured them that Gordon was not leading the expedition. Pasquale had been on a mutinous expedition before, and he knew he had to deal with the festering sore quickly, or perhaps lose everything.

In 1997, Pasquale joined me on a climb up Mount Baker, third-highest peak in the Pacific Northwest. To outfit us we hired a guiding company run by a couple.

The husband-and-wife team were Himalayan veterans. The distaff, a willowy redhead, was on an ambitious path to become the first woman to climb all fourteen of the world's eight-thousand-meter peaks. The Baker climb was uneventful except for getting lost a few times, and for the public bickering between the owners. Not long after the climb, suspicious that his wife was having an affair with another guide, the husband hanged himself in their kitchen.

The next year, the widow set out to lead a commercial climb up an eight-thousand-meter peak in the Karakoram. Pasquale and Brent Bishop—whose father, Barry Bishop, was a member of the 1963 Everest expedition that put the first Americans on top—joined on the redhead's permit, but were ostensibly climbing on their own.

It became evident early on that the redhead had little experience running a major high-altitude expedition. So Pasquale and Brent went ahead and picked up the slack, pushing the route out front, fixing the ropes, setting up tents and camps, and cooking. She would stagger into camp long after Pasquale and Brent, and collapse without acknowledging them or making any contribution.

One day she went to Brent and Pasquale and accused them of not supporting her, of not being team members, of trying to undermine her on the expedition. She blamed them for the brewing discontent among her own members, went so far as to call them mutineers. So Pasquale told her, "You don't understand. I am your strongest supporter. I'm not required to do anything, but Brent and I have put all our efforts into making sure that you and your expedition are successful, and we're not even on your team."

She didn't understand, felt threatened by Pasquale. The delicate balance of the expedition began to topple. Something had to give. So Pasquale quit the expedition before reaching the top, as did several others. A week later, the redhead summited with her photographer and another climber.

While picking his way down the mountain, Pasquale chewed on the difficulties of being an expedition leader, of how it required not only keen physical skills but an ability to retain control of others, and to check one's own sensitivities under stress. It was important, he thought, to be open to disapproval, to be accountable, and to offer solutions. He also decided that a leader couldn't be a chief if he or she wasn't also willing to be an Indian.

Discontent and fear ran deep on the Blue Nile that day, as Pasquale went to Gordon and offered to agree to disagree about the event. Gordon accepted the gesture, and they went to work together on reorganizing the rafts. When they pulled out a dry box from the flipped raft, they saw that it had leaked, so they called a lunch break and dried out the food and their tempers.

Later that afternoon, they came to the last major rapid marked on the map: Butler Rapid, a spinning white frenzy shooting through a black barrel. Though not as big as the earlier cataract, in the eddy below, several large crocs were lurking about.

Michel, still reeling from the last dunking, refused to run it. "I'd rather carry the boat on my back than run this rapid," he said. Pasquale was sitting on a rock surveying the rapid, and finally he turned to Alemu: "Let's go." But Alemu said no, he wouldn't run it. Pasquale looked at Baye, but he too shook his head. Nobody wanted to run Butler Rapid.

So, Pasquale ran his raft down alone. It was a magical run for him, one that combined glissé and grind. As the rest of the crew watched from shore, it seemed the light waves around the raft were bent momentarily, not by the gravity of the situation, but by the sheer force of Pasquale's will. When he swept in to the shore in the eddy below, perspiration gleamed on his scalp. He hiked three hundred yards back upstream to Michel's raft, and did it again.

The next day, they floated down to the Bure Bridge, the last bridge across the Blue Nile in Ethiopia and the spot where they would reconfigure the rafts to accommodate fifteen-horsepower Mercury outboard motors. They were through the white stuff, the wild currents, and downstream the river got flat and fat. Only a handful had ever traveled by boat beyond this bridge, none from the source.

As it turned out they missed Jim Masters, the chief engineer on the '68 British Expedition, by ninety minutes. He had returned to Ethiopia to survey tributaries of the Blue Nile and had heard about Pasquale's expedition. Hitching a ride with the resupply truck, he'd waited for them all morning, but the capsize had put the expedition behind schedule, and Masters ultimately left before they arrived. They just missed a historic meeting, two ships passing in the night.

Pasquale set up camp directly beneath the bridge, and he spent the afternoon mounting motors and rerigging the rafts. He reviewed the gear and found that the trip was wearing on more than psyches. The pots and pans were dented, there were holes in the tents, and tools and utensils had gone missing.

Then the Ethiopians stepped over to Pasquale and said they needed to talk. They circled him ominously, demanding double payment for their services to date. They said the unexpected dangers, the searing heat, and isolation all warranted more, and once again they threatened to leave if the new payment demands were not met. Pasquale argued, but he too was weary and frustrated, and finally gave in. He needed the crew to be with him at least to the border, where he was worried about armed threats on both sides.

It was still 90 degrees out when Pasquale at last retired for the day. He was relieved that his crew was staying, that the rapids were behind them, and that the mutiny had been averted. But as he spun the dial on the shortwave radio, he heard on a German radio program that the civil war in Sudan had reignited. Pasquale's only present reality had been his little tribe at the bottom of a gorge on the Blue Nile, but there was a larger world awaiting them that would have consequences.

Dread of what lay ahead sat in Pasquale's stomach like a stone.

JOURNAL DAY 28

Shitty camp at bridge, so slept on the boat. Everyone else slept outside on concrete under the bridge. Every fish sound all night startled me because of fear of crocs. Finally the end of the big resupply and rigging boats. Now all we have to do is motor to Egypt.

CHAPTER SEVENTEEN

It's not all pleasure, this exploration.
DAVID LIVINGSTONE, APRIL 19, 1873

Again the river canyon was changing, shape-shifting. It grew wider, and fields of corn and cotton spread to the river's edge. The fast water was behind, Pasquale hoped, so he cinched the rafts end-to-end like boxcars. But as he cranked up the motor, the second raft whipped about, so he stopped and repositioned the rafts so they were tied side-to-side, with Gordon's kayak tied on across the top. They decided to name the two rafts at this point. As they were approaching Sudan, they thought it appropriate to christen one *Temsah,* "crocodile" in Arabic, and the other Azo, the same in Amharic.

Pasquale calculated they were moving at about five to six miles per hour and were getting about fifty-five miles to the tank. At this rate they'd make it to Khartoum in a week.

They motored all morning down a river that poured into a haze of heat. The Ethiopian staff fell asleep, and Pasquale had a hard time keeping his eyes open while buzzing along. Gordon was restless and skittered about the rafts. At lunch, taken on the rafts, Gordon announced he no longer wanted to ride the rafts; he intended to kayak all the way to Egypt. "You're nuts. It can't be done," Pasquale tendered his opinion. Michel piped in as well: "*Loco!*" Even the Ethiopians shook their heads at the notion.

"I won't feel as though I really did the Nile if I just motor the rest of the way," Gordon replied.

"This is not the 'Gordon-kayak-to-the-sea expedition.' It's dangerous if you get behind us. And you won't be able to keep up. You've got a whitewater kayak, the wrong boat for flat water. You need a touring kayak with a keel. Look, you'll be a burden on the expedition," Pasquale argued.

"And you're shirking your responsibilities as a cameraman. You're supposed to be shooting video," Michel added.

"You can shoot stills *and* the video," Gordon snapped back to Michel, then squeezed into his kayak and started rotoring downstream.

Almost immediately the expedition spotted a hefty river horse strolling along the far shore. Hippos are proportionately the fattest animals on earth, and this one walked with elevated deportment, shifting his weight as though he had weak ankles. Seeing the kayak and rafts, he slipped into the river, opening his mouth some forty-five degrees, the angle of his jaw starting just behind his eye. Then he sank, and a couple minutes later, a pair of beady eyes and wiggling ears poked from the water not thirty feet from the kayak. The second-largest land mammal after the elephant, the hippo is storied for turning over boats and snapping occupants in two. Gordon was nonplussed, and continued paddling.

Sometime in midafternoon, Pasquale saw a group of fierce-looking Beni Shangul Gumuz people waving an EPRDF flag on the right bank. They were black as night, of Nilotic stock, as opposed to the mocha-skinned Amharas of the highlands. He pulled over and moored the rafts next to their dugouts, knowing the former revolutionaries were usually well-armed and trained to shoot first, ask later. All of them had decorative scar tissue on their shoulders, backs, arms, and faces, and they pressed together like a wall so Pasquale couldn't see behind them, where the distinctive fragrance of marijuana wafted from some cultivated fields. But Alemu and Baye, still wearing their fatigues and wielding their own firearms, spoke with the Gumuz and convinced them the little expedition was no threat, either politically or to whatever enterprises were being stoked up the valley. The Gumuz waved the expedition on.

That night they approximated civilization, the way Samuel and Florence Baker used to do when exploring the Nile in the mid-nineteenth century. They set up a proper table by the river, lit candles, and sipped red wine over a multicourse meal of lentil soup, pasta, and mixed fresh fruit, prepared by Yohannes.

The next morning, Pasquale's circadian rhythms were disrupted at 5:30 A.M. by the sounds of the Ethiopian staff chattering away in the darkness. After breakfast, they started motoring and entered a west-running gorge of metamorphic rock. It was unnamed, so Pasquale appointed it the Western Gorge. The river slipped illimitably between narrow cliffs, convergence waves rippling like the hide of a beast.

As the team proceeded, they encountered several gravel bars and snags. As Pasquale followed Gordon through the channel of one Class II rapid, he caught his stout white-ash oar on a submerged branch. It bent like a banana, then sprung back and smacked Solomon on his right hip so hard that the oar snapped. Solomon was catapulted into the bow of the boat. It was a close call caused by the proximity of the boats. When the next rapid reared, this time a boulder-littered, unnamed Class III, Pasquale broke the boats apart and had Michel row the second raft again. When Pasquale reattached the boats, he tried to navigate a shallow section and bent a propeller. He had one more spare prop, but more than two thousand miles to go.

It was a long, hot slog that day. They stopped once, to photograph a Gumuz man with his four wives, and the man's silly grin made the American crew jealous. Gordon, Pasquale, and the Ethiopian crew had been on the river for more than a month; hadn't seen loved ones for three.

That night, the BBC had a mention of the civil war in Sudan, something about it getting worse, not better. Solomon was in pain from the oar incident, and Pasquale worried that Solomon might have internal injuries. He gave him a dose of the narcotic analgesic Percocet, and

Solomon promptly dropped to sleep. Pasquale then retired to the egglike solitude of the mesh MSR tent he'd been using sporadically for the past month, and he hooked his laptop to a car battery that had been brought in at the last resupply and typed up his notes until 1:00 A.M.

The next day, the entropic logic of Murphy's Law was taken to a new extreme.

About eighteen miles into the day, a big crocodile slithered from the bank and made a beeline toward the back of Gordon's kayak. Gordon was paddling hard, trying to keep up with the rafts, and didn't see or hear the approaching crocodile. But Pasquale, a few yards ahead, happened to turn around and see the beast when it was about fifteen feet away from the kayak. Pasquale started yelling at the top of his lungs and scissoring his hands to indicate a charging croc. Both Alemu and Baye chambered rounds in their rifles—*chuk-chuk*—and took aim. "Don't shoot!" Pasquale screamed, once again fearing they might miss and hit Gordon.

Gordon turned to see the crocodile, its mouth open in attack mode, about ten feet away, and he snapped the bow of his boat about to face the predator. He started his Don Quixote maneuver, as Pasquale had named it: "a croc fighter spinning his blade at windmills."

At about three feet away, Gordon raised his paddle and brought it down on top of the croc's snout. But this old croc didn't frighten. It opened its jaws wider and charged. The croc grabbed Gordon's paddle blade, inches from Gordon's hand, and started to twist, in a move that began to wrench Gordon from the boat. Gordon pulled back in a tug-of-war, finally got his paddle back, and slapped the water again. The croc sank; Gordon braced. Then it burst up again under the kayak, jaws snapping for purchase. Gordon turned once more and pumped his paddle like a piston to get away.

It was the worst croc attack yet.

Africa has many cunning passages and contrived corners, and survival of the fittest is more evident here than anywhere else. Gordon, Pasquale concluded, felt he was above the base rules of the continent.

But before they could process what had just happened, a great gray hulk, water washing from its head like off a whale's back, emerged next to the raft: a huge hippo. Tiny turreted eyes flared as its mouth stretched like some industrial steam shovel with teeth. It lunged toward Pasquale, and he instinctively lifted the ten-foot oar and jabbed the blade into its throat as far as he could. The creature let out a basso profundo bellow, then sank into the depths, leaving just a swirl on the surface as its signature.

Up to this point, the few close encounters with hippos on the Blue Nile had been almost theme-park adventures; the animals popped up and down like rubber toys. Now, though, a line had been crossed. This hippo, likely a gentle giant in most scenarios, had been stirred from its nap with all the screaming, and had taken action.

A little later in the day, the rafts motored ahead of Gordon and pulled over to make camp in a spot where brush fires were not far away. Suddenly the radio crackled to life with Gordon's voice: "Pasquale! I'm under attack! They're shooting at me!"

"What's happening? Where are you?" Pasquale shouted back.

"I don't know. Two bullets hit the water near me. I heard four shots. Have you run any rapids? Can you come back upriver with Alemu and Baye? I'm in an eddy behind some big rocks. Where are you?"

Pasquale had no idea where he was, particularly in relation to Gordon. He vaulted back into the raft and fired up the engine, and Alemu and Baye jumped on with their rifles. They headed back upstream against the current. Just around the bend they found Gordon, white as a ghost, paddling downriver toward them. In a frantic, wavering voice Gordon explained that he'd been paddling along when some men had appeared on a gravel bar and started yelling for him to pull over. He had yelled back, "No," and they crouched and started shooting.

Cautiously, quietly, they all headed downstream, searching the banks for any movement. When they came to a protected campsite, walled on three sides, they pulled in for the night and set up a guard rotation.

Things were tense in camp that night. Gordon was anxious and distressed. He said the crocodile dangers were insignificant compared to being shot at. He wondered aloud who had fired the shots: Were they from shiftas, from the OLF (Oromo Liberation Front), or from any one of the political movements that hide in these knobby canyons; from coal makers, poachers, or marijuana farmers, or just some paranoids or yahoos on the bank?

"Just another reason why you should give up this stupid notion of trying to solo-paddle all the way to Egypt," Pasquale lit in.

"You guys aren't supporting me," Gordon shot back. "I'm the one trying to make this a pure descent."

"Bullshit. Gordon, no one cares whether or not you paddle the entire river—just like no one cared that Hillary used oxygen on Everest." Pasquale was citing the fashionable argument that the "pure" way to climb Mount Everest is without oxygen, though Edmund Hillary's first ascent had been considered no less heroic for its use.

"I can do it. All you guys have to do is leave earlier—get to camp later . . . and slow down by a few miles an hour," Gordon continued.

"C'mon. We have lakes to cross. Long stretches of flat water. It's going to take a lot, lot longer if you try to kayak this whole thing. Our goal is to complete forty miles a day without burning ourselves out. Am I going to fail or have less of a journey because I motored rather than rowed a raft for two years?

"Besides, Gordon, you're the one who wakes up late. You're the one we wait for. I'm up every morning by six trying to get you guys going, and often we have to wake you up and wait in the boats for you to get ready. You're the last one to pack up; you're the last one in the boats. And now you want us to leave earlier?"

Then Alemu and Baye got into the discussion, using Yibeltal as a translator. They threatened that if Gordon continued kayaking, they wanted a letter from the police commissioner in Bahir Dar clearing them of responsibility for his well-being.

Pasquale reentered the fray: "If you want a pristine kayak expedition, come back with kayakers, with the right kayaks, take your time, and enjoy the trip, the experience. Don't torment yourself on this expedition. This was always meant to be a motorized expedition; let's not change it now."

Gordon stood dyspeptically aloof, then stomped away.

Later in the evening, Gordon returned to the campfire and said the rest of the crew was trying to "guilt trip" him into riding the rafts, and they had succeeded. He said he would forgo his kayak.

Even the sunlight looked a little ill the next morning. Smoke was drifting through camp, curling across the beach. Somebody had been lighting brush fires nearby throughout the night. Alemu and Baye were dead tired from sitting watch all night long, but other than a distant campfire, they'd seen no evidence of shiftas or armed insurgents.

Pasquale was getting worried about crossing the border into Sudan at Bombudi; he wanted to beat the cloud of unknowing. Since leaving Bahir Dar he had heard nothing from the film producers, who had assured him they would make arrangements to have proper sanctions to cross the border. Pasquale had phoned and e-mailed them for the past few days, asking for details, and had heard nothing. So Pasquale called Kim, his wife, and asked her to call Mark Krenzien, the line producer. "Tell him unless we get some confirmation in the next few days that we have permits, guards, food, fuel, et cetera, that the expedition will be shut down." Kim called back a few minutes later and said that Mark was unavailable.

"What the hell?" Pasquale cried into the phone. "We're at the brink of Sudan and we can't get ahold of anybody! Who's supposed to be assisting this expedition?"

Kim said she would continue to try, and hung up.

CHAPTER EIGHTEEN

We proceeded on.

LEWIS AND CLARK, 1805

They came to more rapids, one almost a mile in length, and once again split the rafts apart to make it through. Even so, Pasquale busted another propeller. Then, after the confluence with the Didessa, the largest tributary to the Blue Nile, the taupe-colored canyon began to taper and the river broadened once again. There were bloats of hippos in eddies, who when disturbed would rewrite the river in a frenzy of splashes as they dove for safety. And the beaches were riddled with hippo footprints. Hippos spend their days wallowing in the river bottoms, but at dusk they make their way to shore, where they chow down up to two hundred pounds of grass in a night before waddling back to the river at daybreak. Pasquale had to be careful now, to miss not just the rocks but also the hippos.

"It now feels like Africa—deepest Africa. A big, wide, slow, shallow, rocky river—exactly what I hate," Pasquale confessed to Gordon, who was sprawled across the rafts in a sulfurous funk himself.

The river was two hundred yards wide and smooth as glass, and there was no breeze. The thick, dank air pressed down on their shoulders and poured into their lungs. It would have been 110 degrees in the shade, if there was any. Pasquale searched the horizon for some sort of visual distraction, but found nothing. He closed his eyes for a moment and remembered watching a formation of snowy white egrets floating up the Gilgel Abay in the early evening a month ago. They had been shards of cosmic grace, soaring elegance in the rough canyon. For a moment he relished the memory, and he grinned.

Pasquale then stirred Gordon awake and asked him to take a spell at the rudder. But as Pasquale lay down to rest, there was a bump and then a crunching sound. Gordon had steered the metal motor mount on *Temsah* into a rock and damaged it badly. So, they pulled over for an early camp at a sandbar at the confluence with the Sirba Shet, and Pasquale tried to straighten out the bent pipe, to no avail.

And the day was not yet through. No sooner had they unloaded the boats than a group of scar-faced Gumuz carrying guns strode into camp. They were led by Mamacha Kana, leader of the local militia. He was tall, as if half his body was in his legs, and in a bleak mood.

Pasquale shook his hand vigorously and tried to make him laugh, as was his way with all new introductions. But the grins glanced off the grim figure.

"Why are you here?" Mamacha Kana asked.

"We're making a film about the Blue Nile," Pasquale answered, thinking everyone the world over gets excited about movies. Mamacha didn't smile. Yibeltal translated as he barked a reply.

"A group of journalists in rafts came through here a couple years ago and didn't stop. We all got in trouble. You will not leave until the local police commissioner sees you."

The British Army had ended their expedition here in 1968, but that was too long ago to be the group Mamacha Kana had referred to. It must have been the Sobek/National Geographic Blue Nile Expedition of 1999, Pasquale figured. That expedition had finished at Bombudi, not far downstream.

Then Mamacha broke into perfect English: "You need to come to the village. It is three hours away," he stated.

"I'm not going anywhere," Pasquale snorted.

"Then the police will come here," Mamacha replied. "Do you have a permit?" he asked.

"Sure I do," Pasquale lied.

"Okay then, I will return tomorrow morning at nine-thirty with the police. You must not leave." And Mamacha turned and walked away.

Then some Gumuz boys appeared, one wearing a powder-blue leisure suit and white golf shoes without laces. "Where did you get that outfit?" Pasquale asked.

The boy said there were five Norwegian nurses in the village, and one had taken a shine to him and given him the clothes.

Five Norwegian nurses. That sounds interesting, Pasquale thought. He was tempted to march on up, but resisted.

After dinner, Pasquale pulled out the permits he was carrying and quietly showed them to Baye and Alemu just to double-check. "Best burned," Baye said, and pretended to throw them into the campfire. Before heading to bed Pasquale wrote in his journal: "Permits are all screwed up and expired. They're trash. Not sure what will happen."

At 1:30 A.M., Pasquale was stirred awake by hoots and hollers and lights approaching camp from across the Sirba Shet. Alemu and Baye were shouting back, telling the intruders not to cross the tributary. But they were clearly outnumbered, and Baye and Alemu stood down as twelve armed men waded across the river in the inky night and surrounded the camp. Pasquale was getting dressed in his tent when the flap pulled back and Baye leaned in and said, "Pasquale, you must come."

Pasquale stood in front of the uniformed men and listened as Yibeltal translated. The men were from the village of Sirba Abay, about six miles away, and they had come to arrest Pasquale and the team. Mamacha had warned them that the expedition might try to escape before morning. The leader of this band was Tage Dano, and he booked them on the spot.

"All of you must come now," Dano said.

"No, we are not leaving this camp," Pasquale told him.

"Hand over your weapons," Dano demanded.

"No, they are not giving up their guns," Pasquale said.

The standoff continued for an hour, with much agitated discussion between Alemu, Baye, Dano, and the local militia. But in the thick darkness, with occasional sweeps of their flashlights, Pasquale noticed that the visitors were wearing fatigues tucked into their boots and that their AK-47s were fairly new, which perhaps meant they were supported by the government.

"These guys are EPRDF," he blurted.

Baye, in a disgusted voice, replied, "*Ow*," which is "yes" in Amharic.

"Don't they know *you* guys are EPRDF?"

"No, they don't believe us. They think we can be OLF spies," said Yibeltal.

"Give me a break. OLF spies who speak perfect Amharic, dressed as EPRDF, with ID cards, with white American spies in yellow rafts?" Pasquale replied.

He refused to relent, and so the local commander, Dano, angrily agreed to stay until morning, but only if Pasquale would go with him to the local EPRDF headquarters after breakfast. He had his men disarm Baye and Alemu and confiscate Pasquale's knife. Baye looked over to Pasquale and put his hands together as though handcuffed.

Pasquale's blood boiled. He spent the remainder of the night in a restless state, wondering what was in store next. After surviving the rapids, crocodiles, hippos, insects, and injuries, would they be done in by some local yokels? He cast his mind over similar situations of the past, for ideas of how to defuse the situation. This one reminded him of his time in Somaliland back in the early '90s.

Pasquale had been hired by an oil consortium to oversee an exploration project on a 5.5-million-acre tract of desolate land in the Ogaden Desert, one of the most godforsaken scratches on the planet. The colonial penknife had put the region in southeastern Ethiopia, but the nomadic tribes in the region were ethnically Somali, and if oil were to be found, the place would detonate into a political conflagration over possession. Anticipatory sparks had been flying for years. In 1977, Somalia attacked Ethiopia for this parched piece of land, but was beaten back by Soviet and Cuban forces who were assisting Ethiopia at the time. Skirmishes across the dotted line have occurred ever since.

Pasquale's crew had consisted of twenty expats and as many as seven hundred Ethiopians and Somalis at any given time. They were trying to do seismic, gravity, magnetics, and borehole work to determine potential for drilling oil and gas wells. There was no law or order; no governing authority in the region. It was the Wild East.

In fact, when Pasquale had showed up in Addis Ababa in 1991, the crew had been sitting on their haunches for five months because they couldn't even get out of the capital. The roads had been destroyed, the bridges had been blown up, and every time they attempted to head to the Ogaden, they had been robbed and sabotaged by the local Somalis. The helicopter loaned to Pasquale's team had been shot down by an RPG the year before, and the Canadians on board, working on an earlier concession, had been killed.

Pasquale rounded up the seismic crew and got them moving toward the Ogaden, about six hundred miles southeast of Addis Ababa. They rode in big Russian troop carriers with one hundred hardened EPRDF troops, some of whom had been at war for more than thirty years. They had a bulldozer and a grader in front, and en route they repaired the roads and fixed the bridges. Throughout the advance they were repeatedly shot at. As they came into villages, the EPRDF would have to fan out, surround the village, disarm the inhabitants, and set up a cordon. As they went deeper into this completely lawless frontier of Ethiopia, they actually brought it more under control.

The first camp was at an abandoned Cuban air base called Awaray, which in Amharic means "dust." As they rolled in, clouds of red dust billowed, and when the convoy stopped, it took ten minutes for the dust to clear. Hordes of Somali refugees were standing against destroyed buildings that were painted with faded hammers and sickles and communist slogans. Blown-up and abandoned Russian T62 tanks littered the landscape.

Pasquale was met by a British crew chief in Bermuda shorts, who invited him to take an inspection tour. They piled into an old Land Cruiser and started driving about in 120-degree heat with two EPRDF in the back swathed in bandoliers and grenades. At one point they passed a Somali in a white robe and henna-colored beard with an AK-47 slung over his shoulder. The Somali took off running and the EPRDF guys started firing at him, and the Somali turned and started shooting back at the truck. The Brit and Pasquale jumped from the truck into dust six inches deep and crawled under the chassis while a gun battle raged for ten minutes. "This is nuts," Pasquale said to the Brit.

"Welcome to the Ogaden," he smirked back.

The next day they passed through a village, pushing their way through a crowd at about a mile an hour, with scores of Somalis crushing up against the truck. Suddenly one man wedged through the crowd, opened his robe, took out a hand grenade, pulled out the pin and set it on the hood of Pasquale's truck. The guards pointed their AK-47s at the man, and ordered him to put the pin back, which he did. When asked why he did this, he replied that he wanted to get a job. "That's a hell of a way to ask for a job," Pasquale fired back.

The man didn't get the employment, but thousands of others did. Whenever they stopped to employ fifty locals, the warlords and chieftains insisted that they hire five hundred. Though Pasquale resisted, he eventually learned the Ethiopian saying, "It's easier to catch birds with honey than with vinegar," and he hired whole battalions to do the work of five Europeans—though at about the same price.

About a year into the project, Pasquale was assigned a new military chief, a Commander Kalkay. His parents had been killed by the Dergue and he was sent at age four to a guerrilla training camp in Sudan. By the time he was eleven, he was fighting with the EPRDF to overthrow the communist government of Mengistu Haile Mariam. In a firefight with the

Ethiopian Dergue, Kalkay had taken a bullet in the head, which blew away the right side of his face and took out an eye. When Pasquale met him he wore a big black patch over his right eye and a nine-millimeter pistol on his belt. He was fearless.

They were working in an area near a huge refugee camp of about forty thousand, on top of a small mesa. Pasquale's team often set up on mesas so they had high ground for the lookout towers and guard posts. Typically they would circle their fifty or so vehicles around a half-acre common area, and create an additional fortification with sandbags. They were finishing a monthlong oil and gas survey in which they would lay out ten-mile seismic lines, detonate charges, and then record the sound waves to make geophysical maps. Coming up empty, they decided it was time to move on to another grid.

One night, before they were to leave the area, Pasquale was awakened by Commander Kalkay: "We have a big problem," he said.

They were surrounded by hundreds of Somalis armed with AK-47s and RPGs.

Pasquale sent an interpreter out with some troops under a white flag. It turned out that the Somalis wanted a bonus totaling about $50,000 for their work before the convoy moved. They threatened to kill Pasquale and his entire crew if they attempted to leave without paying. Pasquale was stymied. The Somalis had already been fairly paid their agreed-upon wages, and besides, Pasquale didn't have that kind of extra money.

So Commander Kalkay looked Pasquale straight in the face and said, "Mr. Pasquale, I've fought many years as a soldier. You give us the word and we will attack them. We are not afraid to die."

Pasquale paused with this statement, and then replied that he appreciated that, but he personally wasn't ready to die.

So, Pasquale started negotiating. He sent a translator back and forth throughout the day, and finally the Somalis agreed upon a $5,000 bonus, which Pasquale had in his coffers. Pasquale gave them the money as Commander Kalkay stationed troops in the front and back of the convoy and on top of the trucks with machine guns and RPGs. Then they began to drive off the mesa. The crowds of Somalis parted like the Red Sea, and Pasquale's convoy managed to trundle away without a firefight.

Variations on this theme happened again and again. Almost every day there were gunfights, grenade attacks, RPG attacks, people killed. Pasquale had eleven fatalities on his crew during the tour. Finally, after two years in the desert, with much of their equipment stolen and no sign of oil or gas, Pasquale announced an end to the project and prepared to head home. But once more, several thousand agitated Somalis surrounded him and started popping shots at the convoy.

This time Pasquale called the American ambassador, who called the minister of defense, who called the nearest general in Jijiga. The general then called Pasquale and asked how long he could hold on. Pasquale said not long—his troops were running out of bullets. The general advised them to hunker down and said he would do his best.

After about five hours in an Alamo-like siege, Pasquale spied a huge cloud of dust off to the northwest. One of Pasquale's lieutenants, who was out near the front line, called over the radio, "Pasquale, you're not gonna believe this, but it's the cavalry!"

Blazing across the desert in huge, Soviet six-wheeled troop carriers, five hundred EPRDF soldiers came to the rescue. They fanned out and surrounded the Somalis, shooting at them, arresting them, and driving them away. Then one of the troop carriers came in to the perimeter, and a general got off and introduced himself. "I'm at your service," he said.

Pasquale thanked the general profusely, excused himself, packed up, and got the hell out of there.

CHAPTER NINETEEN

*Where the south declines towards the setting sun lies the country called
Ethiopia, the last inhabited land in that direction. There gold is obtained in
great plenty.*

HERODOTUS, *THE HISTORIES*

If you're not living good, travel wide.

BOB MARLEY

One of the lessons Pasquale had learned from the Ogaden experience was that no matter how angry one gets in Africa, it never pays to show anger. The enemy thinks they've won if patience is lost. So Pasquale finally fell asleep on the banks of the Blue Nile vowing to quash his temper the next morning.

In the flat white light of the new day, Pasquale came to coffee to find even more militia, now numbering fifteen. Dano insisted that Pasquale accompany him, along with Alemu, Baye, and Yibeltal. He instructed the others to stay behind.

Gordon was disturbed with this plan: "I knew they were going to try to split us up."

"Gordon, I think it best I go, so we can get this solved," Pasquale replied.

Gordon had no choice. The well-armed militia was in control. So, at 8:30, the four from the expedition, plus ten soldiers, took off walking toward the village of Sirba Abay. The other militia stayed behind to guard Gordon and the rest of the crew.

It was a surreal walk for Pasquale, a sort of perp walk in khakis. As they waded through the four-foot-high elephant grass he noticed that while he was dressed in his usual ex officio khakis, the EPRDF were outfitted in their "official" khakis. The difference was they had the guns.

On the banks of a small stream just down from the village of Sirba Abay, they passed the Norwegian missionary outpost, Mekane Jesus. Pasquale poked his head into several of the tin-roofed buildings, including a clinic and a classroom, but spotted no nurses, no Norwegians at all. Apparently they had all gone to Addis Ababa for a conference; the place was deserted.

Upon arriving in Sirba Abay, Pasquale was escorted to meet a man in white shoes and a brimmed white hat with a twisted smile. He wore a heavy leather Camel-cigarette jacket, even though the heat was stupefying.

The man cocked his head like a vulture and introduced himself as Faisa Ayana, the administrator for Sirba Abay Wereda. He looked like a bad guy in a very bad movie. He told Pasquale, "You are under arrest." Then he called a meeting with the Sirba council at his "headquarters," a wattle-and-daub hut, painted white, with packed dirt floors. When he emerged, he said the council decision was that Pasquale and his team needed a Gumuz permit to travel in Gumuz country. Without it, they had to turn back.

Pasquale wondered if they wanted money, but he had very little left, so he didn't bring it up. Instead he pulled out his Iridium sat-phone and asked if he could make a call. Reluctantly, Faisa agreed. Pasquale began punching in numbers. He called me, and described the situation, and I began to contact friends in the State Department. He called Yohannes Assefa in Addis Ababa, and asked him to call the "Ministry of Defense, the Ministry of Tourism, the Ministry of Everything" to help out. Assefa suggested they divide and conquer, and gave Pasquale the numbers of the federal police commissioner and the minister of justice. As he hung up,

Pasquale noticed that the battery was low, so he called the minister of justice and pleaded his case as concisely as possible. The minister didn't seem to respond, so Pasquale threw in his kicker: "If I don't hear back from you, I'm calling the American Embassy and the U.S. Military. They'll send in troops, helicopters, and this could become an international incid—" The sat-phone died before he knew if his words had made any impact.

A while later, Faisa received a call on his sideband radio. It was from the minister of justice, who reamed the local official for holding up the expedition and said that there might be big trouble with America if Pasquale wasn't released immediately. The minister ordered Faisa to write up a letter of transit, and to "get rid of them" as soon as possible. Defeated, Faisa stepped over to a haggard woman hunched over a primitive desk, and asked her to type up an official-looking document on an old-fashioned typewriter, in quadruplicate, with carbon paper. But the typewriter jammed halfway through. Finally Pasquale dictated what he thought the letter should say, and Faisa handwrote the letter and gave it an official stamp.

At 10:00 that night, Pasquale strode back into camp, his knife back in his possession, and Baye's and Alemu's guns in theirs. As he reached the campfire, he saw that several militia were still there, and he commanded: "You all get out of our camp . . . NOW!" They hotfooted away.

For dinner, Yohannes prepared a goat, and Pasquale pulled out the Johnnie Walker Red, and, in bacchic spirit, got wasted.

They didn't get onto the river until 9:45 the next morning, their latest launch yet. It was Day 35 on the river. They motored for seven hours straight—about thirty-five miles—through an endless maze of rocks, gravel bars, and Class II rapids. Dohm palm trees and baobabs began to appear on the banks. Pasquale pulled over at 4:30 to camp at a wide sandbar, and again he got into a spat with Gordon, who complained that the beach didn't have a place to hang his hammock. "You never think of me when you choose a camp," Gordon carped.

"I'm leading this expedition. There are all kinds of reasons to pick a camp. I think about the safety of the camp, the wind, freshwater, flat tent spots. You're thinking of yourself; I'm thinking of the expedition. Sleep on the goddamn ground," Pasquale growled.

"Sure, if you give me one of the tents. I got the tents donated; they're mine, after all."

Pasquale picked up the tent he had been using throughout the expedition and threw it at Gordon, and then proceeded to set up a sleeping spot for himself on one of the rafts. He sat down and pulled out his journal and made an entry: "Amazing how entire group uses all of my equipment and things I brought over, but things Gordo brought over are definitely his. Made sure to tell me that the two tents are his. Hmmmm. I guess that's just life. Sort of like marriage: 'What's mine is mine, and what's yours is ours.' "

Pasquale also began to think, for the first time, about trying to get Gordon off the expedition. Bombudi, the border town, would be an ideal place for him to exit. He'd been told that the town was replete with restaurants, hotels, and bars, so it would be a fine place for Gordon to wait to be picked up and taken back to Addis Ababa for a flight home. Even though they'd shared a whole gearbox of the expedition's meshings and unmeshings, they were just fundamentally different people, in a different equipoise: same planet, different orbits; same river, different boats.

Later, as things cooled down, they built the campfire. As they sat for dinner, they were approached by a group of naked Gumuz Muslims from the nearby village of Mandeba, carrying a set of large oblong drums made of cowskin stretched over wooden bowls. The Gumuz surrounded the little fire circle, and Pasquale began to fear another arrest. But then they started to beat their drums, and to sing and dance, and Pasquale realized that they had come to entertain. So, they ate their meal to Nile dinner music. Michel took pictures of the dancing Gumuz, but Gordon just sat and shoveled in his food. Pasquale tried to call the producers to see if they had made any progress securing permissions to cross the border at Bombudi, but he got no answers.

For the next two days they just motored down the river, running several Class II rapids, and one Class IV that required uncoupling the boats and going to the oars. Michel again refused to row, and everyone else refused to ride, so Pasquale guided each boat through solo once again. It was, he hoped, the last Last Rapid.

They passed Gumuz women panning for gold along the edge of the river. King Solomon's mines were often rumored to be along the Blue Nile; legend suggests that the Queen of Sheba traveled to Jerusalem and showered the wise king with gold from her land. Herodotus, Agatharchides, Barradas, all spoke of Ethiopia's gold. The Portuguese explorer Juan de Bermudez wrote in his chronicles of Ethiopia that the soil was red, for it was two parts gold and one part earth; that "The precious metal was more common than iron, and was fashioned into wondrous objects by the locals." In the 1920s, a Polish count, Byron de Prorok, claimed to have found an old parchment map in Carthage that showed an ancient slave route up the Blue Nile from Khartoum where Egyptian slaves were sent to mine gold for the pharaohs.

Gold is still a major export for Ethiopia. The Mercato in Addis Ababa heaves with filigree jewelry, bracelets, crosses, and charms made of eighteen-carat gold, much of it extracted from the western region.

But Pasquale didn't stop to seek his fortune . . . he was on a mission.

Finally, Pasquale got through to one of the producers in Spain, who instructed him to call a George Pagoulatos in Khartoum, owner of an old hotel and something of a legend. He was a fixer, an emollient for the media, and the production had paid him to help with the permits. Pasquale was thrilled to at last have someone to help him cross the Bombudi border. He dialed George Pagoulatos.

"This is Pasquale."

"Who?" George Pagoulatos replied.

So Pasquale explained that he was working on an IMAX® Theatre film and was leading an expedition down the Blue Nile. He said he was approaching the border and needed help.

"What border?"

"The border of Sudan."

"Where? I don't know anything about it. I've never heard of you."

"We're approaching Bombudi."

"Bombudi," he repeated. "Where's that?"

"It's on the border," Pasquale spoke loudly into the sat-phone.

"But I don't know anything about it. I have no idea who you are. I never heard of you. And we have a ten-day Islamic holiday starting tomorrow. You are on your own. Good luck, and '*Kulu wiyabeen santi sana*.' "

"What does that last part mean?" Pasquale asked.

"Have a happy holiday, you and your family."

On Day 38 of the river expedition, they pushed off for the final leg to Bombudi, the post at the border with Sudan. Just a half-mile from camp Gordon decided to put his kayak back in the water for some exercise. Pasquale was motoring along at about eight miles an hour, and Gordon was trying to stay ahead, paddling off to the side and out front. But suddenly Gordon darted in front of the rafts. Pasquale looked up and saw Gordon's arm reaching for the safety rope as he was swept under the rafts. Pasquale didn't have time to cut the engine. Solomon and Baye dove into the water on each side of the rafts and grabbed for Gordon. He was still in his kayak under the rafts and couldn't get out. Gordon was dragged the length of the raft, and he just missed being torn apart by the propeller.

JOURNAL DAY 38

Another close call. Everyone is burned out and tired. It is also really hot, somewhere between 110–115 degrees.

By the GPS reading, though, they had but a few miles to go. They could taste the first beer at the Bombudi bar.

On January 30, at 12:30 P.M., in heat that felt like blow-dryers turned to high, Pasquale and his team approached the cable stretched across the river that marked the very edge of Ethiopia, and the beginning of Sudan. They pulled over, tied up the boats, and stepped up the cracked and crumbly bank. The landscape on top could have been drawn and colored by a child. A straight line divided the vast page: on the bottom, a brown barren landscape; on the top, blue sky. They scanned the horizon in all directions. There was no there there. Nothing at all. No restaurants, hotels, bars, no border post. No woodsmoke from cooking fires; no shouts of children playing. There was no town at all. The ground was blank. They were shipwrecked now on the wrong side of purgatory, halfway to no-man's-land in the middle of nowhere.

CHAPTER TWENTY

Men go out into the void spaces of the world for various reasons. Some are actuated simply by a love of adventure, some have the keen thirst for scientific knowledge, and others again are drawn away from the trodden path by the "lure of little voices," the mysterious fascination of the unknown.

SIR ERNEST SHACKLETON, SHIPWRECKED OFF THE COAST
OF ANTARCTICA

As Pasquale and his team stood on the naked, dusty banks of the Blue Nile and scanned the horizon, a wavering mirage appeared in the middle distance. The moving, bending stick figure seemed to be approaching. After a few minutes it assumed some definition . . . it was a camel—no, a horseman—no . . . it was a soldier on a bicycle.

The bicyclist pedaled up to Pasquale and introduced himself as a soldier in the Sudanese Army. Pasquale asked his name.

"Somali."

"No, your name, not your nationality," Pasquale said.

"Somali."

His name was Somali Muza. Pasquale asked him about Bombudi, and he shrugged. Never heard of it. But he said there was a village five miles back up the river, and inland about a mile, called Bamaza. He offered to guide the way, so he jumped on the rafts and they motored back upstream on a section of river so flat and sluggish that it was impossible to tell which way it was flowing.

About forty-five minutes later, they beached on a broad sandbar and marched into the tiny, dusty, nowhere village of Bamaza. At the local bar, Pasquale found a band of shirtless EPRDF and asked about obtaining permissions to cross the border. The soldiers shrugged. They had no authority to grant such permissions and had no idea who might. The last time foreigners were in the area—some French in a truck, three years ago—they waited five weeks for permission, never got it, and turned back. And nobody had ever come down the river, to their knowledge.

The next morning, the Ethiopian staff prepared to leave the expedition. They were more energetic than they had been in weeks. They'd finished their contract with Pasquale and couldn't wait to get home. There was a dirt two-track road out of Bamaza, and Pasquale called Addis Ababa to arrange transport. A part of him wished he could leave with them, and another part feared he would have to.

For lunch Pasquale found his way to a small grass-thatch eatery in the village. It was run by a pretty Amhara woman from Bahir Dar named Fantanish. He sat on a carved stool shaped like an hourglass, and Fantanish shared with Pasquale that she was divorced, that her ex was in Khartoum, and that she had been "stuck" in Bamaza for two years, trying to earn enough money for transport out. "Hopefully *we* won't be stuck here for two years," Pasquale joked, and she flashed her large, lantern eyes. There was enough sublimation in the little restaurant to power a motorboat.

The next morning, Pasquale awoke to see a brush fire raging not far from Bamaza. By 10:00 it was 115 degrees, and very smoky and hazy. Drums were constantly beating somewhere in the distance. "This is what Purgatory must be like," Pasquale wrote. Mostly he waited. He wanted to type notes into his computer, but his mouse pad had melted, as though it had been placed in a microwave, so he sat down and did nothing. Time had no weight here . . . the day passed in a moment. "This whole thing feels like a dream, a bizarre dream," Pasquale said to Michel, who was sprawled in the dirt waiting for nothing.

Finally, Pasquale mustered the energy to hook his computer up to the sat-phone and download e-mail. The first one was from a manager at MacGillivray Freeman Films, and it practically screamed through the monitor: "EMERGENCY—DO NOT GO INTO SUDAN. DO NOT CROSS THE BORDER UNDER ANY CIRCUMSTANCES." *But he didn't say why.*

Pasquale thought maybe the film financing had fallen apart. Maybe the producers had gone bankrupt? Maybe there was all-out war in Sudan? Maybe some larger, global disaster? Pasquale's frustration reached a boiling point. He had no permits, no visas, no documents, no information, no Sudanese money, no place to go.

Pasquale pulled out the Iridium phone, now fully powered from the solar charger. He called the U.S. and spoke with one of the producers. The news was not pleasant. The producer said there was a problem with OFAC (Office of Foreign Assets Control). Sudan, along with North Korea and Libya, is listed as a prohibited country in the Trading with the Enemy Act: U.S. companies cannot operate without special waivers from the State Department. As the expedition was part of a commercial film project, it fell under OFAC controls. The State Department knew of the expedition and had made an official warning that if Pasquale crossed the border without sanctions, all involved would be subject to a $250,000 fine and two years in jail. MacGillivray Freeman Films was appealing for the official permissions, but nobody knew whether they would be successful, or when.

Late in the day, two EPRDF guards came down to the river, where Pasquale sat sulking. One, Daniel Bedry, a good-looking young man, had a very badly infected finger on his right hand. He asked Pasquale for help, as there was no doctor, no clinic, no drugs in Bamaza. Pasquale took a look and saw that the finger was gangrenous, with dead flesh sloughing off, the remains of the nail hanging on by a strand. In several places the bone was exposed.

Daniel said he thought a poisonous insect had bitten him in his sleep twenty-nine days ago, and his finger had been deteriorating ever since. Pasquale cleaned it, gave Daniel several different antibiotics, and told him he needed to find a doctor. . . . The finger, Pasquale knew, had to be amputated, or the infection could spread and perhaps be fatal. He considered attempting the amputation himself, then thought better of it. He just didn't have the experience. "You need to get to a doctor as quickly as you can," Pasquale ordered. But Daniel just looked back blankly, as though it would be easier for him to get to the moon. This dust-filled blotch in the desert was every bit as remote as when James Bruce had passed through on his exploration of the Blue Nile more than 230 years ago.

The following morning, Pasquale hiked up to Fantanish's place for a cup of coffee, and there he met EPRDF Commander Solomon, dressed in ratty civilian clothes, lying on a straw bed in the corner. Pasquale implored the commander for permission to cross the border, but Solomon said no. Permission had to come from higher up, and everyone would wait until then. If they tried to cross without the proper papers, they would be shot.

Pasquale moved to another subject. He explained the condition of one of the commander's troops, Daniel Bedry, and implored Solomon to let Daniel visit a doctor to have his finger amputated. "If not, he could die," Pasquale beseeched. The commander considered Pasquale's words, and then agreed to the proposal. He would get his man to a doctor, some two hundred miles away.

The next day a truck rumbled into the village, and the Ethiopian crew, except Yibeltal, gave hugs, received their last payment from Pasquale, and piled on. Commander Solomon also showed up, escorting Daniel Bedry, and he ordered that Bedry take the last seat. As the engine was fired, Fantanish came running toward the vehicle lugging an old suitcase.

"Please let me on," she pleaded with the driver. But he shook his head no, saying the truck was full. She tried to squeeze in, but was pushed back. Then the driver shifted, and the truck bumped away in a spiral of dust and diesel smoke, leaving a dirt-spattered Fantanish alone in the middle of the road. Pasquale took her suitcase and helped her back to her restaurant, where he spent the rest of the day consoling the displaced woman.

That evening Pasquale spent time considering Sudan. Would he ever see it? Did he want to?

Sudan, the largest nation in Africa, had been mostly mired in civil war since it won independence from Britain in 1956. The central conflict, between Muslim government forces in the North and Christian rebels in the South, began in 1955, abated in 1972, and resumed in 1983. Some two million people have died in what has been called the longest-raging civil war in the world.

In the '90s, the Clinton White House imposed successive sanctions against the Sudanese government, as it had become a haven for terrorists, including Osama bin Laden, who had settled there in 1991. In 1996, President Clinton withdrew the U.S. ambassador, citing terrorist threats against American officials. That same year the United States and Saudi Arabia pressured Sudan to expel bin Laden, who subsequently left for Afghanistan. In 1998, after al-Qaeda's attacks on American embassies in Kenya and Tanzania, Clinton ordered a Tomahawk-missile strike on the Al Shifa pharmaceutical factory, which was suspected of producing chemical weapons, though the suspicion remains unproved. Meanwhile, the Clinton Administration made little progress in curtailing Sudan's civil war. In 1999, Clinton announced the appointment of a special envoy to Sudan, though he never met with the person who filled the post.

President George W. Bush had been more attentive. He rejuvenated a multilateral peace process that had been hosted by Kenya since 1993. On September 6, 2001, he appointed John Danforth, an ordained Episcopal minister and three-term senator from Missouri, as his new special envoy for peace in Sudan. The Bush Administration was also aware that Sudan's oil reserves yielded two billion dollars in annual revenue, although just a fraction of the oil had been tapped. Oil had been discovered in Sudan by Chevron in the 1970s, but because of the civil war it had been exported only since 1999. These reserves, which were being exploited by China, Canada, and Sweden, were off-limits to American companies because of OFAC and a 1997 executive order barring U.S. oil companies from operating in Sudan.

Danforth's overtures were surprisingly well received. The Sudanese government was desperate to end U.S. sanctions and to court American oil investors, and in the wake of 9/11 and the wars in Afghanistan and Iraq, it wished to avoid being added to the Bush Administration's target list. The Southern rebels, who saw that they stood little chance of dislodging the government, were also ready to negotiate.

Sudan's president, Omar al-Bashir, provisionally agreed to share about half the oil revenues with the South, and to permit Christians to escape punishments dictated by Sharia—traditional Islamic law. Bashir even offered to give the South the right to secede from Sudan six years from the signing date, if irreconcilable divisions remained. In return, the rebel leader, John Garang, said he would be willing to serve as vice president in a postwar government.

By December 2003, as Pasquale was beginning his Blue Nile expedition, negotiators were so certain that a deal was imminent that two seats were reserved for Bashir and Garang at Bush's State of the Union address. The stage was set: Bush would have a foreign-policy success in a former terrorist enclave, helping to unite Arabs and Christians; United States businesses would gain access to Sudan's oil; Sudanese civilians would stop dying. And, incidentally, Pasquale and his expedition would have safe passage down the Nile.

But in the days before Pasquale reached the border to Sudan, everything began to unravel. At the same time that the Sudanese government was offering autonomy and oil profits to southern Sudan, people in another neglected region, whose leaders had been excluded from the U.S.-

backed talks, had risen up and demanded political reform and economic assistance. Just when Bashir's regime seemed poised to stop its raids in Southern Sudan, it had launched a bombing campaign in Western Sudan, in a region called Darfur. As Pasquale sat in the roiling heat of Bamaza, Darfur caught fire, and prospects for peace in Sudan went up in smoke. Pasquale, at that moment, was trying to enter one of the most incendiary and dangerous countries in the world.

Before Pasquale went to bed, he got on his laptop and tried to send some e-mail, but he struggled. He sent me one e-mail asking for help, then typed: "I neeed to sign off. My mouse pad has meltted and with the wind bllowing there is now so much sand in the keyboard tht several of the keyyys will no longer wrk."

That night the hot wind wandered across the desert, bringing with it an indefinable sense of dread. The air it carried was different: thirstier, older, bending with mists. Even with Gordon and Michel just a few yards away, Pasquale felt alone with the night. There was nobody in the world, it seemed, inclined to help with his predicament. He was orphaned by indifference.

As Pasquale rolled about in his sleeping bag, unable to sleep, an ineluctable sense that his expedition was under siege crept over him. He began to think this might be the end of the road. After all his public pronouncements of intentions, after all the press, all the awe, all the hubris, he might fail—as every other attempt before him had. He had staked so much on this enterprise, had spent so much of his time and energy, that he seemed destined to make it. But not now. He might have to slink back in defeat, the task undone, the whole of the Nile unrun. And as he tossed about, listening to the acerbic wind, he remembered the last time he had organized and led a risky, high-profile expedition, one so outlandish that to most it seemed doomed from the outset. He remembered when he tried to lead a blind man to the summit of Mount Everest.

The source of the Blue Nile, or Gilgel Abay, as it is known to locals, is a muddy stream. This photo is taken a few feet from the source, at the Springs of Gish Abay at Sakala, Ethiopia. The Gilgel Abay drops 3,300 feet in 102 miles, flowing through lush green valleys and steep cedar-lined gorges before reaching Lake Tana.
Photo by Pasquale Scaturro.

An elderly Ethiopian Orthodox priest at the Church of St. Michael and Zera Baruk, located just up from the source of the Gilgel Abay. The church was erected in the seventeenth century on the ruins of an earlier one built by Emperor Yohannes. Custodians of the Holy Waters of Gish Abay are the only people allowed to draw from it. *Photo by Mike Prosser.*

A rainbow at Tissisat Falls on the upper Blue Nile (upper Abay) below Lake Tana. Descending 153 feet in two large drops, the Falls are the second-largest in Africa and among the scenic wonders of the world. *Photo by Michel L'Huillier.*

Gordon Brown lowering himself in his kayak over Tissisat Falls at the beginning of the expedition. *Photo by Michel L'Huillier.*

Mohammed rappelling off Tissisat Falls, with an expedition raft waiting below. *Photo by Michel L'Huillier.*

An Amhara girl along the banks of the Blue Nile in the Ethiopian highlands near Lake Tana. *Photo by Michel L'Huillier.*

Large Nile crocodiles constantly harassed the expedition, especially in the Black Gorge of western Ethiopia, where Gordon Brown was attacked by a twelve-to-fourteen-footer. These aggressive crocodiles are considered among the most dangerous in Africa. *Photo by Michel L'Huillier.*

Two Amhara farmers poling a reed *tankwa* across the upper Blue Nile in the early-morning mist, only meters above Tissisat Falls. *Photo by Michel L'Huillier.*

A lone Amhara man about to cross a homemade log "bridge" spanning the Blue Nile as it crashes through the Class VI rapids of The Gauntlet at the beginning of the Northern Gorge. The entire Blue Nile squeezes into a crack in the earth less than ten feet wide. The river was so narrow here that the rafts would not fit through the canyon and had to be "ghost-boated," or sent through without people aboard. *Photo by Pasquale Scaturro.*

Mike Prosser runs a Class V waterfall in the upper Blue Nile below Lake Tana. There were many such rapids and waterfalls in this section of the river, and many had never been run before. *Photo by Kurt Hoppe.*

As Gordon Brown kayaks by, a fifteen-foot python stands guard at the entrance of the Grand Canyon of the Blue Nile in the central Ethiopian highlands. *Photo by Pasquale Scaturro.*

Pasquale Scaturro and Gordon Brown scouting Jordi Falls, a Class IV rapid on the upper Blue Nile. Jordi Falls is the first major rapid on the Blue Nile as it spills out of Lake Tana and rushes toward Tissisat Falls and the Northern Gorge. *Photo by Michel L'Huillier.*

Scaturro rowing one of the heavy gear-laden rafts through Island Rapid in the Western Gorge. Because of low water in the dry season, the expedition was faced with hundreds of Class III and IV rapids in the Black Gorge and the Western Gorge. *Photo courtesy Pasquale Scaturro.*

Scaturro guides an expedition raft through the Class V Island Rapid, with its many large steep drops. This is the last major rapid on the Blue Nile before it enters Sudan. *Photo by Michel L'Huillier.*

A hippo in the Western Canyon. Because of hunting, there are not as many hippos in the Nile as there were in the past, but sufficient numbers to cause concern.

Photo by Pasquale Scaturro.

An expedition raft floats by the Pillars of the Grand Canyon of the Blue Nile in central Ethiopia. The Pillars are erosion remnants left from the carving of the canyon through thick basalts that cover much of the Ethiopian highlands. *Photo by Pasquale Scaturro.*

Entering the Gorgeous Gorge section of the Grand Canyon of the Nile in central Ethiopia. This section of the Blue Nile is in scale with the Grand Canyon of the United States, eighteen miles wide and more than 5,000 feet deep. *Photo by Pasquale Scaturro.*

Scaturro guides one of the expedition rafts down a Class V–VI rapid that is part of the Arafami Falls on the upper Blue Nile, below Lake Tana. This was the first known descent of Arafami Rapid. *Photo by Michel L'Huillier.*

Baye Gebre Selassie (right) and Alemu Mehariw, the two Ethiopian People's Revolutionary Democratic Front Special Forces soldiers who accompanied the expedition from Lake Tana to Bomaza, on the border with Sudan. There is no established authority along the Blue Nile corridor in the lowland western reaches of Ethiopia, and Baye and Alemu helped protect the expedition from *shifta*s and local militias. *Photo by Pasquale Scaturro.*

The Great Confluence of the White Nile (light-colored waters on the left) and the Blue Nile at Khartoum, Sudan. Here the combined flows of the river are called the Nile proper. The Blue Nile may be shorter than the White, but it supplies eighty-six percent of the water and silt of the river. *Photo by Pasquale Scaturro.*

Pasquale Scaturro and Gordon Brown study a map of the Blue Nile in eastern Sudan. Very few maps of the Nile were available, and the expedition had to rely on large-scale maps with little usable detail.
Photo by Michel L'Huillier.

The view from the top of Jebel Barkal, three hundred feet off the Sahara Desert floor, at Napata in northern Sudan, looking toward the ruins of the Temple of Amun.
Photo by Pasquale Scaturro.

A silhouette of camels carrying the expedition members to the seventh-century Monastery of St. Simeon on the west bank of the Nile, opposite Aswan, Egypt. Surrounded by desert sands, the monastery is one of the best-preserved original Christian strongholds remaining in Egypt. *Photo by Michel L'Huillier.*

OPPOSITE

The African sun setting across Lake Nasser, viewed from the end of a dock at Wadi Halfa, Sudan. The expedition members camped out here, once released from custody by the Egyptian military after an unsuccessful attempt to enter Egypt through Lake Nasser. They were forced to await formal permission from the Egyptian Ministry of Defense to continue on their own power across Lake Nasser and past Aswan High Dam. *Photo by Pasquale Scaturro.*

An Egyptian police patrol boat escorts the expedition into Cairo and past some of the huge buildings that line the Nile for miles in northern Egypt. Cairo is the largest city in Africa and the Middle East. *Photo by Pasquale Scaturro.*

Pasquale and Gordon in front of the Sphinx, near the pyramids of Giza. This picture was taken prior to the expedition, shortly before the two flew to Ethiopia to start the first full descent of the Blue Nile and Main Nile. *Photo courtesy Pasquale Scaturro.*

The expedition rows out into the Mediterranean Sea, on the Rosetta Branch of the Nile, thus concluding the longest raft trip in history and the first complete descent of the Nile from source to sea, 3,253 miles in 114 days. *Photo by Michel L'Huillier.*

CHAPTER TWENTY-ONE

*Climbers, as a species, are simply not distinguished by an excess of prudence.
And that holds especially true for Everest climbers: when presented with a
chance to reach the planet's highest summit, history shows, people are surprisingly quick to abandon good judgment.*

JON KRAKAUER, *INTO THIN AIR*

D im lights glowed through the thin yellow nylon, rending the
darkness with an eerie glow. A wailing wind rose and fell,
squealing over knife-edged ridges and carrying a charge of
spindrift. Intermittently, stabs of lightning illuminated Pasquale's sur-
roundings . . . sleeping bags rimed with frost, water bottles, climbing gear
left behind. A disembodied voice came to him in bursts, almost buried by
static and the howling jet stream, a call of panic as from the depths of the
sea, or a dream. "I can't breathe! There's something wrong!"

But Pasquale wasn't underwater, and his dreams were not those of
sleep but of fever. He was at twenty-six thousand feet above sea level,
where the air was too thin to support human life for any length of time
without supplemental oxygen. The Death Zone.

He was racked by a 104-degree body temperature, but he shivered
with cold. His bones ached as if compressed by strong unseen arms. Two
hours before, he had been climbing well toward the highest summit on
earth, paying a return visit to the top of Everest, when suddenly he felt
there was something very, very wrong.

Pasquale dragged himself out of his nightmare and rolled over. The expedition radio was next to his ear, popping and hissing in the darkness. He recognized the anguished voice as that of Jeff Evans, one of the climbers he was guiding to the summit. Propping himself up on one elbow, he switched on the phone and said, "Calm down. Take a deep breath. Ang Pasang and Sherm Bull have extra regulators; find one of them and you'll be fine." Then Pasquale fell back into a febrile sleep, tormented by thoughts of failure, of death.

It was May 25, 2001—late in the season for climbing Everest, and the last chance for his team's summit attempt. For the past two years he had been planning for this day, gathering sponsorship and gear, training his own body and those of less-experienced climbers to endure the hardship of long days climbing into an ever-more-airless atmosphere, drawing up plans and fallback plans. But all of his plans were now falling apart, not because of the weather—though it was bad—nor because of the weakness of the equipment or the team.

What was falling apart was his own body, betraying him when he needed it most. The malaria he had contracted decades before on his earliest forays into Africa had come back, resurrected by his stress and exhaustion. Tiny parasites that had lived quietly in his liver for years were now multiplying, invading his bloodstream, destroying the very depleted red blood cells he needed to carry the little oxygen available at this altitude to his organs, his muscles, his brain.

This was not the first time he'd been on Everest, nor was it the first time he would fail to summit. Pasquale knew, even in his delirium, that it was fear of failure that was perhaps the greatest enemy of climbers on Everest, climbers who keep pushing for the Third Pole—as the summit had been known since its discovery in the late 1800s—even when all rationality argues against continuing. Five years earlier, eleven people had lost their lives on a morning like this, including Rob Hall and Scott Fisher, mountain guides who should have known better than to press on. That horrific day—May 10, 1996—made global news, and became the subject of Jon Krakauer's best-seller of "bad luck and worse judgment," as *People* magazine called it.

Now, half-mad, Pasquale wondered if his own expedition would go down in the books as yet another tragedy, one that could have been averted if only more caution had been exercised; if more reasonable minds had prevailed. For this expedition was saddled with an even greater liability than inexperienced climbers or overweening pride . . . one of their climbers, and their very reason for being on the mountain, was Erik Weihenmayer. And Erik was blind.

Pasquale had met Erik at the Outdoor Retailer show in Salt Lake City in 1999, introduced by their mutual friend Sobek guide Jim Slade. At first Pasquale thought of Erik as "a blind guy who did some climbing," but that was shorthand for who Erik was, and what he had accomplished. Though born sighted, Erik developed retinoscheses—a degenerative eye disease that gradually destroyed his vision—and by the age of thirteen he lived in a world of darkness. But as a natural athlete, he refused to be limited by his liability, and against the advice of just about everyone, he pushed himself ever further into physical accomplishment.

He became a wrestler while in high school; later he took up skydiving, running, skiing. At some point, climbing got under his skin. He learned how to feel his way up a rock face by handholds, how to listen to the sound of ice so he could plant pitons in frozen walls. In 1996, he participated in a high-profile ascent of the Nose, a classic 3,300-foot vertical rock climb up El Capitan, in Yosemite. Then he began climbing mountains: Mount Rainier, Mount McKinley, Aconcagua—South America's highest peak—and Kilimanjaro in Africa. A series of "Seven Summits" seemed within reach, an extraordinary accomplishment for any athlete, but unheard of—indeed, unconceived of—for a blind climber.

Jim Slade's recommendation was good enough for Pasquale. After only a few minutes of talking with the tall skinny man, flanked by his Seeing Eye dog, Seigo, and his wife, Ellie, Pasquale popped the fateful question: "Did you ever think of climbing Everest?" Ellie Weihenmayer shot Pasquale a look "that would melt the Tin Man," but the hook was in. The next day Erik called up Pasquale, after doing some research of his own, and they began to lay plans to put the first blind climber on top of the world.

Erik is the kind of guy who doesn't give up easily. He has to be, to have accomplished so much already. Using his connections with the National Federation of the Blind, he put together a meeting between the NFB head Dr. Marc Maurer and Pasquale to discuss sponsorship. Arriving there, Pasquale was startled to find the NFB headquarters in Baltimore windowless and pitch-black. It was a building suited for the blind, such as Erik and Dr. Maurer, but disorienting for Pasquale.

Still, Pasquale was glad he and Erik had done their homework. They were armed with an expedition proposal, even a timetable and budget, with an eye toward getting Erik to the summit of the world's highest peak. Pasquale handed over the proposal—converted to Braille, so Dr. Maurer could read it—and patiently answered the questions that the NFB staff posed.

One of them, however, caught him off guard. Dr. Maurer rocked back and forth in agitation and asked, "I have one question, Pasquale. Can Erik die on this expedition?"

Pasquale took a moment to think through his answer, but only a moment. "Sure he can die."

"Good. That's just what I wanted to hear," said Dr. Maurer. "I want to know that Erik is going to climb this mountain like anyone else. No tricks. He's not going to be carried up like a child; he's going to climb this mountain all on his own."

"I'm not going to carry anyone up that mountain."

"Great. How much do you need?"

With $350,000 from the NFB, and their unconditional support, Pasquale and Erik began assembling their teams. Though Erik had reached the 22,840-foot summit of Aconcagua in 1998, climbing above

26,000 feet in the Himalayas was a different bucket of ice altogether, and both men knew it. Erik agreed to supplement his core team of good friends Chris Morris and Jeff Evans, ice-climber Mike O'Donnell, and Eric Alexander. Pasquale signed up several Himalayan veterans he was comfortable with, like Luis Benitez and Didrik Johnck, team doctor Steve Gipe, and his closest climbing partner from Colorado, Brad Bull. Pasquale also signed up Kami Tenzing Sherpa, with whom he had climbed Everest and Cho Oyu, as *sirdar* overseeing porters and logistics.

But first, some hard lessons had to be learned. The team gathered for a warm-up expedition, an ascent of Ama Dablam. Although its elevation was almost exactly that of Aconcagua, at 22,486 feet, to climb to this peak was a classic Himalayan effort, requiring Sherpa support, long-term planning, equipment and supplies management—and technical rock and ice climbing in thin atmosphere. Ama Dablam is also a beautiful peak, its sharp, sculpted profile dominating the horizon like a Nepalese Matterhorn. But, like the Matterhorn, it has claimed its victims. It would be no cakewalk.

The team arrived in Kathmandu in the spring of 2000, and immediately those who had never been to Nepal before got sick. After a few toilet-bowl days, health returned, and they set out to the Khumbu region of the Himalayas and attacked Ama Dablam. They pushed their way up the mountain's near-vertical face in spite of the bad weather. Pasquale recalled, with some irritation, "We led the mountain. There were four teams on the mountain and we fixed the entire route all the way up. No one else did a thing." But despite their aggressive attack, the mountain was not to be broken.

They had only twenty days scheduled to climb this mountain, and they were hammered by weather. At Camp Two, just over twenty thousand feet, a storm started to blow in. Pasquale decided that Erik would remain with Eric Alexander, with radios, and the rest would return to Base Camp. It was deemed the best chance for group success. The wear on Erik getting up and down would be greater than that of remaining at altitude, and it would be slow. The others could get down, conserve the strength needed to help Erik summit, then return when the weather cleared. It turned out to be a seven-day snowstorm, and Erik was sitting on a three-foot-wide ledge at twenty thousand feet in a blizzard for a week.

Finally the main team could return to Camp Two and begin the summit push. But the long delay had eaten into the food and fuel reserves. No more delays were possible without threatening the lives of the team members. They made it up the steepest, most dangerous ice wall on the mountain, and were within five hundred feet of the summit when, again, the weather turned. Big black clouds wrapped around the so-close summit and came straight for them.

Once more, Pasquale had a tough decision to make. It was possible, just barely, that they could make the summit and return safely, but it was as likely a scenario for disaster. They were out of fuel, out of food, and out of time. They couldn't go up any farther. Pasquale was afraid that if they failed, perhaps the NFB would pull their funding. It was the hardest call he'd ever made in his life.

Pasquale, climbing lead with Chris Morris, radioed down to the team ascending below him. "Guys, you're gonna hate to hear this, but the expedition's over." They returned to camp, packed up, and began the descent even as the storm hit.

But they hadn't avoided fate altogether. Eric Alexander, who had spent the long week with Erik Weihenmayer at Camp Two, slipped on some loose rock and fell 150 feet down a slab, landing on a small ledge. Though his helmet and pack saved him from greater injury, he went into shock during evacuation and his lungs began filling with fluid, the dangerous high-altitude condition known as pulmonary edema. Eventually all the team returned home safely, even though the summit had eluded them.

There are trials by fire . . . this was a trial by ice. Unspoken was the belief that even if they didn't make the summit of Ama Dablam, if Erik

Weihenmayer could survive this weeklong blizzard at twenty thousand feet, he was ready for the big one. They had proven themselves as a team—as Erik wrote in his book *Touch the Top of the World*, "We had stuck together, made good decisions, and taken care of each other to the end. The mountain had erected a powerful barricade, forcing us to cross through it, and on the other side we found our strength."

Dr. Maurer at the National Federation of the Blind was unreserved in his support of Pasquale as expedition leader, grateful that Pasquale had made the right choice at the right time. They spent the next year training, making the media rounds, accumulating sponsors, and training some more. More sponsors came on board, including Mountain Hardwear and other equipment manufacturers, helping to reduce costs. Key was the addition of the pharmaceutical company Aventis, manufacturers of the antihistamine Allegra. Aventis ponied up for an advertising campaign, a major Web site, and a film crew, headed by climbing filmmaker Michael Brown, younger brother to Gordon Brown and an Everest summiteer. An added dimension to the "first-ever" nature of the trip was the decision by Brad Bull's sixty-four-year-old father, Sherm, to join the Everest team. If he were to make the summit, he would become the oldest man to stand on top of Everest. And Eric Alexander, after months of recovery from his fall on Ama Dablam, finally decided to join the expedition and give Everest a shot.

But the attention they were getting was double-edged—there were detractors as well. Jon Krakauer wrote to Erik, discouraging him from making the attempt. "I am not at all enthusiastic about your trip to Everest next spring. It's not that I doubt you have what it takes to reach the summit . . . it's just that I don't think you can get to the top of that particular hill without subjecting yourself to horrendous risk; the same horrendous risk all Everest climbers face, and then some. It's a totally different world above 8000m."

Ed Viesturs, himself a climber of the Seven Summits and of Everest several times, was also discouraging. "More power to him, and I support his going," Viesturs wrote in *Men's Journal* magazine. "But I wouldn't want to take him up there myself. . . . When I guide, I like people to become self-sufficient. With Erik, they'll have to be helping him, watching out for him every step of the way. For me, the risks are too great. It will be the hardest ever guided ascent of Everest, if they pull it off."

If they pull it off. For Pasquale and others on the team, the doubters only reinforced their drive. For them, it became a mission, a calling, a dream. Pasquale had dreamed, literally, when they'd first started their planning, that he and Erik were summiting Everest. When they got above the Hillary Step and looked up, he knew there were only two hundred feet left, and it almost brought tears to his eyes because he knew how difficult it would be. He knew that if they got to that point, it would be the most difficult thing he'd ever done.

Erik, too, was even more motivated to prove himself yet again. He answered his critics, not without bitterness, "I had always prided myself on being one of the reasons for the success of my past expeditions. I had never been short-roped and hauled to the summit, to be spiked in the snow like a football."

The 2001 NFB Everest Expedition reached Base Camp at 17,500 feet on April 5, 2001, after trekking for eight days up the Khumbu Valley. Word of their attempt was widespread—monks in Kathmandu who gave them *kata* scarves for good luck were amazed, villagers along the way were disbelieving, fellow climbers at Base Camp were alternately encouraging and skeptical. Some even doubted that Erik was blind at all, thought it was a stunt. At one point Erik called Kami Tenzing Sherpa into a tent and popped out one of his glass eyes. "Shall I take out the other one?" he asked. Shaken, the *sirdar* quietly spread the word: This guy was for real.

The hard work was just beginning. The first obstacle—some would say most dangerous, aside from the conditions of extreme high altitude—was the Khumbu Icefall. The team would do several practice runs through it, retreating to Base Camp after each one. The Khumbu Glacier spills down the south flank of Everest, and as it levels out above Base Camp, it breaks up into a maze of crevasses, seracs, boulders, and confusion; an ever-shifting landscape of chaos. To add to its dangers, as the day progresses the icefall shifts ever more unpredictably, warmed by the sun. Climbers try to begin their ascent through the icefall before dawn, hoping to reach Camp One at twenty thousand feet well before noon.

For sighted climbers it's a challenge; for Erik, it was virtually impossible. Despite his experience in mountains and on treks, he had to be talked through every step he took—which chafed at his hard-won sense of independence. At several places in the route, rigged ladders spanned deep crevasses, and it was necessary to balance carefully or risk a fatal fall. The tension was unnerving for Erik, who had to do it all by feel and the shouted advice of his partners; after making it across each crevasse he would collapse and hyperventilate from stress. By the time he reached Camp One, darkness was falling. "I wasn't sure which was more exhausted," he wrote, "my body or my mind. Never in my life had I faced terrain so totally patternless."

Erik's climb from Base Camp to Camp One had taken much, much too long. Pasquale was angry and discouraged, though he greeted Erik with a hot meal and a place to rest. He met with the team and confessed his fear that Erik simply wouldn't be able to do it at the current pace. Unbeknownst to him, Erik was listening. It didn't piss Erik off, but it didn't make him feel any better, either.

Over the next several weeks, though, Erik's time through the icefall improved and his confidence—and Pasquale's—returned. Soon he made it from Base Camp through Camps One and Two up to Camp Three, gaining altitude higher and climbing stronger than other members of his own team. Every step he took added to his own altitude record as highest attained by a blind climber, a record he'd set on Aconcagua three years earlier. Spare tents, fuel, food, oxygen bottles, and other supplies were cached at Camp Three in anticipation of the eventual summit push, putting the team within striking distance of their goal. The accomplishment was rewarded by a return to the lower altitude of the Dingboche Valley for some much-needed rest and relaxation and the thicker atmosphere of 14,500 feet.

At Dingboche, they heard the news that Babu Chiri Sherpa, the most famous climber of his clan, had died on the mountain. Babu Chiri had been to the summit of Sagarmatha, as the Sherpas call Everest, eleven times without oxygen. He once climbed from Base Camp to the top in sixteen hours, setting the world speed record; once, he spent twenty hours on the summit, when bad weather prevented his descent. Yet he had died ignobly, stumbling into a hidden crevasse outside his tent at Camp Two.

The news was sobering, a bad portent not only to Pasquale, who had known Babu Chiri from previous expeditions, but to everyone on the mountain. "It didn't matter how much experience you'd had or how strong a climber you were," Erik wrote, "if you let your guard down for just a moment, the mountain would be waiting." They returned to Base Camp in time for a moving ceremony in honor of Babu Chiri.

The devastating news affected the Base Camp population in a strange way: Everyone seemed to be waiting for Pasquale's team to take the lead up the mountain. Other groups of climbers were convinced that they were the strongest team, that they had the best rope, and the best facilities, and that they were going to put in the fixed ropes up the entire mountain that others could then use.

Pasquale had a meeting with the other expedition leaders and said to them, "Guys, I understand what your reasoning is, but keep in mind, *I have a blind climber.* I don't think it's fair for you to wait here in Base Camp for us to fix the route all the way to the top of the mountain, with a blind climber, so you can crawl in our footsteps."

The situation soon resolved itself. After an aborted run for the top in early May, called off when the weather turned, Erik got sick at Base Camp. During this three-day delay, the weather took a turn for the better, and the other teams made a run for the summit. Several groups got a head start on the NFB team, and soon rope was fixed higher and higher up the mountain, while Erik recovered.

Finally, on May 19, their final summit push began. Erik's strength had returned, and with it, he set a record pace for the high camps, reaching Camp Two in a personal-best four hours. They made Camp Three, at almost twenty-four thousand feet, the next day, and on May 21 they headed up to Camp Four, two thousand feet higher. That's when some of the problems started.

Camp Four had been established at the South Col a week earlier, before bad weather had sent them back to Base Camp. Now, they found that the weather had left a sheet of ice six inches deep inside the tents. First to reach the camp and climbing without supplemental oxygen were Pasquale, Didrik Johnck, Brad Bull, and several Sherpas, and they had to spend over three hours chipping ice out of the tents and setting up the spare tents, while the wind blew at sixty-five miles per hour and the temperature dropped below zero.

Erik and the rest of the team were much slower, and by the time they reached the South Col it was almost 5:00 P.M. The original plan had been to leave for the summit at 10:00 P.M., climb through the night, and reach the South Summit with daylight. But everyone was exhausted, and the prospect of sleeping for just three hours at best not only wasn't appealing, it wasn't smart. Pasquale decided to do a layover day and head for the top a day later.

But there was a problem with this plan. The South Col is well into the Death Zone. Above twenty-four thousand feet, the body can no longer acclimate to altitude, nutrition can't be absorbed, and the lack of oxygen means the body literally cannibalizes its own cells to keep itself alive. Supplemental oxygen is needed, and Pasquale's plans had not covered an extra night at this altitude.

Pasquale got on the radio. Fortunately, he had a lot of good friends at Base Camp and was able to locate expeditions with spare oxygen. He bought another twenty-five bottles of oxygen, hired a bunch of Sherpas down the mountain, and gave them a bonus. They carried the oxygen all the way up the next day. Pasquale's team was able to spend the night with an adequate flow of oxygen, knowing there was more on the way.

The next day, May 24, they took it easy, regained their strength, and hiked around the South Col. Among the sights were several bodies of climbers who had died on the mountain, including one Sherpa laid out on a rock, frozen solid. He still wore the Gore-Tex suit he had been climbing in, though his boots were missing; his black hair was exposed to the elements. It was a sobering reminder that Everest is a killer: A thousand people have reached the summit, but close to two hundred have died, and Nepalese porters and Sherpas have always borne the brunt of the mountain's wrath. More than one hundred bodies are thought to litter the highest slopes of Mount Everest.

After darkness fell, the team prepared for the final assault on the summit. They set out at about 8:30 P.M., a bit earlier than originally planned, but taking into consideration Erik and his team's slower pace. Brad Bull and Pasquale led Erik with the first group.

Then, as the evening's wind died down and the way to the top looked at last possible, Pasquale began to feel strange.

He noticed that he was starting to sweat and get chills, and his bones felt weak. He kept walking, but it was evident as he got into the rock band and above, at twenty-seven thousand feet, that something was wrong. He didn't know what it was at the time, but in retrospect, it was obviously a malaria attack.

He'd had a malaria attack on this very mountain in 1995, and it had prevented him from summiting, though he'd reached the top on his subsequent 1998 expedition. Now, the wasting fevers had appeared again, threatening his dream of reaching the top with Erik.

Pasquale asked Brad to check his regulator, thinking perhaps he wasn't getting enough oxygen but secretly knowing that the problem lay within. When his climbing partner told him that his oxygen was fine,

Pasquale had to confess that something was wrong with him; after a few more steps, he announced he had to go down.

When he heard his decision, Erik said, "What!?"

Pasquale told him to relax, that he was in great hands. Then he gave them his best, turned around, and did one of the hardest things he'd ever done in his life. Period. He had been the driving force behind the expedition—not only with all the preparation, planning, and training for the past two years—but on the mountain itself, leading the charge up to altitude, setting up camps, doling out encouragement and guidance with every step.

Down at Base Camp, Kevin Cherilla was handling communications with the team. In Michael Brown's movie *Farther Than the Eye Can See,* the moment when Erik radios down Pasquale's decision is telling: Kevin's jaw literally drops.

Rather than have another climber sacrifice his own summit attempt, Pasquale headed down on his own. Erik remembered the first rule of safety on a climb like this, and radioed down to Camp Three that Pasquale was climbing alone. Dr. Steve Gipe picked up the message and headed out to find him. An hour later he found Pasquale staggering down the mountain, burning with fever. He took him back to a tent, fed him water to keep him hydrated, surrounded him with hot-water bottles, and put him inside four sleeping bags.

The whole time, Pasquale insisted on having an expedition radio at his ear, so he could stay in touch with the progress of the team as it endured its most crucial hours. He had refused the wishes of others to retreat with him, ordering them to continue with Michael Brown and Brad Bull, both previous summit climbers, as their leaders. Everyone had worked so hard, he didn't want anyone to lose the opportunity to summit. He was not going to sacrifice himself or anyone else to get someone up the mountain. He knew Erik was safe. Some of the best climbers on earth were with him—young, strong, faithful.

As the long night eroded onward toward dawn, the fever began to abate and Pasquale came out of his dreams to hear Jeff Evans's plea for a new regulator. He found out who had the spares and radioed up the information—he was still taking care of his team, even while bundled up like a kitten in a tent two thousand feet below. As he drifted in and out of sleep he heard other radio arguments, about bad weather that had created a whiteout above the Yellow Band at twenty-seven thousand feet.

He lay in his tent, shivering—so cold, and yet sweat was pouring off his body. The wind was blowing, so the tent shook wildly. It was such a strange feeling, suffering malaria on Everest. Pasquale was drifting in and out of consciousness. He was dreaming. His brain felt like it was going to explode. So in this delirium, this netherworld, he could hear things that were going on but was not conscious. Then for a moment he became lucid and, hearing about the snowstorm, started wondering if they were going to die. He was thinking that he had failed. He wasn't able to summit; Erik might not summit, the whole team might not summit, and there was not enough oxygen left to do another summit attempt. He was thinking the whole expedition was a failure, because he got sick.

High above, the group was hunkered down saving their strength, without a leader, in the darkness of a high-altitude, pre-dawn whiteout. In a sense they were all blind, equalized by the mountain.

Then word came from below that the storm was lifting, and stars were visible. Sherm Bull, a month shy of his sixty-fifth birthday, got up and said, "Guys, the weather's bad, but it ain't that bad. If you want good weather, go to Central Park. I'm going to the summit." And he headed up.

Sherm Bull and his son Brad summited first, just after sunrise. Finally, a little after 9 A.M., Erik Weihenmayer became the first blind man to stand on the top of the world. He later wrote, "The course of one's life is like the ascent of a mountain," and he had reached his ultimate summit.

Now, two years later, Pasquale tossed and turned in his sleeping bag once again, this time at a border crossing in Africa. He remembered his darkest hour on Everest, and the persistence and judgment he'd learned. Sitting there at the border, he was devastated because all the plans, all the work, the money, the time, the rapids; everything he had done to get to this point was now in jeopardy.

That dreadful night on Everest had turned out better than anyone had a right to expect. Just as Erik had achieved his own personal summit through perseverance, so Pasquale began to think that he could realize *this* dream, this epic descent of the Blue Nile, if he followed his will as much as his dreams.

He would go ahead. He would go forward to Khartoum, permit or no permit, camera or no camera. If necessary, he would do the whole damn river by himself.

CHAPTER TWENTY-TWO

The Sudan is a useless possession, ever was and ever will be. Larger than Germany, France and Spain together, and mostly barren, it cannot be governed, except by a dictator who may be good or bad.

GENERAL CHARLES GORDON IN KHARTOUM

On February 2, after Pasquale and Gordon had been on the expedition for forty-one days, I was in Seattle at home when I got a call from Pasquale on his sat-phone. "I've got good news and bad news," he said.

"Tell me."

"The good news is we're in Sudan. The bad news is we don't have permission; we're here illegally."

Pasquale had awoken after days of waiting and decided to take matters into his own hands; decided to take the risk. The expedition was carrying several hundred thousand dollars' worth of camera and telecommunications gear into one of the most unstable countries in the world, with no permission whatsoever. Everyone was nervous, especially given the firearms the local soldiers carried.

Late that day, Pasquale, Michel, and Gordon pushed the rafts out into the river, fired up the engines, and began to motor downstream. The river ran copper, like an ember on the hearth. They quietly passed under the cable that marked the border, passing from the churches of Ethiopia toward the mosques of Sudan. They puttered past an old cement-and-stone structure, the first of the Great Nilometers. With a series of concrete steps, engraved in Arabic, the Nilometer gauged river height during the annual floods so those downstream could be alerted.

Pasquale had also brought Somali, the Sudanese soldier, with them. A mile inside Sudan, Pasquale called me with the news. At mile two he was waved over by about twenty Sudanese Army troops fetching water on a gravel bank. Gordon yelled, "Soldiers . . . here they come. Shit, I knew it. We're screwed." The soldiers recognized Somali, and gave him a warm greeting, but asked Pasquale to accompany them up to the nearby Arada army post.

Before Pasquale could even start up the hill, however, a Commander Khalil walked down to inspect the invading flotilla. He checked passports and examined the boats, and Pasquale held his breath, waiting to see if they might again be arrested. But Commander Khalil pulled out his pen and handwrote a letter to the other army commanders along the Nile to allow the expedition through to the Sudanese town of Damazine, adjacent to Rosaries Dam at the far end of Rosaries Reservoir. Pasquale was overwhelmed: "Commander, you are an honor to Sudan. We want to thank you very much!"

The commander grinned from ear to ear, and said he had heard all about the expedition from a woman friend across the border. In fact, he confessed, he himself had crossed the border illegally the other day to visit his favorite bar—the one owned by Fantanish—as he enjoyed a good drink every now and then, and alcohol was illegal in Sudan. Fantanish had filled the commander in on the expedition, and had spoken of the character of the participants. The commander said he supported the effort but was concerned for the expedition's safety. He ordered Somali and another army troop to escort Pasquale all the way to Damazine.

Delighted with this turn of luck, Pasquale and team headed downstream, carrying the letter of permission. He still had no exit visa from Ethiopia, entry visa to the Sudan, sanctions from any government ministries, film permits, or customs clearance for the gear. But they were on their way.

The orange sun floated like a balloon on the rim of the sky. Pop, it went down. That night, camping three miles inside Sudan on a beach of fine white sand, Pasquale received an e-mail from the producers in the U.S.: "Good news. We received the waiver from the State Department. As soon as you get local government clearances you can proceed to Sudan."

Pasquale began to do some calculations. In the forty-two days since the expedition began it had descended 7,308 feet in 750 miles, from the source of the Blue Nile at Sakala in the highlands of Ethiopia to the frontier deserts of Sudan. The river had transformed from a trickle to a raging torrent pinching through narrow gorges to a flat, fat bastard of a river. Scrubby vegetation had replaced hardwoods, and the river was lined with small wooden boats tied up at thatch-roofed huts.

Michel wandered over and sat next to Pasquale.

"According to Somali, Damazine has hotels, restaurants, and an Internet café," Michel said in delightful anticipation. "Can't wait to finally get a hot shower and check my e-mail. If they have a Hilton, let's stay there."

"Give me a break," Pasquale replied. "We'll stay at the Sheraton right across the street. I have a Starwood Gold card."

Two more days of motoring and they reached the southern point of the nearly half-century-old Lake Rosaries. The reservoir was silted in by the never-ending runoff of rich Ethiopian volcanic soil that had fertilized Egypt for thousands of years. The maps and GPS said that they were supposed to be in open lake water, but in fact they were slogging through a basin of oozing, stinking mudflats cluttered with water reeds and stinging plants. They struggled to find a camp, but at twilight the land seemed drowned beneath a weight of water. Finally they discovered a small, muddy, bug-infested inlet leading to a bluff no more than fifteen feet high. Most of it was planted with vegetables, someone's garden. They squeezed their tents into what little space remained and, for lack of wood, had a cold dinner of crackers and bananas. They immediately retreated to their tents to escape the swarms of mosquitoes and other bugs that engulfed the night. The gibbous moon poured a flood of violent light into the bowers of the tents.

The next day they set off early, assuming they would spend one more night on the river and then reach the Rosaries Dam and Damazine. No sooner had they launched than a hard, bitter wind kicked up, sending two-foot waves crashing over the raised bows of the rafts. They were stalled in a smelly, swampy maze of mudflats and reed beds that stretched to the horizon, with no sign of hard shoreline or possible camps for the evening. Between an outdated map showing where the lake should have been, and the GPS pointing toward a dam they couldn't reach, they were lost. They backtracked, found another course, inched forward, bumped into cul-de-sacs, retreated, tried again, and slowly progressed toward what they didn't quite know. They were floating through the ghost of a world, a lost world.

After they'd spent a few hours probing various labyrinthine channels, the dusk began to thicken to darkness. The team was about resigned to spending the night on the boats when Pasquale spotted the faint lights of the dam in the distance. Immediately a frantic debate broke out. Somali argued against approaching the dam in the dark. He was scared that the expedition would be mistaken for terrorists approaching the dam and be blown out of the water. It was only recently that the government had wrested back control of the dam and its province from John Garang and the SPLA (Sudan People's Liberation Army, the Christian rebel group in the south).

Pasquale, however, insisted that they proceed. Then they watched as a small boat turned on its spotlight and swept a beam across the water.

"We have to go back. They will shoot us!" Somali cried in the darkness.

"Listen to him, Pasquale," Gordon's voice cut like a bright blade over the din of the engine.

Pasquale idled down. Reluctantly, he agreed to find a spot to sleep on the lake. For the next hour he motored in circles trying to find a suitable place to moor for the night, and at last they came across a dry and crooked acacia whose branches spread across a dark pool. Its rough foliage, structured in horizontal layers, gave it a heroic air, like a full-rigged ship with sails clewed up. Carefully avoiding the sharp, two-inch thorns, Pasquale tied up the rafts. The crew spread sleeping bags across the thwarts, curled up to keep warm in the night air, and fell into sleep just a mile from the Rosaries Dam.

The sun shot up and decanted a vast, hard light. Pasquale fired up the motor and steered toward the dam. The Rosaries Dam was about a half-mile wide, with the central portion made of aging gray concrete grading into basketball-sized angular boulders. Through binoculars, Pasquale could see a large battery of old antiaircraft guns positioned on the crest of the dam, just to the right of the main works. As they approached, camouflaged soldiers rushed out of squat dark-green buildings adjacent to the guns, some heading toward the top of the dam and others into a patrol boat that sped out to intercept them. Soldiers were motioning Pasquale to pull over to the right side of the dam, but he ignored them and just kept puttering toward the main wall.

"We have to stop . . . Now!" Gordon yelled to Pasquale above the drone of the motor.

Pasquale worried that Gordon might be right, but he swallowed and kept on going, believing that the soldiers would not fire at boats filled with a combination of white men and a Sudanese soldier.

When they reached the dam wall, Pasquale ordered the others to remain in the rafts. He leapt out and walked toward the uniformed man who appeared to be in charge. He tried to radiate a confidence he didn't feel.

"*As-Salaam-Alaikum,*" said Pasquale, using the standard Arabic greeting. It literally means "Peace be unto you."

"Salaam." The uniformed man nodded back. Then Pasquale began to explain the expedition and its purpose, but the officer held up his hand to silence Pasquale halfway through the pitch.

"We've been here all night waiting for you," the officer said. "Commander Khalil radioed instructions to meet you and give you help. We were so worried last night when you didn't show up that we went out looking for you with our patrol boat and spotlight."

The army officer radioed into town and requested that the local security chief come out to talk with them. As soon as the security chief showed up he started asking questions in broken English.

"Who are you?" he asked, while taking Pasquale's hand and leading him away from the rest of the group, behind a truck.

"My name is Pasquale. What is your name?"

"My name is Osama."

Great, Pasquale thought. "Osama, what a wonderful name," he said.

"How did you get here?" Osama asked in a genuinely puzzled tone.

"What do you mean?"

"How did you get here?" he repeated.

Pasquale paused, then replied: "By boat."

Now Osama was really perplexed.

A third time he asked. "No. Perhaps you do not understand. I mean how did you get *here?*" He pointed to the dam.

Grabbing Osama's hand, Pasquale led him over to the dam wall and pointed down at the two yellow rafts tied together in the water at the base of the dam.

"You came in *those?*" Osama asked incredulously.

"All the way from the source of the Blue Nile."

Osama stared at the rafts for a while, trying to grasp what he'd just heard.

"This is not possible. The water is too big. Impossible," he said, stunned. Then, "Where are your papers?"

"We don't have any. We just have this letter from the commander back up at Arada army post." Pasquale pulled out Khalil's scribbled letter and handed it over.

"You have no papers?" Osama again sounded dumbstruck as he looked over the letter.

Taking Pasquale by the hand, Osama walked back to the main group. He announced that they would all go into town to check in with the local police and get another permit. When they were finished, he would bring them back and help move the boats around the dam.

Soldiers were ordered to stay with the boats, Pasquale and crew piled into a truck, and off they rode to Damazine, where they would find sanction and temporary sanctuary at the bar and hotel.

En route Osama quizzed Pasquale on the journey from the far-off mountains. After listening to the tales of steep cataracts, deep canyons, and man-eating crocodiles, Osama spoke:

"My whole life I have lived along the Bahr al Azraq [Arabic for the Blue Nile]. I have watched every year as it floods, and every year as it dries to a trickle. And I have always wondered where it comes from, and where it goes. For me, that is the mystery of this river. And you have told me the answer."

Damazine turned out to be a squat, dusty, trash-littered Sudanese frontier town. So much for Michel's Hilton. The office of the police chief functioned as customs, immigration, and just about everything else official that happened in this part of Sudan. Housed in an old Italianate building built in the era of the Rosaries Dam construction, it was now run-down and chinked, a shadow of its former imposing self.

Sudanese Arabs wear white turbans, rather than the checkered *kaffiyehs* of the Palestinians and other Arabs. Their *galabiehs* (traditional robes) too are white, and with an outer cloak, they make a costume that is both cool and democratic, indicating the equality of all men in the eyes of God. But the towering, massively built, jet black Sudanese who met them in the police office was clearly more equal than others, even in his flowing galabieh.

"I am Yusef," he started, "chief of Damazine security. We welcome you to Sudan with open hearts. You are very welcome here and praise Allah that you are visiting us."

Pasquale and the others were thunderstruck. Was this the Sudan about which they had been so overwrought? The Sudan of Islamic fundamentalists and terrorists?

Yusef glanced at the passports of the expeditioneers, holding some of them upside-down—it was evident that he could not read—and declared them in order, despite the fact that all the visas had expired. "We have never heard of anyone coming down this river. We are honored to meet you," Yusef concluded.

When they returned to the dam, Osama ordered his soldiers to help move the boats into a requisitioned dump truck. With all the military assistance, this turned out to be the easiest portage Pasquale had ever experienced. The rafts were rerigged and ready to go well before dark. Despite the lack of a Hilton, they were in a joyous mood. It seemed, at that moment, that they would actually make it to Khartoum, some five hundred miles away, where the Blue Nile ends and the Nile proper begins. If they succeeded that far, Pasquale and Gordon would become the first people in history to navigate the entire length of the Blue Nile.

CHAPTER TWENTY-THREE

Before the Congo, I was just a mere animal.
JOSEPH CONRAD

For the next several days, Pasquale and the others pushed on, deeper and deeper into Sudan. Although they had stopped at the Arada military garrison just inside the Sudanese border and at police headquarters in Damazine, they still had no official Sudanese documents, passport visas, customs documents, or filming permits. Officially, they didn't exist in the country through which they now passed.

No mountains were to be seen now, not even in the distance. The riverbanks rose to twenty feet on either side, composed mostly of brownish-gray mud and sand. They moved through the washed-out glare of too much heat trapped in too little space. Shards of dead branches stuck out in frantic directions, like bones broken through skin. The land felt drained of life—cracked and brittle, like a piece of old leather.

After a few days, though, they began to pass some banana and papaya trees. There were now small plots of subsistence farms with mud-brick and thatch-roof villages every few miles. There were girls and young women down by the river washing clothes; men were seen tending the old Indian-made single-piston diesel motors with small irrigation pumps used to water the subsistence crops that lined both shores.

Day by day more villages appeared, then small towns with mosques and abandoned ornate colonial buildings, relics of some past prosperity. Where once this part of the Blue Nile bustled with schemes to create vast fields of high-quality cotton and other cash crops, now little remained but dust, and trash blowing in the wind.

Herds of cattle jostled with camels for space to drink at the river's edges. More people and animals and fewer sandbars meant that good camping spots were becoming rare. Firewood all but disappeared, which meant cold meals were often the norm. When they did pull over for the night, the noise—the disharmonic Arabic music, chickens squawking, trucks blatting, the calls to prayers from the mosques—was grating after the quietude of the upper river. Everyone was feeling a bit short-tempered and ill in the new environment. Yibeltal, especially, seemed to be suffering. He had been quiet and sluggish for days, and his frame was looking rawboned and thin.

Pasquale kept wondering how a river could change so much in such a short span. Crossing from Ethiopia into Sudan had been more than just an international boundary; it had been an abrupt change of culture, religion, scenery, and topography. It wasn't just a residual demarcation from the colonial penknife; it was a boundary between worlds.

The corridor through which they now moved wrinkled into dry ridges, like a badly healed wound. The landscape remained monotonous: mud banks, hard red termite mounds, trees with finger-sized thorns—a sun-fried furnace under a bleached sky. Dust devils whirled up like great columns of smoke. The river was sluggish, and the rafts seemed to hang motionless on the water like junks in a Chinese painting. They could shut their eyes, and open them an hour later to the exact same scene. Not only were there no signs of life or current, there was the smell of death in the air. At regular intervals, they saw the carcasses of dozens of wild and domesticated animals, dumped or fallen into the river. The hot sun scooped up the smell and spread it like a thin mist.

JOURNAL DAY 47

Long, long day. Mostly sat in boats trying to read, sleep, or look at what scenery there is. One bend in the river pretty much looks like the next. This is no longer an expedition of challenging rapids, steep canyons, crocs, hippos, shiftas, etc. This is now just a trip of mental endurance. Mile after mile—day after day—week after week—the drone of the 2-stroke Merc, hot blistering sun, occasional cooling breeze, endless expanse of river ahead of us occasionally narrowed by sand bars. This will be our routine for the next 2 months . . .

That evening they pulled into a spit of sand and called camp. To find some relief from the heat and blowing sand, they all stripped and swam in the Nile, splashing one another, in water hot as tea. But when they reemerged on shore, they found their little camp surrounded by an aggressive group of young, blue-black galabieh-clad Sudanese men. A thin, scholarly-looking man of perhaps thirty stepped forward, and in halting English he introduced himself as Abdu Osman of Abu Zoor village.

"Do you have equipment to look underwater?" he asked.

Pasquale was puzzled at the request. "Why do you ask?"

"One of the boys of the village has drowned today in the Nile and we cannot find his body. We have sent men downstream and cannot find him. Perhaps the crocodiles have eaten him."

Pasquale and the others were surprised. It had been a dozen days since they had seen any crocodiles, and now with so many people along the river—many with Kalashnikovs—it was hard to fathom that any crocodiles survived in this stretch. And, of course, they were keenly aware that they had been swimming in these waters just moments before.

"I am sorry, but we do not have such equipment," Pasquale replied.

"There will be a funeral tomorrow and you must come," Abdu firmly stated. "No, no, we must go on downriver," replied Pasquale. But as he spoke, he was fearful of countermanding what might be Sudanese Islamic fundamentalists. When Abdu continued to insist, Pasquale relented and promised to attend the morning service.

Perhaps four hundred people scratched out life in the dustbin village of Abu Zoor. The next morning, as the team approached, they could see armed men sitting on mats in congregations of twenty to thirty, talking while chopping the air with their hands. But when Pasquale and the team stepped onto the hard dirt of the village commons, all conversation abruptly stopped. Dark eyes followed Pasquale as he moved slowly to the center, as though walking underwater. It was dead silent. Pasquale was worried—it would be so easy to disappear here.

After what seemed an eternity, one of the elders at the axis of the village stood up, a watery-eyed, white-haired, toothless man, his black face deeply lined with wrinkles. He reached for Pasquale's hand, and before Pasquale could protest, the old man kissed the back of it, and said, "My son is gone." Pasquale felt tears form in his eyes.

Then as Pasquale searched for words of condolence, the other men jumped up and rushed forward to express gratitude for their attendance at the funeral. To them it elevated the somber ordeal, and made the boy special, blessed by visiting angels.

For the next several hours Pasquale and the team watched the funeral. One man read from a copy of the Koran that was bound in goatskin parchment. Another man blew a crude, single-note tin trumpet, with a sound so evocative it caused the hairs at the nape of Pasquale's neck to prickle. Another man, wrapped in a homespun tunic and jodhpurs, was striking a cow-skin drum with a quiet but insistent beat.

Involuntarily, the team felt their own bodies responding to the rhythm, and they swayed a bit with the villagers. Some members of the village keened and wailed. Boys pressed their hands together like butterfly wings. Every few minutes the men paraded in a sobbing circle.

The funeral march continued, stopping in the shade of parasol-shaped thorn trees every few minutes for Koranic readings and antiphonal chanting. The crowd of men seethed and eddied like a foamy sea. Noting that only men were participating in the rituals, Pasquale asked Abdu why. He was told that, according to the strict Islamic Sharia law that Sudan officially embraced, women were not allowed in public when outsiders were present. All of the girls and women were grieving in their homes.

Gender segregation notwithstanding, Pasquale couldn't help but compare what he was witnessing with the Western rituals of grief. Long, complex obsequies are starkly simplified here, resulting in a deep sense of community, of collective grief and purging. Everyone shared the sorrow and anguish.

Back on the river, they neared Sennar Dam, the second impoundment on the Blue Nile. Sugarcane fields spread along the buggy mud deposits, and occasionally the team would pull over, slice off a stalk, and suck on its sweet juice as they motored across the bleak and monotonous floodplain. Every now and then the thought of abandoning the quest squirreled into Pasquale's mind, but he shook it away. It took a certain mental toughness to soldier on, and he bent his will to the task.

Sennar was the first dam built on the Nile in Sudan, constructed in 1925 by the British hegemons eager to develop the vast, raw, fertile land that the Nile watered. Built as part of the Great Gezira irrigation scheme, it was meant to irrigate millions of acres of cotton—which was then in great demand for the huge textile mills of Europe. The Anglo hydrologists and engineers knew that the great silt load of the Blue Nile—which provides over 90 percent of the silt load for the Nile proper—would fill most dams in short order. So they imagined a dam with a flush system that would allow the silt to pass through, making the dam immortal.

Their vision was not realized, though. Today a sea of mud ten miles in width stretches behind the dam. A torrid channel a hundred yards wide is the only approach through the almost-filled reservoir, and the banks are a slimy, black oozing muck just a few inches off the water. It was impossible to stand on this quagmire, much less set up a camp.

It was middle afternoon. Time seeped like syrup. The sky was a metallic dome, white with the heat. The temperature clambered up to more than 120 degrees, and as Pasquale buzzed along he had time to think; too much time. He remembered the last time he was in heat this brutal, two years back, exploring the Fish River Canyon of Namibia.

In the jigsaw puzzle that is Africa, Namibia is the piece that got left behind. The barren state, larger than Texas, lies north of South Africa's western border, and most of its eastern edge abuts Botswana. Like Papua New Guinea, Namibia was a German colony until the end of the First World War, when the League of Nations entrusted South West Africa, as it was then known, to South Africa as a mandated territory. The country gained independence in 1990, yet it remains one of the least-explored domains on the continent.

Pasquale and I and a few friends wheeled south from Windhoek, the capital, into the vast, rocky ocean that is the Namibian desert, an endless retreat of buttes and ravines, ridges and terraced escarpments, the compacted age-lines of the earth as deep and hard and revealing as the dark, weather-carved face of an aged German miner.

Our host was Louis Fourie, a former South African wine farmer with sun-pinched eyes. When he was fourteen, he'd had a dream to own land so vast that he couldn't see the borders. Prodigal with his plans, he'd purchased thirty-six thousand acres for a song, including the upper Fish River Canyon, some nine years before. He had fashioned a modest lodge, which served as our base camp. The plan was to spend a few days hiking the upper canyon on Louis's land, then do a trek into the main Fish River Canyon National Park. A couple flyovers of the river had been planned, too, for aerial recces to see if the Fish River might be navigable by raft. Nobody had ever tried it, despite the fact that the Fish River Canyon was promoted as another Grand Canyon of Africa.

Timing seemed spot-on; until a few days before, all the canyon had seen were what Louis called "bankruptcy clouds," the high, wispy, rainless streaks that will cause a waiting farmer to go under. But by the time we boarded the plane stateside, it had started to rain, the first water in the canyon in ten months. "The river floods this time of year," Louis warned. "It can get up to 250,000 cubic feet per second." That seemed a bit of a stretch—ten times the flow of the Colorado through the Grand Canyon, which drains the western slopes of the snow-coated Rockies— especially given that there's no snow in Namibia. Louis also said that we could drink the water untreated, but none of us took his word on that.

At midafternoon, the Land Rover tires crackled into Louis's hardscrabble oasis, a cozy former farmhouse that his wife, Riette, had decorated. We started to pack for our first foray into the canyon the next day. Our team included *Outside* magazine editor-at-large Tim Cahill; Dr. Seth Berkley, president of the International AIDS Vaccine Initiative; Peggy Dulany, chair of the poverty-fighting institute Synergos; Lisa Conte, CEO of Napo Pharmaceuticals; and several other rogues and scalawags. Louis's garrulous mother, Gerty, had flown up from South Africa to be our cook, and she grilled up tasty servings of klipspringer and gemsbok, which we washed down with Windhoek lagers, supposedly brewed to German purity rules. As the sun fired a gorgeous sunset against an oxide-red cliff, we went swimming in a pond fresh from the rains. Then we sat on the porch talking and sipping fifteen-year-old Glendronach whiskey. At one point a giant scorpion, looking like the creature in *Alien*, scuttled across the floorboards, and Riette jumped on the table and screeched. It was a wind scorpion. "Lots more of those in the canyon," Louis said gently.

We decided to do a shakedown hike, an eleven-mile tramp in which we would drop into an unnamed fissure, climb out the other side, then descend into Lion River Gorge, which in turn descends into Fish River

Canyon. We would then hike downstream several miles to first-night camp, which was accessible with a four-wheel-drive vehicle, and Louis would arrange to have our tents and bags trucked around, along with iced drinks, steaks, tiki lamps, plastic chairs, and a box of Cuban cigars. So, all we would need for the day would be water and a day pack.

"You taking the sat-phone?" I called to Pasquale as we loaded into the trucks, referring to the Inmarsat mini-M satellite telephone Pasquale had brought for emergencies.

"Nah . . . it's just a day hike. I'll have it shipped around to camp."

"Makes sense," I agreed. The phone was heavy, and this was just the warm-up: a chance to test our hiking boots, to acclimatize to the heat, and to set our pace for the next several days. We wouldn't even need our 1:50,000 topo maps or GPSs.

Louis decided to manage the moving of our gear to camp, so Riette volunteered to be our guide, though she had never done the hike. Nonetheless, her attire alone instilled confidence. Although we were decked out in candy-colored Mountain Hardwear and brand-new Leki trekking poles, she wore a tennis outfit and sneakers, as though this were a stroll to the courts. She bobbed down the trail, not so much hiking as sailing.

The hike began simply, down a mountain zebra path. Mud, crisped into a lattice of flakes, crunched under our feet. The landscape was dotted with quiver trees, weird aloes that looked like hangovers from a Dr. Seuss book. The Bushmen used their hollow branches to hold arrows. Everywhere klipspringers, tiny-horned wraiths, made serpentine leaps along the blistered cliffs. There were heart-shaped leopard-paw prints. A pair of green parrots, local love birds, flitted across a canyon wall. Then we ascended the other side, and stooped on pieces of shale and gulped water and chewed springbok jerky. Across from the shaded bench, a kestrel rose from a lookout rock and wheeled with motionless wings ever higher on the thermals.

The team then climbed out of the small canyon, worked across a wind-scored plateau dotted with daisies and delicate pale-yellow, pink, and blue wildflowers. If it wasn't so hot, this would be a lovely place.

Soon the team began its plunge to the Lion River, down a Precambrian staircase, a journey of a billion years or so. In the mists of geological time, a seabed here had been lifted miles above the level of the ocean and had weathered into ranges of table mountains. Then, some five hundred million years ago, a fault had opened up. Fifty million years ago a river began to flow.

The canyon was steep and narrow, and the rocks were loose. "What do we do if it flash-floods?" someone asked. "We'll have time to get out of the way," Pasquale offered, remembering flash floods down tributaries of the Grand Canyon. "There's warning—it sounds like a freight train coming. Then we head for high ground." All then glanced at the steep walls to map a route upward.

By midday, several in the group weren't feeling well; one stopped to vomit. Another had turned his ankle on some wobbly rocks and was limping a bit. Still another was developing a rash. When the team pulled off boots to jump into a limestone pool, about half the feet were angry with blisters.

After the dip, Pasquale, feeling energized, strode out to the front of the pack with Riette and Peggy and a couple of others. They crossed a layer of red-brown quartzite and intersected with the Lion River, and began to make way down toward the Fish, when suddenly they heard the shouts from behind. "Hold up! Hold up! Seth broke his ankle!"

At first Pasquale thought it was a joke, but the tone was too severe. He turned to Riette, they exchanged glances, and then they took off running back up the trail with a couple others.

Pasquale scrabbled up the scree, and came to a sandstone shelf. There sprawled Dr. Seth Berkley, his shirt stained with tram-lines of sweat. Tim Cahill was crouched over Seth's left foot, firmly holding it in place. Seth described his fall, wherein he'd stepped off a ledge, twisting his right ankle, then fallen hard over onto his left one, which had made a shattering sound. His left foot was turned in a 90-degree angle, dangling with no support on the medial side—likely a multiple fracture with torn ligaments. He had called to Tim, who was hiking a few paces in front. Following instructions from Seth, Tim held the twisted foot in a viselike grip, and Seth turned to reset it.

Hot snakes of pain were running around Seth's legs. He refused painkillers, citing the increased possibility of shock and wanting to keep a clear head. We had a SAM splint, or pocket cast, and Pasquale formed it to the bottom of Seth's leg, ankle, and foot, but Seth's ankle needed side support. The team looked around for something flat—a branch, a stone—but could find nothing appropriate. Then Tim Cahill pulled out his two elongated journalist's notepads, just the right size, and offered them. He sacrificed his thoughts of the last few days, the currency of his livelihood, for Seth's sake.

With Seth's ankle stabilized, it was next imperative to get him out of the canyon. The sat-phone was at camp, so the team had to try to carry the two-hundred-pound man out. Going back up the canyon was ruled out—it would be too hard to lift him—so that left downward, and it was another five miles or so to camp. Pasquale, the strongest member of the team, was the primary carrier, with Seth's right arm slung over his shoulder, while three others took turns at his left arm. It was slow going, as his other ankle was also injured and he couldn't handle much weight on it for long.

Slowly, slowly he limped down the widening canyon. Pasquale tried various ways to carry him—the lifeguard carry, the fireman's carry, hoisting by his belt—but nothing worked for more than a few yards at a time. And it was now midafternoon, the sun at its zenith, the temperature over 120 degrees. "It may be hot, but at least it's steep," Pasquale quipped, in his signature mode of cheerful pessimism.

Seth's rush of adrenaline in the aftermath was gone, and he was hanging like a rag doll. It was very hard to carry him more than a few feet at a time without a respite. So the team stopped beneath a camel-thorn tree.

Its branches, more gray than green, shone with a metallic glister and gave little shade. Pasquale put a day pack under Seth's neck as a pillow and propped his leg on another. It was clear he couldn't be carried all the way out in a timely fashion; it would take days at this rate.

"I've got a plan," Pasquale offered. "We leave him here for ten days until he's down to a hundred and ten pounds, then we come back and carry him out." It was exactly the type of joke Seth needed, and he smiled for the first time in over an hour.

Pasquale looked around to see if we could fashion a stretcher from tree branches and packs, but the scratchy vegetation wasn't sturdy enough for poles. The sun was merciless and seemed somehow personal, staring like a snake's eye. The team was on the edge of the muddy, fulvous Lion River, the water hot as soup. A solution was needed, and quickly.

Lisa Conte, a marathon runner, volunteered to jog to camp and fetch the sat-phone. It was five miles each way over ground as inhospitable as the moon, three hours at best in the poisonous heat. The exercise had the potential to feed oxygen to the firestorm of the accident with yet another. But when Seth said he thought he had just a couple hours before gangrene might set in, a strong light burned behind Lisa's eyes. As she took off, a troop of baboons barked, and a flock of Egyptian geese flapped up the canyon, as though alarmed by the craziness of the scheme.

The air was hot, dry, breathless. Seth lay in the scant shade of the thorn tree and fell back into a funk. "I might lose my leg," he mumbled aloud. "I could die here." Then he held his breath, as though the least movement might snap the thread of his being.

At 4:00, Pasquale looked up the canyon and followed its contours. Something waved into view: a desert mirage, something jinking toward us, like a klipspringer. He watched transfixed as the image grew from a blur to something with features. It was Louis, carrying a black bag—the sat-phone. Not far behind was his assistant, Peter Brandt, from the tribe of Nama, carrying fence posts, rope, and a tarp to fashion a stretcher.

As it turned out, Lisa had made it to camp, dug the sat-phone out of a pack, and given it to Louis. Louis knew the fastest way to the bottom of the Lion River was from the rim, so he picked up Peter, drove to the rim, and hiked down.

Now there were options. Pasquale unpacked the sat-phone and started climbing up the cliffs to find a clear view of the Atlantic satellite. The others put together a stretcher with Peter's materials.

Phoning a rescue helicopter from the Fish River Canyon on a Sunday evening was no easy task. It took an hour just to lock in to the satellite, and then Louis tried calling various friends and neighbors who might find the number of a Medevac service in Windhoek. Nobody could. So, Pasquale tried calling friends and relatives in the United States. He called Kim, his wife, and had her search his computer, to no avail. He called the operator, and got a woman's voice in London. "We're in Namibia, and we have an emergency."

"I've never heard of Namibia," she replied, and hung up.

While making the phone calls, Pasquale watched the battery-indicator bars reduce, as well as the silent movie of the team below attempting to use the stretcher. They carefully moved Seth onto the makeshift gurney and lifted him up. They struggled to carry him over the rocks for just a few yards before being forced to stop and rest. A couple of times they almost spilled him. Tempers were running high. The fading sun was turning the canyon walls blue-black, menacing and separate. Pasquale went down the hill to tell the group to head to camp, to race the darkness. In the last light, a fish eagle floated down the canyon.

The sat-phone battery died. Pasquale slipped in the spare. Louis connected with a neighbor who had found the number of a helicopter pilot in Windhoek, and Pasquale dialed through. The pilot said he would try to find a chopper, but that he needed coordinates. Because the GPSs were at camp, Pasquale could only describe the location: five miles up Lion River Gorge from the confluence with the Fish River. That wasn't good enough, the pilot said, as it would be a three-hour flight from Windhoek, and it would be dark soon. The pilot said he might try a midnight rescue, but he needed the coordinates before an attempt. Louis said he would call back.

The second battery was almost dead, probably enough for one more call. Louis decided to call his mom and ask her to find the coordinates on a map, and then call the pilot. But as soon as he got Gerty on the phone, she started to chatter, dominating the conversation, blithely telling him about the minutiae of her day. "Shut up, Mom, and listen," Louis yelled into the phone, just as it went dead.

It was hard to pick a way down the talus to where Seth sprawled in a heat-induced stupor on his abandoned stretcher. Tim Cahill, Pasquale, and I stayed behind while the rest of the group headed for camp. Even though the shutters of the day were nearly closed, Louis volunteered to head down the canyon, as he knew the way and could then take a vehicle to his lodge, where he could use a landline to coordinate. If he was lucky, he would arrive by midnight.

So, Louis borrowed a pair of socks from Pasquale and struck out into the night. Letting Louis go felt like throwing away the compass. The remaining trekkers were trapped in the pit of an African canyon, distant and unconnected from the world.

Pasquale figured to make a series of campfires, and use flashlights to wave in the helicopter if it made the midnight run. Tim, Pasquale, and I picked through packs looking for matches, but we couldn't find any.

We moved Seth to a level spot in the lee of a large granite rock far up from the river, near a cluster of sacred datura. Since we couldn't make a fire, we spread out on the sand and watched the stars and talked. I recounted a Danish Dogme film I'd recently seen, *The King Is Alive*, with Jennifer Jason Leigh, in which a group of tourists gets lost in the Namibian desert and decides to put on a performance of *King Lear* to distract themselves from their fate. Down by the river the frogs started to sing, and Seth moved into a remarkably good mood, helped in part by the two-milligram tablets of Dilaudid he finally swallowed. He told brittle jokes, then pondered his life's latticework and tangles.

Fireflies spun about, and every now and then we lifted our heads to see if one of the bugs was really an approaching rescue light. About 11:00 the talk dried up. Silently, we watched the silver pinpoints of the Southern Cross.

About midnight, an owl swooped over the makeshift camp. Then a dry, warm wind began to scuffle up the canyon. At first it was just a breeze, and its night smells seemed to wash the camp clean. But it grew and we could feel the sting of grains on our cheeks. It began to blow away the stars, lightning flashed in the distance, and there was that indefinable smell of tension that precedes rain. Pasquale stood up, gritted his teeth. "A storm's coming. No helicopter tonight."

A flashlight swept across Seth's face, and he looked scared. He had a prison pallor and a web of hairline cracks around his eyes. "What about a flash flood?" he asked.

"Nah, not here . . . the canyon is too wide," Pasquale lied. Then he looked about for a flat spot up the sheer walls where Seth might be repositioned. There was nothing.

The unit of exchange here was a full quart of water, and we were all low. Pasquale stepped down to the bank of the river and pumped filtered water into all the bottles, came back, and distributed them to the bodies lying in the sand. Then he noticed a series of caves just above the roost, and borrowing a flashlight, he went up to check them out. They were tiny, tortured holes, with flinty, sharp-edged rocks as the floor, littered with rat turds. These were probably dens of scorpions, spiders, snakes, blister beetles, and other toxic creatures that have pushed the envelope of adaptability, but they were also shelters from the hostile wind, and some were just big enough to squeeze into.

Pasquale wrapped Seth in a tarp, anchored the edges, and moved to the caves to weather the storm, along with Tim Cahill and me. It was kicking into high gear, and sand was racing along the black earth like rapids, spraying like BBs, blasting a layer off exposed skin. "I've got sand up my urethra," Seth yelled.

We folded and contorted ourselves into the caves. Pasquale found an upper entrance and twisted in above my head. Then the skies opened; the rain came down hard. Lightning flashed, thunder rolled. The wind began to make a singular, animal-like howl, and the rain was so loud it sounded like a freight train coming. "No, dude," Pasquale yelled down to me. "It can't flash flood here . . ."

We had a clear view of Seth from where we crouched in the caves, and the flashing light illuminated his wrapped form. We waited until there was a lull in the rain, then unfolded, and ventured out into the sand-laden wind to check on Seth. "You okay?"

"Are you kidding?" he said in a feeble voice, grinding sand between his teeth. "Two broken ankles, sandstorms, windstorms, lightning, thunder, rain, flash floods. What's next, locusts?"

We laughed into the talons of the wind, then stumbled down to the river to see if the flash-flood nightmare might be coming true. But no, the river had barely changed. We breathed a sigh of relief, and headed back to the cave.

Once curled back inside, lying on a bed of broken rocks, the ceiling an inch from our heads, Pasquale's foot on my neck, we drew feet up into fetal positions. A tree outside creaked like an old rope. "At least it's dry," Pasquale consoled. But then the cave began to leak, and rivulets of rainwater poured onto our necks, thighs, and exposed legs. There was another round of lightning and long, trembling salvos of thunder. The wind outside seemed to celebrate a new depth of misery.

Since sleep was not forthcoming, Pasquale and I talked. We recognized that despite the travails and Seth's misfortune, we were realizing some sort of explorers' solace. Stripped of all layers, decocted down to an essence, it felt somehow comfortable and real; life was here, not through a window or on a screen. And there was a sense of being unbounded by geography or history. Not reconciled, not resolved. Not free of fretting about Seth. But free of trappings. And if accessories are a species of idleness, then free of sloth.

In the pale, infected light of daybreak we unfolded from the cave. Our mouths and throats felt made of tin. The air, doubly still now after the departure of the storm, was like something drawn up from a well, fresh and cool. We stepped down to Seth's stretcher. His face was cracked, like a crocodile's belly, with dust rings around his eyes. There was no helicopter. No rescue party.

"That was the worst night of my life, bar none," offered Seth, who had spent a career traveling to hardship posts.

"You didn't have it so bad," Pasquale quipped. "My cave was so small I had to go outside to change my mind."

Seth managed a smile. "What do we do now?" he asked, his voice sounding small in the immense morning. "I don't know if I can take another day of this heat."

"We wait," Pasquale advised. "Someone will come soon." Already the heat was pricking the backs of our necks.

Minutes later, we looked across the river to see some sort of vehicle working its way down a mesa. With binoculars we saw it was Louis's Unimog, a relic of the South African border war. It ground to a stop several hundred feet up the canyon, and Louis hopped out and sprinted down to the river, then crossed over to us.

"Where's the chopper?" Pasquale asked.

"I don't know. Never made it back to the lodge last night. I just slept a bit, grabbed the truck at camp, and worked my way here."

An hour later, a black cormorant near camp flapped up into the sullen sky. Suddenly, a Bell Jet helicopter whooshed up the canyon. Louis started to cry. But it continued up-canyon, apparently missing our waving red jackets and space blanket, and vanished around a bend. The canyon filled with a roar of nothingness. Had the pilot given up on us? We waited three minutes, five, ten, and began to fret. The desert seemed to have inhaled and was holding its breath.

Then a sound split the silence into fragments: the distinctive *whop,*

whop, whop poured down the gorge. After a couple passes the helicopter made a landing, almost twenty hours after the accident.

A medic wearing a flight suit stitched with a logo that read NAM POWER hopped out, hustled to Seth, and took control. He pulled out an aluminum splint and, to the great relief of Tim Cahill, replaced the notebooks that had supported Seth's left ankle. Minutes later we were saying goodbye, and the chopper lifted off from Seth's battlefield to the meadows of some hospital.

Soon Lisa and Peggy showed up, having hiked down from the rim with food and supplies, and we resumed our hike to camp. Tents and cold beer awaited there, and we would begin to put the layers of civilization back on. But for a few more miles, we were still clean and uncluttered.

CHAPTER TWENTY-FOUR

The Nile comes out of the Garden of Paradise, and if you were to examine it when it comes out, you would find in it the leaves of Paradise.

Mohammed, the Prophet of God

I t may be hot, but at least it's humid," Pasquale said to his Blue Nile crew, who were stretched out on the rafts, lolling, near-motionless. If they heard him, they didn't respond. Pasquale's temples felt as though they'd been bound with rope; his head felt both too big and too brittle.

As the temperature and humidity increased, so did the insects. Clouds of malaria-bearing anopheles mosquitoes and other biting and stinging insects engulfed them. Adding to the physical irritations was the constant tug-of-war between Pasquale and Gordon, a jousting for leadership and power.

JOURNAL DAY 48

Yet another argument with Gordon, who has a very unpredictable temper. He has very little understanding of expedition behavior or dynamics. Perhaps this is because he is used to small, self-contained expeditions, where there is no need to be concerned with others or planning.

225

After what seemed an eternity, they spied the outline of the Sennar Dam. Pasquale agreed to avoid a direct approach, in case the army guards this time around had no advance warning of their arrival. But the one-hundred-yard-wide channel led them directly to the main sluice gates at the middle of the dam, exactly the approach they had hoped to avoid. They had no choice. It was impossible to get out and walk across the mudflats.

The dam was an old gray lady perhaps two miles long and sixty feet high in the middle. There was a series of rusting ten-foot-wide closed steel sluicegates, perhaps thirty in all. As they approached to within fifty feet of the middle of the main concrete wall, they saw, directly to their left, a small gravel island rising over the boggy lake. On top of the gravel mound was a small, peeling building—evidently the army post guarding the dam. Pasquale motored directly up to the dam wall and waited. Nothing.

Hydrodams, of course, are among the most heavily secured structures in any country, as they supply critical power. Yet Pasquale and the team saw nobody patrolling or watching or moving. So, after several minutes, they jumped out of the rafts and walked to the guard post. They looked inside the dark, doorless building and found an entire squadron of Sudanese Army guards . . . asleep.

"Salaam," Pasquale whispered, and the closest soldier stirred, rubbed his eyes, then sat up erect, grabbed his rifle, and pointed it at the doorway. Pasquale put up his hands, and gently explained his presence, and the soldier backed down. He, too, had heard of the Blue Nile Expedition and been advised to give it a warm welcome.

The soldier escorted Pasquale and the others up the dam ladder, across the rim walkway, and to the adjacent town of Sennar, the dirtiest hole of a way station Pasquale had yet to encounter. The combination of heat, putrefying garbage, and steaming urine was virtually unbearable. Of Sennar, James Bruce wrote in 1772: "No horse, mule, ass, or any beast of burden, will breed, or even live at Sennar, or many miles around it. Poultry does not live here. Neither cat nor dog, sheep nor bullock can be preserved a season there . . ." A once rich and powerful empire stretching a thousand miles along the Nile during the reign of the Fung Dynasty in the sixteenth century, Sennar was now a crumbled and decayed backwater.

Pasquale decided that they would spend the night in Sennar to resupply and recharge, then leave early the next morning to push for Khartoum. But Gordon protested, saying the place was uninhabitable. They got into a shouting match.

JOURNAL DAY 49

Gordon is worried about mosquitoes and bed lice in his room in the only hotel in Sennar. He won't sleep on the bed. He either wants to go to the boats to sleep or put up a tent in the room.

As Gordon complained about the conditions of the hotel in Sennar, Pasquale learned of potentially more serious problems. Yibeltal came to Pasquale and confided that he had just discovered that he had a large tapeworm in his intestine, most likely the result of the raw meat called *kitfo* that the Ethiopians love to eat. He was certain it was what was making him ill.

"How do you know you have a tapeworm?" Pasquale asked. "Can you feel it inside your stomach?"

Yibeltal looked around and answered faintly, embarrassed: "When I go to the bathroom it is sticking out of my anus and crawling down my leg . . ."

"We need to get you to the doctor in Khartoum," Pasquale replied.

The Sennar Dam diverted large amounts of water into the desert, so when the expedition reloaded below the dam, it was as though the river had been stolen. It was so low, a trickle winding through white, wide sandbars, that Pasquale wondered if the expedition might have to end for lack of navigable water.

This was the dry season in East Africa. When the rains come in the summer months, usually June to September, more than 95 percent of the precipitation for the entire year inundates the highlands of Ethiopia. For these months, the Blue Nile is huge beyond belief, often flooding vast sections of land in Ethiopia and Sudan. These floods last until mid-October, and by January the river is a shadow of its rainy-season flow.

Pasquale had been eager to run the Blue Nile in the low season because it would make running the rapids in the upper and northern gorges more navigable. But he hadn't anticipated the effects of the dams in Sudan.

They scraped along, often in water only a few inches deep. After a time they began to pass abandoned brick water-pumping stations on either side of the river. These prodigious buildings were several stories high, with steel-pipe intakes often two feet in diameter reaching far out into the main flow of the riverbed. And yet they all appeared broken down and deserted; it was as if the rafts were floating through a museum of broken schemes.

In *The Blue Nile*, Alan Moorehead wrote of grandiose private British irrigation projects from the Sudan border to Khartoum. The industrial world was ravenous for cotton to feed the textile revolution, and the capacious and fertile flood plains of Sudan and endless waters of the Blue Nile were there for the picking. Now it was all derelict and deserted. With the end of the British colonial era and subsequent mismanagement of the postcolonial dictatorships, most of the commercial cotton farms and pumping schemes had been shut down and forgotten. Where once millions of acres of cotton waved in the wind, irrigated with elaborate pumping stations and hundreds of miles of pipeline, now barren land ran to the horizon. The brick stations were ruins, slowly crumbling back into the Nile the sand and silt from which they had come.

JOURNAL DAY 50

All day there are white sand beaches many miles long on both sides of the Nile. Very shallow water. Greenish water. Pure white sand beaches. Blue sky—small waves—feels just like the Bahamas. Thousands of small single-stroke diesel pumps alongshore continue to pull water from river. It may just be possible that the river does dry up before the confluence in Khartoum. After 8–10 hours' continuous motoring we are exhausted. Starting to feel like zombies. Gordon is moody—very short fuse.

As they wound toward Khartoum the wind began to whip, blowing the fine white sand in little puffs. Gusts of fifteen to twenty miles per hour became common. For the first time, temperatures began to drop, a funneling consequence of the winter storms pounding Europe.

Slowed to a crawl, they tried using both outboard motors at once, but found little augmentation in speed for twice the noise, twice the fuel consumption, and the increased hazard of running the boats aground in the shallow river. The motor blades were starting to wear down due to constant hangups on sandbars and gravel shoals.

For the next three days and nights the winds turned cold, mounting in speed and duration. The continuous gusts kicked up whitecaps, and two-foot waves broke over the bow, soaking the team with spray. Temperatures dropped into the fifties and lower. They put on all their fleece, Gore-Tex, life vests, everything they owned. Without jackets, Yibeltal and Michel wrapped themselves in shade cloth. To Gordon, who lived on a boat back home in Marina del Rey, California, it felt like nothing less than sailing. "This reminds me of the ocean, the cold open ocean," he said.

Then all color disappeared. It was as if someone had taken a brush and painted all the Blue Nile and Sudan in shades of gray and white, blotting out the green of the river, the yellow of the sun, and the blue of the African sky. What started as a low cloud of light-brown dust and haze in the far distance now became a cloud of fine white pulverized sand rolling over them, blasting their ears, noses, lungs, and pores. The sandstorm swallowed them like pills.

This was the first of the *haboobs* that would torment the expedition for the next two months and two thousand miles. The name "haboob" is rooted in the Arabic word for "phenomenon." It is a form of monsoon/dust storm generated as a thunderstorm produces a downdraft of cold air. It can last for upwards of three hours, and can rage along at over fifty miles per hour.

For the next several days they lived in a world of white, a world where the African sunsets no longer blazed with ochres and oranges. The pallid haze hung in the sky like a London fog. Occasionally the sun would emerge like a white ball suspended in the sky. The minarets of mosques that began to appear along both banks were cloaked in white shrouds. Yibeltal, too, was turning pale; his normally dark skin looked like rice paper. And there was the smoke, and smell, from burning dung, used for cooking-fires along the banks. Whatever faith one had in the Sudan, it was certain that they were in some sort of white hell.

As Pasquale and team finally motored into Khartoum, they passed under the steel expansion bridges built by the British decades earlier, and past the colonial headquarters where Gordon of Khartoum was speared to death. They steered into a dock at the Blue Nile Sailing Club, decelerating so abruptly that Pasquale felt nauseated.

It all somehow seemed anticlimactic. Pasquale and Gordon had just made the first full descent of the Blue Nile from font to finish, yet there was no merriment, no celebration. They still had a quarter of a continent to cross, and Yibeltal was sick. They tied up and caught a bus to the Acropol Hotel in downtown Khartoum.

There are moments in expeditions when one can actually feel culture shock, when passing from one world to another is so sharp and deep as to stagger the senses. As they rode the bus, Khartoum suffused them, getting in their eyes and nostrils and ears. The alien atmosphere was dustier, mustier, and thick with scents that battled one another in the nose—the sharp-sour smoke of Turkish tobacco and the saccharine-flower miasma that lurked in places where perfume was easier to come by than showers; the smell of cooking meat, and tea brewing. Once checked in at their hotel, they walked across the tiled lobby past furniture covered with antimacassars, dropped their packs in their ceiling-fanned rooms, took hot showers, and drowned themselves in a couple of cold beers with the owner, George Pagoulatos.

Pagoulatos was the same fixer who had not fixed their border crossing. Though Greek by birth, from George's appearance he might have been a descendant of one of the *effendi*s who had administered this chunk of the Ottoman Empire before the Mahdi drove most of them away. Though proud of his accommodations, he did not shy away from telling about how in 1988, a grenade attack on the hotel killed seven people, including two British missionaries and their two infant children.

That event seemed distant now—Pasquale had other matters to worry him. He finished his drink, then took Yibeltal to the doctor.

CHAPTER TWENTY-FIVE

When you have passed this portion of the river in the space of forty days you go on board another boat and proceed by water for twelve days more, at the end of which time you reach a great city called Meroë, which is said to be the capital of the other Ethiopians.

HERODOTUS, *THE HISTORIES*

I am dreaming of finding the lost city of Meroë, but reality reveals that I have lost nearly all my teeth.

DAVID LIVINGSTONE, JOURNALS, 1873

The name "Sudan" originated with the medieval Muslim geographers' term *Bilad al-Sudan,* "Land of the Blacks." Ethnically, however, one-third of the populace is Arab. Arabic is the lingua franca, and Arabs control the government and most of the country.

Gaunt and pale, his form thinning from the intestinal parasite feeding from within, Yibeltal collapsed against Pasquale, who held him tight around the waist as he ushered him into the doctor's office in Khartoum. The Arab doctor scratched his head, saying he was not familiar with tapeworm.

"I need to go back to Ethiopia," Yibeltal confided to Pasquale. "I need to see an Ethiopian doctor who understands these things. They eat strange food here, and they don't know how to cure the kitfo disease."

Pasquale wondered if the nondiagnosis might have been more than incompetence. The Khartoum doctor was Muslim; Yibeltal was a Christian Amhara who spoke no Arabic. From years of trying to coax Ethiopian Christian and Somali Muslim workers to cooperate, he knew how formidable that challenge was.

Pasquale had wanted his trusted aide Yibeltal to travel the whole of the expedition with him. But it was not to be; Yibeltal could go no further. Gordon had several times demanded that Yibeltal leave the expedition, and now he got his wish. Pasquale and Yibeltal parted ways in Khartoum, and Yibeltal headed home for treatment.

Michel, who had joined the expedition at the Second Portuguese Bridge just below the Northern Gorge, also decided to leave the expedition at Khartoum. He was tired, and he found the endless motoring boring, so he caught the first flight back to Spain. That left only Pasquale and Gordon to continue on to the Mediterranean.

Pasquale hoped things would get off to a better start with Gordon on the second half of the expedition. But during a shopping sortie to a local market, Gordon became agitated and contentious, and once again Pasquale felt his leadership threatened.

JOURNAL DAY 55

11:00. Gordon and I had a blowup during the food buy at the Amaret Store in Khartoum. Gordo—bizarre behavior at store, passive/aggressive—excessively so. Ran around grabbing things off shelves like a kid—totally unorganized. Kept saying that everything I want to buy is bullshit: "I would never eat THAT . . . but buy it if you want."

Now that they were down to two, Pasquale hoped to scale back to one raft, potentially speeding up the trip down the Nile proper, saving fuel and time. Yet the latest outburst from Gordon convinced Pasquale it was best to keep both rafts on the water for the "breathing space" they'd provide. Each could pilot his own boat, in his own silent world, and rarely have to interact with the other.

One evening behind the crenellated walls of a party in Khartoum, over plates of eggplant and raw lamb kidneys in hot sauce, Pasquale met the U.S. Embassy chargé d'affaires. Jerry Gallucci was a career diplomat and the highest-ranking U.S. diplomat in Sudan, since no ambassador had yet been reappointed. Pasquale and Jerry conversed late into the night, and Jerry confided that he was keen to join the expedition for a few days downriver to Shendi, a small town about 120 miles north of Khartoum. Pasquale was thrilled with the prospect, and he signed the diplomat on.

Pasquale wanted to source another interpreter and a cook to join the expedition, and he asked Jerry's advice. Jerry promptly recommended two able bodies: a multilingual kitchen aide, Ahmet Ali, from a village in the northernmost province; and one of his personal cooks, Raum, a forty-eight-year-old Catholic from the Dinka Lunyanja tribe in southern Sudan who had two wives and nine children.

The civil war in Sudan, essentially between the Christian south and the Muslim north, had been raging intermittently since independence in 1956. There were an estimated two million non-Arab Nilotic Sudanese refugees—mostly Christian Dinka and Nuer tribesmen from the White Nile region between Uganda and Khartoum—living in often squalid conditions in and around Omdurman, Khartoum's sister city across the Nile on its western shore. These non-Arabs often assumed the menial and servant jobs for the powerful in Khartoum. Raum was one such refugee, and Pasquale wondered about the wisdom of taking a southern black Christian into the north, deeper into fundamentalist Sudan. But he wanted to keep an open mind, and he had no other immediate options.

Upon meeting Raum the next day, Pasquale harbored even deeper doubts as to whether the cook was the right man for the job.

JOURNAL DAY 56

Raum talked too much and appeared combative, and I was concerned that he and Gordon might not get along. The worst thing would be to have yet another helper on the trip that clashes with Gordon. Even though I asked him to bring his kit, Raum showed up with absolutely nothing but the clothes on his back. Nothing at all. No jacket, blanket or pillow, toothbrush, plate, cup . . . nothing.

Not wanting to offend the acting ambassador, Pasquale hired Raum anyway, and hoped for the best.

The next day, Pasquale set out to find some detailed maps of the route ahead.

JOURNAL DAY 57

10:30. Mapping office to buy maps. Huge old office—many lights and drafting tables, map cabinets. All abandoned. Old maps piled every-where. What a shame. Old English two-story colonial complex.

Completely dilapidated.

General Director eating lunch. I was told I must wait.

Director says: "We don't have the right maps; it will take three
months."

I ask "Why so long?"

"We don't have paper."

"Can I buy you paper?"

"No, it will take three months."

"Can I look at the maps on shelves?"

"No, you don't need them."

I walked out, disgusted.

Before departing, there was one last matter to attend: their legal status. They still had no formal permissions, and they would next need visas to exit Sudan and enter Egypt, the most notoriously bureaucratic country in Africa.

Pasquale and Gordon shuttled among government agencies and ministries: Customs, Immigration, Finance, Trade, Defense, Communications, even Tourism. So often the authority to sign a particular document fell between two stools. Power didn't coincide with the titles in the chains of command, and ministers, undersecretaries, and directors-general often didn't know the extent of their authority or were unwilling to go out on a limb and grant the expedition permits. Though every meeting was rich with hospitality, optimism, and mint tea, the request was unprecedented. Nobody in Sudan could recall an attempt to navigate the Nile from Khartoum to Aswan, in Egypt. As far as the bureaucrats in Khartoum knew, the border on the Nile to Egypt was closed.

Awash in the dead-end warrens of civil service, Pasquale turned to the fixer, George Pagoulatos, who led him through the labyrinthine beadledom of Khartoum, finally landing with his old friend Osman Abubaker, of the External Information Council. In the furbelows and folderol of chat between the first cup of tea and the second, between the exchange of cigarettes, each observed the small signals—the way a glass of tea is stirred and sipped or the offer of a match—in order to know how to proceed. Some money was exchanged, and then a letter was composed and stamped, ostensibly sanctioning the expedition and giving permission to exit Sudan and enter Egypt. They were set, or so they thought.

On the first day of March, Pasquale, Gordon, and the new expedition members met at the Blue Nile Sailing Club, reinflated and rerigged the rafts, and slid them back into the river. With the skyline of Khartoum to the south, they motored to Tutti Island, the spit that marks the actual confluence of the Blue and White Niles, reaching it at 12:05 P.M. For the next mile, the light greenish-blue waters of the Blue Nile commingled with the milky light-gray waters of the White Nile, and they rode the crease of two of the world's greatest rivers. After a few miles the divergent currents and colors blended until there was but one flow, the River Nile.

Once again the air seemed superheated, as though they were motoring through the open door of an oven. The ground and the water seemed to melt to a kind of infernal liquid that scorched with every breath.

Two days out, they came to the first significant natural obstacle on the Nile, Sabaluga. It was the Sixth Cataract of the Nile, considered the most notorious of the series that begins with the First Cataract, just below the Aswan High Dam. Like the other great cataracts of the Nile, Sabaluga was formed when hard, dense Precambrian rocks of the Nubian Swell were thrust to the surface, at first blocking the Nile, but weathering away over eons to form a section of granitic bedrock that cut the river so it bled white.

Legends abound of boats tossed against these rocks, but it wasn't until halfway through the rapid that Pasquale was even aware they had entered Sabaluga. After nearly eight hundred miles of Class IV to VI rapids in Ethiopia, the Great Cataracts of the Sudan and Egypt, in Pasquale's estimation, would not require much derring-do.

That night at camp, Raum, the cook, appeared lost, asking for help with the most basic of tasks. His lack of experience was quickly noticed by Gordon, who expressed his dissatisfaction by taking control of the kitchen and cooking up something on his own. Raum pleaded that this was his first day on the job; that he needed some time to learn the ways of river cooking. Pasquale and Jerry both calmed Raum down, saying that of course he would have time . . . lots of time.

During the next several hundred miles, the pace and scope of the expedition differed little from day to day. The wind would stir early in the morning and gain strength throughout the day, peaking in the late afternoon with gusts up to forty miles per hour. They were at the start of the *Hamseen*, a season of hot, dry desert winds that blow from the north in early spring. "Hamseen" is Arabic for "fifty," as the winds supposedly last for fifty days.

When the Hamseen winds blew directly upriver, the temperatures would average 100 to 110 degrees, but as wind or river shifted direction even slightly, as they often did, the wind would blow directly off the blistering Sahara Desert bordering both banks of the Nile. Then temperatures would spike to 120, even 125 degrees.

In the evenings the weather was even more oppressive. As the winds died down late in the day, the humidity would creep to 90 percent, and the thick, dank air pressed down on their shoulders and poured into their lungs. When the temperature dropped below eighty-five degrees, moisture would condense and precipitate, drenching everything with dew.

Three days down from Khartoum, they reached the frowzy, dog-eared desert town of Shendi, once the hub of Sudan's slave trade. In 1814, the Swiss explorer Johann Lewis Burckhardt estimated that about five thousand slaves annually passed through the Shendi market before being exported to Egypt and Arabia. It was the end of the road for many black Africans captured in their villages by Arab traders.

This was also the end of the river road for Jerry Gallucci; he had to get back to work trying to douse the tinderbox that was Khartoum. Waiting for America's top representative in Sudan, parked along the shore, were three white steel-armored American Embassy Suburbans, replete with muscular armed security agents and guards.

For an instant Pasquale was struck with the contrast. They had just floated three days down the Nile with no bodyguards or armaments whatsoever, and Jerry had been like a regular buddy on a camping trip. Now Jerry stepped back into an insular world of protection and paranoia. His little armada would be driving on a paved road back to the capital that had been Osama bin Laden's safe haven along the Nile in the early '90s. For all anyone knew, bin Laden, or his followers, could now be hiding in that very region.

As Jerry drove away in a roar of dust, Pasquale felt a sense of loneliness closing back in. Though Gordon was still his companion, a fellow

American with a common history, a shared love of adventure, and a mutual goal, he was also a stranger, and sometimes an adversary. They would spend more time in earsplitting silence than in talk, and Pasquale's only real conversations were with himself.

For the next several weeks, Pasquale and his team ground the small flotilla deeper and deeper into the brown belly of the Sahara Desert. In the distance they could see palisades of blue, blunt mountains, or *jebels,* boiling out of the earth. On the shores were sand dunes born of the constant northerly winds, long ridges that butted and intersected and overlapped in complex patterns, a network of ridges and dips, crescents and curls, that from the river resembled the whorls of gigantic fingertips.

At one stop, off the eastern bank of the river, they encountered one of the most magnificent sites of the Nile, yet one rarely seen: the fifty royal pyramids of Meroë, the largest collection of pyramids in the world. In the mid-sixth century B.C., Meroë became the central city of the ancient Nubian Kushite dynasty, the "black pharaohs," who ruled some 2,500 years ago in the area from Aswan to present-day Khartoum. The Nubians were at different times both rivals and allies of the ancient Egyptians and adopted many of their northern neighbors' practices, including burying members of the royal family in pyramid tombs.

Some of the pyramids were partially buried by the orange sands of the Sahara. Others were simply decapitated, the consequence of activities of an overzealous treasure-seeker. In 1832, an Italian doctor named Giuseppe Ferlini came to Sudan in search of gold. According to his published account, he employed a very "efficient"—today we would say "barbarous"—method of conducting his treasure hunt: he blew off the roofs of some forty pyramids with dynamite. He found but one royal cache, yet in the process committed one of the greatest archeological crimes of all time.

The team decided to shoot some IMAX® Theatre footage of Meroë. Moving the heavy gear to a high vantage point again precipitated a tiff.

JOURNAL DAY 67

Big argument with Gordon. He threw a fit because we didn't jump to when he wanted to start carrying IMAX equipment up. "I'll carry it all myself," he said, as if he does all of the work. He really doesn't have enough to do—doesn't write or read. Doesn't have a laptop, goes to bed really early so has lots of time to think and brew and torment over things. I must be careful what I say because what I say and how I act and react, my attitude, my negative statements fuel his reaction and attitudes. In many ways he seems tortured.

Farther downriver, the team came to the confluence with the Atbara River, the largest and the last tributary to the Nile. About thirty million years ago, it had been the source of the early Nile.

The Atbara begins as the Tekeze River in the Ethiopian highlands, the next watershed north of the Blue Nile, and flows around the flanks of the Simien Mountains until it enters the Sudan, where it is renamed the Atbara. Pasquale knew the river very well. In 1996 we organized and coled an expedition to make the first descent of the Tekeze. But Pasquale almost didn't make the trip. One of the greatest tragedies of his life threw itself in his path.

It was December 14, 1995. Pasquale and Kim were enjoying a late dinner in their home in Colorado when the phone rang. It was Jody, Pasquale's ex-wife, who also lived in town. She was sobbing, trying to say something about their son, Adam.

Finally she blurted: "I'm in the car going to the hospital. Adam broke his neck and can't move."

"What do you mean?" said Pasquale. "What happened?"

"A bunch of the football guys were wrestling with each other and one of his buddies threw him down and broke his neck," she bawled. "He can't move anything below his neck. Hurry up . . ."

Pasquale met Jody at the door to the emergency room, where she was wailing like an ambulance. As he rushed inside, Adam let out a low-level howl that echoed down the ward. His entire body and head were duct-taped to a portable wooden gurney. A mob of doctors and nurses rushed about. Adam was trying desperately to move his body below his neck as the nurses struggled to keep him immobile. Pasquale tried to reach his son and hug him, but the nurses held him back.

After a time, a female neurosurgeon approached Pasquale and Jody: "Adam's broken his neck at C6-C7. We need to get some X-rays, but we know what happened."

Pasquale's head spun as if he were in some sort of psychotropic dream. This was the sort of thing that happened to *other* people's kids, not his own. "What's going to happen to him? Is he paralyzed?" His voice choked with emotion.

"I've seen these injuries many times before, and they are usually permanent. He'll probably be paralyzed for the rest of his life," she stated matter-of-factly.

Pasquale's emotional ship was wrecked, his compass spinning. Adam was the youngest of his three children and a star athlete in high school. He had turned seventeen ten days earlier. His older brother and sister, Tim and Sarah, were both overachievers, athletic and academic stars, and Adam was following in their footsteps. Looking at Adam strapped to a wooden board, probably paralyzed for life, Pasquale was stupefied, numbed. He held his hands to his face and fled the room. Outside the hospital, in the icy cold night, Pasquale wept for what seemed an eternity, wishing he could take the place of his son. Adam's life had barely begun.

For the next two and a half months, Adam was a patient at Craig Hospital in Denver. Pasquale and the rest of the family spent long hours helping Adam adjust to the new reality, a reality that included wheelchairs and almost constant medical attention. After the operation to repair and fuse the broken vertebrae in his back, Adam gained back a little movement. A C6-C7 injury (to the sixth and seventh cervical vertebrae, in other words) was not as serious as the C1-C2 injury that had befallen actor Christopher Reeve a few months earlier. Adam was still a quadriplegic, but the injury was low enough in his spinal cord that he was able to breathe on his own, with perhaps 50 percent of his original lung capacity. He was also able to recover some movement in his arms.

After a few months, Adam regained some hypersensitive feeling in his lower body, a rarity that would help him move around in his wheelchair with some freedom. The doctors were amazed. Adam's determination was almost superhuman; his defiance of the odds a near miracle.

Pasquale's life changed after Adam's injury. While Adam was growing up, Pasquale had been away from home for extended periods of time working as a geophysicist in some of the far corners of the world. When he'd had the chance, he'd often taken his sons on climbing and rafting expeditions. In 1991, when Adam was twelve years old, Pasquale had taken him to Bolivia to climb the 19,347-foot Cotopaxi. While coming down the mountain, they'd made promises to one day climb together on Mount Everest.

In Pasquale's mind, these adventures were now no longer possible. He resigned himself to spending the next few years devoted to Adam, trying to help him cope with his new world. It seemed the right thing to do.

Up to that point, Pasquale had seen adventure as the finest expression of freedom and self-validation that existed. He believed that the American idea of freedom was Huck rafting the Mississippi, or Thoreau going up the Merrimack, or John Muir climbing the Sierras. He had seen firsthand the transformational power of adventure, the lightness it brought to life. But now he saw the dark side. How could fate snatch away a life so full of promise, charity, and happiness? What sort of Faustian bargain had he struck? He had amassed more than his share of thrills and spills. Now, guilt and shame ran through him, and rafting down a river seemed a frivolous exercise. Everything was like a photographic negative of the way he had seen it before; everything white was black.

Thinking this way, Pasquale felt he could no longer be involved with the Tekeze Expedition, which we had been planning for years. He called me in a sulfurous funk to say he had decided to pull out of the project. We spoke at length, and I told him not to let his spirit be hijacked. I counseled that it would be better to move on with his life, celebrating life, continuing to explore and discover, than to surrender to a bad twist of fate. Adam was in good hands, and Pasquale had always inspired him. If Pasquale continued to push his own limits—to prove that the impossible was not so, to pioneer in places where others refused to go—he would continue to inspire his son. Perhaps that inspiration would make a difference.

Pasquale listened hard, and he said he would get back to me. He went and spoke with Adam, who encouraged his father to keep pursuing the unattainable. And Pasquale leaned down and hugged his son hard, and they both wept.

The next day, Pasquale was packing for a scout of the Tekeze. It would be his first introduction to the watershed of the Nile. It changed his course, and the course of history. And it made his son proud.

Adam and Pasquale's dream to visit Everest together was also to come true. On an acid-cold, wind-torn day in April of 2001, Pasquale, with the help of several Sherpas, set about moving and chipping at the huge pile of boulders and ice blocks that comprise the frozen Khumbu Glacier on which Everest Base Camp sits. Several days later, on May 4, Pasquale watched with tears clouding the view as Adam arrived at Everest Base Camp. For the previous two weeks he had been carried in a traditional weaved basket by a group of Sherpa porters from the village of Lukla at the crux of the Khumbu Valley. When Adam was unloaded, he looked around at the high mountains, grinned in the rarefied air, and through a shutter of flying snow he said, "Dad, we made it!"

CHAPTER TWENTY-SIX

The further one goes
The less one knows.
LAO-TZU

On the Nile, it was sand, not snow, that flew. For the next several days, the winds of the Sahara whisked the sand like flour. The sky turned a hazy yellow, blurring the sun. Sand gritted in teeth, turned the team's eyes the color of beer. The dunes smoked, and the wind made a scratchy drumming sound, caused by the piezoelectric properties of crystalline quartz. The Sahara seemed to be shifting, migrating. As they motored, they drew kerchiefs across their faces and cast their eyes downward.

At times the hot breath of the Sahara blew so hard that white grains spun thousands of feet into the air. Sand beat on the rafts with a sound like heavy rain. The particulate haze was so thick that there was virtually no color anywhere, near or far. They could stare straight at the sun with no eye protection, the sand filters were so solid. It was as though they were living in a black-and-white movie.

Then the misery set in. As darkness set over the Nile one night and dinner was being prepared, the temperature dipped below 100 degrees. Pasquale was writing in his journal when the worst *haboob* yet roared in. It was a tempest of dust and dirt and ground quartz, one that hissed and crackled, pummeled and polished like a living thing, a shifting, capricious, willful entity, obliterating all in its path. It was everywhere. It was relentless. Pasquale crawled to his sleeping bag on the deck of his raft, covered his face with a towel, and spent the next seven hours trying to breathe without inhaling dust. By morning, Pasquale's sleeping bag was filled to the top with sand the color of old ash. He felt as if he had swallowed the whole of the Sahara.

North of the desert town of Berber they passed through the eight-mile-long Fifth Cataract of the Nile. There, the river broke into a dozen different channels, separated by large boulder-covered islands. They picked and poked down a series of Class III rapids, passing several wrecked ships piled up in heaps on the rocks, some more than a century old. At the north end of the cataract, the branches merged back to two channels that circumscribed the black-schist El 'Usheir Island. They spied an old fort at the high palisade at the far end of the island, a magnificent garrison surrounded by walls of mud brick fifty feet tall.

Pasquale couldn't find the fort on any of his maps, including a 1937 British topo. He figured that he and his little band were perhaps among the few to have seen this remote fastness in perhaps half a century or more. In fact, for the next six hundred miles Pasquale and the others were to see what very few humans had ever seen. Mile after mile, they passed ancient Pharaonic, Roman, Turkish, and Arabic ruins, the monuments of conquests by almost every civilization that ever dashed against the African littoral.

But amidst the awe of the testaments to crushed ambition and the relics of a hoary history, there were widening cracks in the foundation stones of the trip. Raum the cook was vocal about his hatred for the Arab northerners: "Arabs are dishonest and lazy," he would rant. And he was a lousy cook. Gordon began to lose patience with Raum, and he increasingly yelled at the cook, citing ineptitude. Pasquale began to consider dropping Raum off at one of the villages along the way, rather than risking a major blowup.

One day Gordon decided to teach Raum and Ahmet some river safety.

Gordon lined them up on shore and began his lesson: "Now, if there's an emergency and someone goes into the water, first you need to assess the situation, get your feet downriver, relax. Throw a life preserver . . ."

Raum and Ahmet, whose English was rudimentary, stared back at Gordon.

"Do you know what Gordon is talking about?" Pasquale asked the Sudanese men.

Raum and Ahmet shook their heads no.

Gordon's eyes welled in anger. "I'll teach them on the boats, then."

So as they motored downstream, Gordon would throw a life preserver in the water as though a man were overboard, and instruct Raum to take the tiller and maneuver the boat around to make a retrieval. Yet Raum would steer around the jacket in circles, failing to reach it with each pass. After every botched attempt, Gordon would grab the motor handle and fetch the jacket, seething and cursing at Raum's clumsiness. Pasquale, too, wondered about the abilities of the man recommended by the acting U.S. ambassador.

JOURNAL DAY 70

As soon as we launched, Raum had another tantrum. He's complaining that he has to get up earlier than us when it's cold and make a fire, and he doesn't feel good—blah—blah. I am really very sick and tired of him. I asked him if he wants off the trip and he said yes, then complained about money, etc. I told him that I would let him off at the next village, called Kurt. Of course he didn't understand, so when we got there he didn't want off—said that his contract was to Wadi Halfa. "This is very dangerous out here, I do not know where to go. I am Christian. These people are animals. They will kill me."

Pasquale was distraught. Unable to put Raum off the expedition or shield him from Gordon's temper, he worried that yet another blowup might be brewing.

JOURNAL DAY 71

Gordon and Raum were at each other's throats all day. I should pull them apart but I'm tired of trying to take care of the children. In some ways I do sympathize with Gordon, but he must learn how to control his temper. My own anger is coming too easy. Can't wait to get to Wadi Halfa to get new crew of workers. What an incredible difference between the Ethiopians and the Sudanese.

After refueling in the railroad depot of Abu Hamad, the expedition turned toward the southwest and into the great S-bend of the Nile, the two-hundred-mile-long Abu Hamad Reach. For the first time in weeks they had the wind at their backs. The river tucked into a tight black gorge, reminiscent of the Ethiopian canyons upstream. There were many small, exquisite villages built into the pink boulders and lined with lush green date palms and fields of wheat. It was the most handsome section of the Nile they had seen—and it was scheduled to be entombed under yet another reservoir. The Meroë Dam, slated to close walls in late 2007, just downstream from the Fourth Cataract, will drown an estimated one hundred miles of Nile corridor, displacing some forty-eight thousand people, and inundating an area rich in antiquities dating back five thousand years. Financed by Middle Eastern sheiks, the state-owned China International Water and Electric Corporation is the main contractor, in cooperation with the German firm Lahmeyer International. The ten turbines are being supplied by the Paris-based firm Alstom. There have been no environmental assessments, nor any considerations given to the rights of the farmers who have lived for generations along the fertile banks.

JOURNAL DAY 72

Many people along both banks of the Nile—solid with people and villages. Where will they go? What about their culture, farms, proximity to the river, history, way of life, heritage?

Strangely surreal motoring down such a stark and beautiful river lined with villages and farms with locals constantly waving hello to us, knowing that the people will soon be engulfed by a permanent flood.

Beyond the Fourth Cataract, the expedition moved into the heart of Nubia, the legendary kingdom of Kush. Beginning with colonization by the Egyptians in about 2000 B.C., a string of pyramids, forts, and cities were built all the way up the Nile to Jebel Barkal, a tremendous dun-colored flat-topped mesa that punctured the desert's skin. In 900 B.C. a Sudanese kingdom arose at Napata, and these "black pharaohs" were able to conquer and rule Egypt for about one hundred years, from 747 to 656 B.C. The Romans came through in 23 B.C. and sacked Napata. Then in about A.D. 542, Nubia was Christianized, and it stayed so until about 1340, when the Turkish rulers of Egypt turned the kingdom of Kush to Islam. Pasquale reveled in this ancient history as they floated through lands where wars had been fought, and empires had risen and fallen. But he kept being pulled back to the vicissitudes of the present.

JOURNAL DAY 73

Slept till 7:00. Bitter cold night, especially with wet sleeping bag. Good start today but a terrible fight between Raum and Gordon over burning plastic in fire. Raum is incredibly stupid, hard of hearing, or hardheaded. He just is incapable of following even basic instructions, and you must show him something ten times for him to get it and do it right.

I find myself having to control my temper continuously, and I do so by reminding myself that his time with us is limited.

Put on the river at 8:30 after the huge yelling match between Gordon and Raum.

Gordon wanted to kick Raum off at Dongola. I told Gordon that Raum had to stay, mainly because of his association with Jerry Gallucci. Jerry has been helping us tremendously with our permits to get across Lake Nasser, and I do not want him to think we are having these sorts of problems. Gordon was not happy . . .

I am starting to tire of dealing with Gordon and Raum. Both are unhappy with each other. I'm sure that Raum wants off the expedition also. It is another very windy and cold night, and I fear that Raum will do something intentional to set Gordon off. Should have chosen another campsite, as the blowing sand makes it hard to set up camp and cook. Raum tried to cook some sort of soup. It was just terrible, almost inedible.

Just north of Kerma and the Third Cataract of the Nile, the expedition came upon the largest piece of whitewater on the Nile since Ethiopia. Called Dal Rapid, it was a series of significant Class III and IV cascades that plunged through a maze of whirlpools and toothlike piles of sharp, jagged rocks. Unable to scout from shore because of a thick copse of camel-thorn trees, unable to judge the drop or length of the falls, Pasquale decided to stow the engines atop the rafts and row through. Gordon planned to get an IMAX® Theatre shot of the largest rapid on the main Nile, and in fact the last rapid before Lake Nasser, only a few miles downriver.

Pasquale tied the bowlines around a scraggly driftwood log and asked Raum to watch the rafts to ensure that they stayed put as Gordon and he unloaded and set up the IMAX® Theatre camera. As the tripod was being telescoped, Pasquale cast a glance back at the mooring and saw that one of the rafts had loosed itself and was in the main current floating away. Raum was looking the other way, and he hadn't noticed.

Pasquale ran to the other raft, untied the bowline, and jumped in. He rowed out to the middle of the river and lassoed the runaway raft. As he began to tow it to shore he looked up just in time to see Gordon running toward Raum while letting loose a yell. Then, as if in a scene from a kung-fu film, Gordon rose into the air and kicked Raum in the chest. As Gordon's two hundred pounds of force exploded square into his torso, Raum's head snapped forward and his body flew backward, collapsing into a pile in the sand. By the time Pasquale got back to shore, Raum lay crumpled on the ground, covered with sand and sobbing. "He almost killed me!" he cried through his tears. "He struck me just like this yesterday, and we never told you. He is mad. I'm going to kill Gordon," Raum blurted, doubled over in pain.

For the rest of the day Pasquale kept Gordon and Raum apart. After recovering, Raum repeatedly threatened to contact the authorities in Khartoum to inform them of the atrocities being committed by the expedition. Pasquale knew the gravity of the situation. If the wrong word got to the wrong people, the expedition could be in jeopardy—it could be an embarrassment, maybe even an international incident. Pasquale was crushed, and at a loss. He called me that night and spewed for a long time, saying he wanted to kick Gordon off the expedition. He called the producers and made the same plea.

Everyone Pasquale spoke with told him to tough it out; to try to get along with Gordon; to try to make the peace. It used to be that Pasquale would head to the desert to be healed; to find solace. But now he was as distressed as he ever was, anxiety permeating him. He and Gordon had crashed into some sort of Hegelian dialectic. In Gordon's estimation, Pasquale was irrational, too quick to make decisions, unsafe. Pasquale was now thoroughly convinced that his partner was unhinged and daft, possessed of an uncontrollable rage. After seventy-eight days and 2,200 miles, the enterprise was in serious trouble—not from crocodiles, hippos, bandits, diseases, or even bureaucracy—but from simple human conflict.

CHAPTER TWENTY-SEVEN

We are all travelers
In the wilderness of the world
And the best we can find
In our travels
Is an honest friend.

ROBERT LOUIS STEVENSON

They made it to the Promised Land, but they had to turn back.

For the next few days, Pasquale did all he could to keep Gordon and Raum apart, having them travel in separate rafts, camp on opposite ends of the beaches. He motored as fast as he could toward Wadi Halfa, on the Egyptian border, 175 miles away. Raum continued to attempt to cook in the evenings, but no one was in the mood to eat. Talk dried up. Morale was wrapped in a blanket. There was no attempt to disguise the fact that Raum and Ahmet wanted off the expedition as much as Gordon and Pasquale wanted them off.

JOURNAL DAY 77

Weird. Nobody speaks to one another. It's been especially bad since Gordon struck Raum. Similar situation to what happened between Gordon and Yibeltal during the first part of the expedition, although this is much worse.

Other than chargé d'affaires Jerry Gallucci, they hadn't seen a single Westerner since leaving Khartoum, and Pasquale was aching to converse with someone, to share his thoughts, and the moments of terrible beauty and boredom.

The ruffles and flutes of the Nubian sands blazed with gold and orange against the hard blue sky. The rafts dropped into a deflation basin, an oval lowland scoured by constant wind. They meandered through a forest of "ventifact," rock carved and polished by sand into far-fetched shapes. It was like motoring down a griddle beneath a heat lamp. Pasquale felt cooked and spent, pummeled by the sun. Heinrich Barth, the German explorer who passed through the Sahara in the mid-nineteenth century, noted that "It is indeed very remarkable how quickly the strength of a European is broken in these climes."

When the sun was at its zenith, the heat seemed nuclear. They droned past a plain of lag gravel cemented by gypsum deposits and dotted with black slablike stone . . . it was like skulking through a graveyard.

The flow of the Nile vanished about seventy-five miles short of Wadi Halfa, where the dead waters of Lake Nubia (as Lake Nasser is called in Sudan) swallowed the current's life. At the lake's beginnings, Pasquale called Romany Helmy, proprietor of Mery Ra Travel in Cairo and a well-known Egyptian fixer. Romany had been retained by Jordi Llompart weeks before to secure filming permits, and he had performed magic then. Now Pasquale hoped he could do the same to secure their permissions to breach the border and to cross Lake Nasser in the rafts.

"It is impossible, my friend. Military High Intelligence will not allow your boats to cross Lake Nasser. You must take the big boat to Aswan," Romany stated, referring to the once-a-week government ferry.

"What do you mean? We haven't come all the way from Ethiopia to take another boat across the lake."

"The problem is there are no towns at all on Lake Nasser in Egypt until you get to Aswan," Romany replied. "This is the official border crossing. You cannot go on the lake by yourselves. It is forbidden."

Pasquale had always felt that a true "source-to-sea" Nile expedition had to be done unsupported, under its own power. So far they had achieved that goal. During the two thousand miles traveled so far they had received no assistance on the portages of waterfalls, rapids, or dams, or across the Ethiopia-Sudan border. He intended to maintain that linear purity all the way to the Mediterranean.

In the hours before reaching Wadi Halfa, they pulled to the lakeshore to recover from the relentless winds for a spell. There they discovered a snowy-haired man rowing a weathered wooden boat in a cove. He was Mohedine Mohammed Hassan, sixty-eight, a fisherman from Wadi Halfa who spent his waning years rowing up and down the edges of Lake Nasser on the Sudan side of the border, scraping out a living with his tattered net. When Pasquale explained his own mission, Mohedine said that in 1958, three kayakers came down the Nile River before it was dammed. They had come from Lake Victoria far to the south, following the White Nile. He remembered meeting one Scotsman and two Englishmen. They had been paddling three red-and-white wooden kayaks. When Pasquale asked if he was certain of the dates, Mohedine said he was sure because his mind was good back then. The kayakers were the only other people he had ever seen or heard of who had come down the Nile, and he was positive that no group had ever attempted to cross Lake Nasser after the construction of the Aswan High Dam in 1971. "If you cross this lake by yourselves, you will be the first in history, of that I am sure," the old man said as he rowed off into a fog.

At Wadi Halfa the banks were brown as pottery, baked dry as straw, and brushed over with a gilding of thorn trees, smelling of dust and honey. The water was ablaze from the sun's torch, and Pasquale shielded his eyes as he steered the rafts toward a long concrete-and-wood pier that jutted perhaps a thousand feet into the lake. Several bulky, rusting barges were tied up, waiting to be unloaded. Pasquale motored past the barges and the stares of the Sudanese workers and up to the beginning of the pier. As he moored the rafts, a small army of armed and uniformed Sudanese security officials stomped down the ramp.

They had been expecting Pasquale and team: George Pagoulatos had contacted a local Nubian fixer named Magdi Bushara in Wadi Halfa and asked him to grease any wheels that might allow them to leave Sudan and enter Egypt. Magdi reached through the press of the crowd, took Pasquale by the arm, and escorted him up the ramp and into a dilapidated Customs and Immigration shed. Mud plaster was falling from the walls inside, leaving the supporting poles exposed, like the skin falling away in tatters from the dried ribs of some dead animal.

"Please give me the Form 25 that you have received from Sudanese Customs when you entered the country," Magdi requested.

"I don't have one," Pasquale replied.

"How did you get into the country?"

"We just crossed into Sudan with a letter from the army commander on the Ethiopian border, in Bombudi," Pasquale replied.

"Well then, they must have given you a Form 25, because you brought your equipment in," he insisted. "No one can bring anything into Sudan without a Form 25. This is the law."

Pasquale presented his letter from Osman Abubaker of the External Information Council in Khartoum. "I was told this letter was all we would need to enter Egypt."

Unlike Bombudi on the Ethiopian border, the Nubian town of Wadi Halfa was a major entry-and-exit point for the country. It was well traveled by people who took the weekly ferry crossing to Aswan to work and visit relatives, a direct consequence of Lake Nasser.

Lake Nasser was created in 1971 by the completion of the 364-foot-tall Aswan High Dam, a project eight years in the making. It backed up the Nile for almost three hundred miles, creating one of the largest man-made lakes in the world, with 162 billion cubic yards of water in storage. It ended up drowning the original town of Wadi Halfa, once one of the great date-growing regions of the world, and dislocating more than fifty thousand Nubians. To this day it is considered one of the largest human-rights abuses in the history of dam building. It destroyed a major wedge of Nubian culture and separated by hundreds of miles the Nubians living in Egypt from the few that remained south of the new reservoir. Many Halfawi Nubians were moved hundreds of miles away to the Atbara River in eastern Sudan, where they scratched out a living alongside an intermittent stream far from their homelands.

Magdi inspected Osman's letter and glowered: "I am sorry, this will not do. There are many Egyptian Army posts inside Mossir [Egypt], and they have speedboats with guns and will arrest you or shoot you if you try to enter. These boats are very fast. No one ever goes in." According to Magdi, *everyone* was required to take the weekly Egyptian ferry to Aswan, no exceptions. Magdi conveyed this with a hint of empathy, and then he invited Pasquale and his team to his home to discuss matters, while the customs officials impounded the rafts and all the gear.

They left the pier and dusted into Wadi Halfa. Described as beautiful and a kind of Arcadia by early travelers—Cleopatra was supposedly born here—Wadi Halfa was now a huddle of rhymeless mud-brick buildings on a windswept plateau. The new town of Wadi Halfa sat several hundred feet above the old town, entombed in fathoms of darkness beneath the reservoir. There were really no roads, just collections of sand tracks that zigzagged into the desert. There were no tourist or traveler facilities, and only the most rudimentary stores and places to eat. The only significant edifice was the train station.

The weekly train from Wadi Halfa to Khartoum was scheduled to leave that day, so the first task was buying tickets for Raum and Ahmet. Pasquale took Raum aside and peeled off his full pay, and then doubled it by way of a tip, asking that he keep quiet about the incident with Gordon. Raum counted the money, and scowled.

"This is not enough money. I have been treated very badly and

Gordon tried to kill me. I do all of the work and it is very hard. I am very tired and my body hurts. You will give me more money," he demanded.

Pasquale had had enough. "Raum, I'm fed up with you. Take this money and get out of my sight. You are not honorable or honest. Take this money and get the hell out of here."

Raum was stunned. He had hoped the fear of what he could say about the expedition in Khartoum would have forced Pasquale to cave. But even though Pasquale very well might need extra support from Sudanese officials in Khartoum, and from the U.S. Embassy, he wasn't going to give in to extortion. He would call Jerry Gallucci, explain everything, and hope for the best.

The phone call was terse but cordial, and Pasquale explained the best he could what had happened between Gordon and Raum. Jerry seemed to understand, and he said he would handle the matter; not to worry. He also volunteered to contact the U.S. ambassador in Cairo to ask if he might use some influence to gain permissions for them to cross Lake Nasser on their own steam and enter Egypt.

In the meantime, Magdi contacted Osman at the External Information Council and asked for the infamous Form 25. It would take two days, but it was faxed to Wadi Halfa, then stamped as an exit sanction, and one piece of the puzzle was solved: They could leave Sudan. But not long after, Pasquale received a call from Romany in Cairo. "There is very bad news from the American Embassy. They say that you and Gordon have to go to Khartoum and have your passports stamped with visas from the Egyptian Embassy and then return to Wadi Halfa to take the ferry across the lake to Aswan. The Egyptian government will not let you enter Egypt without visas and will never let you take your boats across the lake."

"We can't put all of our shit on a cruise ship like a bunch of tourists," Pasquale said. "It'll destroy everything we've worked for. We've come two thousand miles—we can't give up now."

"I am sorry; you have no choice. This is Egypt."

Pasquale suddenly felt terribly alone, without an ally or advocate, stuck in a world apart.

That twilight, Pasquale went to the uncertain edge of the lake and sat by himself. The lake, he thought, looked like a sleeping giant. Time itself seemed frozen. The surrounding thorn trees, the cracked mud, the warm yellow sands, the lake itself, were all motionless as in a snapshot, caught in a continuous Now, living in the warmth of the setting sun with neither past nor future.

In the midst of this reverie an undefined, vague disquiet crept over Pasquale. He realized, perhaps for the first time, that during much of the expedition he had made most of the decisions regarding logistics, schedules—everything—almost unilaterally. It dawned on him now that he had been wrong in thinking that Gordon was somehow not entitled to be involved in the decision-making, despite the fact that he felt Gordon hadn't had enough African experience. Perhaps he had significantly contributed to the problems that had ruined their relationship. For the first time, Pasquale felt the need to bare his soul to Gordon and let him know he wasn't sure what was going to happen to them.

Pasquale got up and went to find Gordon.

"Gordon, you need to tell me what you think. I haven't been able to get permits to get into Egypt. I've tried through the American Embassy, through Romany, through contacts in the U.S. Everyone says we won't get permission to cross into Egypt on our boats. This is your decision as well as mine. If we try, it could be dangerous and we could get arrested, maybe shot. But I don't want to take the ferry. It'll mean that we've failed to do the entire Nile by ourselves. I just don't know what to do."

Gordon was silent for a while, staring to the middle distance. Then he turned to look Pasquale in the eyes: "Pasquale, we've come a long way and I know we've had problems. But I've never thought of giving up, even when I disagreed with you. I'm not giving up now. I don't care if they stop us. It's you and me . . . all the way to the ocean."

CHAPTER TWENTY-EIGHT

Without adventure civilization is in full decline.
ALFRED NORTH WHITEHEAD

A brazen sun announced the arrival of morning as they pushed their boats from the pier. Pasquale called Romany on the satellite phone to let him know the plan. "Romany, we are leaving for Aswan."

"Egyptian High Intelligence knows you are coming and they will stop you at Line Twenty-Two," Romany squawked through the phone. Line 22 was 22 degrees north latitude—the border between Egypt and Sudan established by treaty in 1899.

"How do they know we're coming?"

"There are Egyptian spies everywhere in Wadi Halfa and they have been following you. High Intelligence reported that two Americans, with boats full of electronic equipment, are going to enter Egypt illegally and try to go to Aswan and the High Dam. They think you are terrorists determined to blow up the dam and wreak havoc on Egypt."

"We're not stopping. What will they do if they catch us?"

"I do not know. They may take you to Abu Simbel. They may take you to Aswan. They may just send you back. Or they may arrest you or shoot you."

"What do you think, Gordon?" Pasquale conferred.

"Let's go for it."

As they motored along at six miles an hour toward the Egyptian border, the two of them in separate rafts just a few yards apart, the lake was mirror-smooth, the sky clear and blue. Pasquale hoped if they stayed in the middle of the ten-mile-wide lake, they might get through undetected. Other than a few sere islands scattered about like leopard spots, they saw nothing in their path.

The day passed uneventfully, until at 6:10 P.M. Pasquale noticed a couple of small boats off to the front and left. He pulled his binoculars from his jacket, and saw there were actually four boats filled with armed uniformed men. The GPS read N21°58.500', barely south of the 22nd parallel. Minutes later the patrol boats fanned out in formation in front of Pasquale, effecting a blockade.

Pasquale steered his boat toward the eastern shore, away from the oncoming boats. But the patrol boats just repositioned, linebackers jockeying to intercept a runner. Three times Pasquale turned away from the boats, seeking a way through, and each time the patrol boats followed suit, spreading out into a wider arc. Pasquale was now at N21°59.999 feet, technically still in Sudan. Though the armed boats prevented further progress, there was nothing else they could do out of their jurisdiction—or so Pasquale figured.

But suddenly the black patrol boats crossed the 22nd parallel and sped toward them, boxing them in a semicircle. Pasquale looked back at Gordon in the other raft and was shocked to see that he was shooting video of the scene. Pasquale yelled back to hide the video camera, and Gordon stashed it just as the boats cordoned them in. Surrounded by thirty armed soldiers with automatic weapons raised, Pasquale and Gordon shut down the motors and threw their hands up in the air. Immediately, several soldiers jumped from the patrol boats onto the rafts, shoved Pasquale and Gordon to the thwarts, restarted the engines, and took control, motoring toward Egypt as though hauling animals to the abattoir.

A stern-looking officer moved to the bow of the largest patrol boat, pistol in hand, and asked, "Who are you and why have you come?"

"We are going to Aswan," Pasquale replied in a merry tone, trying to defuse the situation.

"No, you are not. You are coming with us. You are in Egypt illegally," he replied.

"No, we're not. We are still in Sudanese waters." Pasquale held up his GPS and pointed at its readings.

"It does not matter. We have been waiting for you for four days. We have been sleeping on the boats for the last two nights because we did not want you to get past. Now you are under arrest and you will come with us," he declared.

The soldier on Pasquale's raft gunned the motor, and they sped toward the western shore of the lake while two other soldiers tied Gordon's raft to the larger patrol boat and followed.

They landed at the Argeen Egyptian Army Base and were ordered to wait at the rafts under guard. Unbeknownst to the guards, Pasquale had hidden his sat-phone in his jacket, and three hours later, when the guards stepped away for a smoke, Pasquale dialed a number.

"Richard, it's Pasquale," he whispered into the mouthpiece.

"Hey, Pasquale, speak up. What's going on? How you guys doing?" I replied, thinking they were blissfully heading into the final stretch of the expedition.

"Listen, we're under arrest. We're in Egypt near the border at this place called Argeen. See if you can contact someone, the ambassador—anyone—about the situation." Pasquale hurriedly hung up, not wanting the guards to see the phone.

I went online immediately and sent out a flood of e-mails describing the situation to all our contacts in Egypt, Sudan, and the U.S. State Department, and asked for help or advice. Those who replied shrugged electronically and said, "Good luck."

While waiting on the boats, Pasquale remarked that it was impolite not to invite visitors to the base for a cup of tea. Ever since Herodotus, Egyptians have welcomed foreigners with a mixture of banter, hearty browbeating, effusiveness, and the sort of insincere familiarity associated with people trying to become intimate enough to pick a pocket. Therefore it was an insult of the highest order to suggest that the countrymen were inhospitable, and one of the young troops ran up to fetch the commander, who returned forthwith.

Commander Mohammed Mohammed apologized for the wait, saying he had been on the radio to superiors in Aswan requesting instructions on what to do with the raiders. Some suspected they were al-Qaeda terrorists set to destroy the Aswan High Dam, the vital pumping heart of Egypt.

Inviting a thorough inspection of the rafts and all the gear, Pasquale presented the case that he and Gordon were not terrorists but rather adventurers. He told the commander that they were traversing the length of the Nile carrying a bottle of holy water from the sacred source of the river that they hoped to present to President Mubarak in Cairo. Commander Mohammed Mohammed said that he believed them, and he invited them to sleep in his home while things were sorted out.

Pasquale turned in his sleep . . . there was something wrong. The usual choir of night insects had stopped dead. The silence was so intense it was suffocating, a negation so absolute it had become a positive presence, pressing not only upon his ears but his mind. He turned, and felt his sheet drenched in his own sweat. And he began to shiver in the cold. Then, at last, he fell asleep.

At the cusp of dawn, in a swirl of dust motes, the commander told Pasquale the bad news. "My commander in Aswan said he knows what tricks you are up to. You will not go forward on your own. You can either go back to Wadi Halfa or go to Aswan in handcuffs." He fixed Pasquale with a cold stare.

They had no choice. Pasquale and Gordon were escorted back to Line 22. There they were released and watched by the Egyptian troops as they chuffed back into Sudan, once again without entry visas.

Inside Sudan, about three hundred feet from the border, they pulled over to the first village, Argeen—named the same as the Egyptian army base across the border, as the village once stretched that far. It was a ghost of a town that until five years ago had harbored several thousand Nubians. But a flood in 1988 had backed Lake Nasser to record levels, and the town was flooded and abandoned. The tall mosque, the shops, the administration buildings all remained, but there were no residents—except for some thirty Sudanese soldiers who bloomed from the tamarisk wielding AK-47s.

Despite their threatening appearance, however, the Sudanese were in fact great hosts. For the next three hours Pasquale and Gordon were fêted and feasted with the local commander. A glance at their passports told the commander they didn't have valid visas. "No problem!! You are our guests and this is not a problem. You must stay with us and have dinner. Relax, nap, you must be tired, so please spend the night."

The next morning, Pasquale and Gordon set out once more for the south. They needed resolution, and Wadi Halfa was their only hope.

As they wearily motored along past the poured geometry of the high sand dunes, the surface of Lake Nasser shone rose-red in the morning light. Gordon navigated adjacent to Pasquale and bent over in a sort of confessional posture: "You know, I'm a little homesick. I've never felt like this before. Perhaps I miss the green . . . the ocean . . . I don't know. It seems like we're at the end of the earth."

"We are," Pasquale replied. "Look at a map. We are."

CHAPTER TWENTY-NINE

You can check out any time you like, but you can never leave.
THE EAGLES, "HOTEL CALIFORNIA"

Arriving at the Wadi Halfa pier, they were met again by Magdi, who informed them that they had new problems. Since they had checked out of Sudan the previous day, they no longer had any of the documents required to reenter Sudan, including a valid Form 25.

Customs Commander Hassan personally came down to the port to meet with Pasquale. He said there was no way he could allow them back into the country, though he would let them park their rafts between the anchored river barges and camp out on the end of the pier for the next three days, waiting for the weekly Egyptian government ferry that would hopefully take them and their equipment to Aswan.

As the shadows slanted into evening, Pasquale and Gordon felt more like refugees than adventurers. They were betwixt and between, without valid visas for either nation. They set up a makeshift camp and built a cooking fire at the very end of the fifteen-foot-wide pier, their own little piece of purgatory.

As night fell, they were surrounded by a vast cloud of strange insects with long, soft, velvety bodies, gauzy wings, and pale, green-white dragon faces. Pasquale went to find refuge in one of the barges, and he befriended an old barge captain with a face wrinkled and brown as a walnut. He was Mohammed Wahabe Abbas, and within minutes of introducing himself he confessed he was suffering from a severe case of constipation. Pasquale gave him some Ex-Lax from his kit, and the captain pulled out a bottle of whiskey. They spent the next several hours together drinking and sharing stories of the Nile's personalities and quirks. When Pasquale said he had come from the source, far up in the Ethiopian mountains, the captain said the tale was the most mysterious he had heard. Like most Egyptians, he knew where the Nile went, but not from whence it came.

"I would like to go to the Nile's beginnings," the captain interposed.

"I would like to go to the Nile's end," Pasquale replied. "I would like to cross this lake on our rafts to get there."

"No, no, no, you don't," the captain warned. "It may seem calm here, but there are many storms in this lake. Many, many small boats have been swallowed by this sea. It would take a miracle for you to cross."

"I believe in making my own miracles," Pasquale said.

Two days later, the old German-built passenger ferry *Sagalnaam*, powered by dual 850-horsepower diesel engines, churned out of Wadi Halfa bound for Aswan, Egypt. On its crowded deck were two disheartened Americans, some five hundred Sudanese laborers, and a dozen Egyptian soldiers deployed to guard the foreigners. In its hold were two yellow rafts and one yellow kayak that had traveled more than two thousand miles down the Nile.

JOURNAL DAY 87

So strange to be confined in this little smelly cabin with 500 other people after spending the last three months on our boats under our own power, in the open, with complete freedom.

The "toilet" is just down the hall—rusting away, filthy. One of the sinks is clogged with some sort of tobacco shit, full of spit and over-flowing onto the floor. People are packed like sardines on benches. People are sleeping in aisles, sleeping all over the decks—and they tell me this ship is nowhere close to being full. What a nightmare. Dirty, bloodstained sheets on beds in our cabin. Argued with the guy taking care of the cabins, and he agreed to change them. This isn't what we came here for. I want to be on the river again.

I stayed awake all night trying to figure out how we are going to get across this reservoir. Didn't feel good. I think something may be wrong with me.

At 10:00 the next morning, the *Sagalnaam* pulled up to the dock at the port of Aswan. Immediately Romany was ushered onto the ferry by Egyptian military police. He had flown from Cairo to meet Pasquale and Gordon. "We must hurry. I have been told to get you and your equipment off the boat first. I have your visas."

"What about all of the other five hundred people on this boat?" Pasquale asked. "We can't just make them wait."

"Forget them. I have been dealing with State Security all morning and they want you off the ship," he replied. "Forget the other passengers. This is Egypt and this is the way it works."

Romany was built close to the ground, a busy, bald Egyptian, in his early fifties, with large eyes that seemed about to pop out of his head and eyebrows mobile as a hummingbird. Though he was perhaps the best fixer in all Egypt, even he had been thwarted by the request to raft across Lake Nasser.

They slipped eight liters of duty-free whiskey to the customs manager and moved the equipment into storage in a customs shed. Then Pasquale turned to Romany: "Look, Romany, I am not going to give up—not yet. Let's leave the equipment in customs and Gordon can guard it. You and

I fly to Cairo tomorrow morning, and do whatever it takes to get a permit to cross Lake Nasser. I don't care if we have to go to every single ministry in Egypt. We have to get a permit."

"You mean you want to go back to Wadi Halfa to start over?" Romany asked incredulously.

"You're damned right," said Pasquale.

In Aswan, they checked into the Old Cataract Hotel, built by Thomas Cook in 1899, where Agatha Christie famously wrote *Death on the Nile*. Gordon and Pasquale retired to the 1902 Dining Room, with its vaulted ceilings and Moorish arches, overlooking the three-thousand-year-old garrison ruins on Elephantine Island. It was all very disorienting, dining in luxury where Tsar Nicholas II, Tutankhamen tomb discoverer Howard Carter, and Churchill had all eaten from bone china while sipping from Waterford crystal. Especially after three months of eating lentil soup, couscous, and freshly slaughtered goat cooked in its own fat, all generously mixed with river silt and sand.

That day they also met Gordon's stepfather, octogenarian Leo Hargrave, and his wife, Ellen, who had flown in a few days earlier to spend some time with Gordon. Leo explained that Gordon's mother had divorced his biological father when he was three, had married Leo and moved to his ranch west of Kalispell, Montana, on the Thompson River. Leo raised Gordon, teaching him to run cattle, ride horses, and appreciate the wilderness. And they had remained close to this day. "And look at him now . . . he leads major expeditions." Leo beamed, and held his glass up for a toast. Pasquale raised his glass as well—in front of his face to hide a grimace.

The following day, Pasquale took Gordon aside before heading for the Cairo-bound flight with Romany. "Gordie, make sure you keep in touch and let me know your whereabouts. I'll be back in a few days . . . hopefully with a permit." With that, Gordon and Pasquale separated, for the first time since they had begun the expedition three months previous.

CHAPTER THIRTY

However much you and all of us may desire it, there is not much hope of redemption without the shedding of blood.

HENRY HIGHLAND GARNET

JOURNAL DAY 88

Cairo, largest Arab city in the world—22 million people sprawling to the horizon in every direction. Cloaked in smog and dust. Traffic—even on a Friday, the Muslim holiday. Incredible culture shock coming from Nubia and the Sahara Desert.

During the next week, it seemed as though Pasquale and Romany visited every single ministry and Egyptian security office in Cairo. With Romany's magic wand, and some generously applied grease, permissions were obtained from National Security, the Ministry of Defense, the Ministry of Interior, the Ministry of Information, and the Ministry of Tourism. What eluded them, however, were permits from State Security and Army High Intelligence, the most critical sanctions. They continued to lobby, and they thought they were making progress when the weekend interrupted their efforts.

On his seventh morning in Cairo, Pasquale was awakened from a deep sleep at 2:00 A.M. by a phone call from Romany. His voice was frantic. "State Security has just called me. Gordon has disappeared and they cannot find him."

Pasquale sat up. "What happened to him?"

"The State Security guards who were guarding him say he snuck away somehow and they don't know where he is. They went to his room at the Cataract and all of his belongings are gone. They are very upset."

"Will this hurt us getting a permit?"

"It will if we cannot find him. They are responsible for his safety and security, and this may cause big problems for us. You must call someone to find out where he is."

Pasquale was furious. He had been working ceaselessly to obtain the permits to cross Lake Nasser, and now Gordon was potentially capsizing the efforts. Pasquale called Kim in Denver and asked her to call Gordon's ex-wife, Allison, and his biological father, Roger Brown, to see if Gordon might have contacted them. But she called back saying nobody had heard a word. Pasquale then called producer Greg MacGillivray in California, the man who had hired Gordon for the IMAX® Theatre film job, but he too had heard nothing. By daybreak, Gordon's disappearance was on the verge of becoming an international incident, with friends and family back in the U.S. fearful that he had been abducted by Islamic terrorists.

Pasquale and Romany caught the first flight back to Aswan. When they'd landed and were picking up their bags, Pasquale's phone rang.

"Hey, what's going on?" Gordon asked blithely.

"Where the hell are you?" Pasquale fumed. "Everybody on two continents is looking for you. State Security is pissed. Your dad and Allison are frantic . . . everybody thinks you were kidnapped by al-Qaeda!"

It was quiet for several beats on the other end of the phone. "Uhh . . . I'm in Luxor with Leo and Ellen, about to come back to Aswan. After you left we decided to get out of the hotel and head north and see some of the temples. We checked out of the hotel and walked out the back door. Damn. Sorry if I caused any problems."

"Problems!? You may have fucked up our last chance to finish this expedition, you asshole!" Pasquale hung up, anger coursing through him.

P asquale transferred to the cataract and headed to the patio bar. A few hours later Leo came in and ordered a beer.

"You know Gordon, probably better than anyone," Pasquale said to Leo.

"That's probably true."

"Has he always been like this? His behavior has been pretty erratic on this trip."

Leo took a long draw on his Stella, then looked into Pasquale's eyes. "You know about his brain cancer, don't you?"

Pasquale stared back, stunned; then he slowly shook his head no.

"About five years ago, they discovered a tumor in the middle of his brain. He went through six months of chemotherapy. He wasn't expected to live. The doctor said he administered the highest dose of chemotherapy he'd ever heard of and was amazed when Gordon pulled through. He's a survivor. Some people think he's changed; his moods more pronounced, his patience shorter, his energy lower. But Christ, he beat back cancer. He deserves some slack. And he continues to do amazing things. I'm really proud of my boy."

The substance of Pasquale's wrath collapsed. Since Gordon's disappearance, he had come to believe that Gordon was some sort of apotheosis of darkness. He now reviewed the entire expedition and Gordon's role, his words, his actions. Suddenly all his own criticisms, all his rebukes, seemed cruel and unjustified in this new light. Pasquale excused himself, went to his room, and gave me a call.

"Yeah, I knew about the cancer," I told him. "I do think it has changed him. I worked with him on a film project in Sulawesi in the early nineties, and he was the hero of the shoot. Once when I collapsed on a hike out of a steep, steamy, tropical canyon, he was the one who took care of me, got me back to camp. Yeah, I think he's changed a bit, maybe a bit more emotional, maybe not as tolerant—at least I thought that when working with him on the first part of the IMAX® Theatre film shoot. I've heard others say the same, even Greg MacGillivray. But you know, he's still solid as a rock. He's still got a huge heart. He's still the same Gordon Brown."

Pasquale went to seek out Gordon in his room.

"Gordon, I'm sorry."

"About what?"

"Leo just told me about your cancer, and some of the aftereffects. I'm afraid I misjudged you."

"Hell, Pasquale. I appreciate that, but I don't think the cancer has changed me. I'm still taking supplements, and they may affect my moods a bit. I trip over my own words a little more than I used to. But I don't really think about it. I'm happy to be alive; happy to be here."

After traveling together for weeks and months, through hell and low water, Pasquale and Gordon at last broke open their cauterized confidence, opened up to each other their own private Niles. They moved from touchstone to touchstone, through sublimity, danger, fear and grace, alighting where they had begun, knowing the place for the first time.

They drank and talked deep into the night. Pasquale discovered that Gordon's mother, like his, had been diagnosed schizophrenic; she had spent time in a state hospital, leaving Gordon to chase a path of independence. Gordon talked of the fact that in his kayak he had found the happiness he was cheated out of in so many other places. And Pasquale saw that the more he ran down Gordon the more he ran into himself. They were very much the same in so many ways: their strengths, their liabilities. They were tough, stubborn, resilient, skilled, impatient, impulsive, hot-tempered, resourceful, tenacious, and fair. Leaning downstream with an appetite to know it, battened to each other, they were, perhaps, the only two-person team that could have made the first full descent of the Blue Nile, and beyond.

"You know, you were right about a lot of things on this trip. About not paddling the whole way; about the crocs; about how to deal with the various authorities and situations. I have a lot of admiration for my teammate," Gordon said after too many beers.

"Me too, my friend," answered Pasquale.

CHAPTER THIRTY-ONE

All men dream, but not equally. Those who dream by night in the dusty re-cesses of their minds wake in the day to find that it was vanity; but the dream-ers of the day are dangerous men, for they may act their dreams with open eyes to make them possible.

T. E. LAWRENCE, *THE SEVEN PILLARS OF WISDOM*

Like a tightrope walker who must keep moving forward to stay aloft, Pasquale simply could no longer wait for a Lake Nasser permit.

His head thrummed; his body cricked and panged as he unfolded with the morning—the consequences, he figured, of the all-night binge with Gordon, or perhaps it was an oncoming flu. Pasquale had no time to rest or worry about how he felt. There was too much to do.

After several cups of black coffee, Pasquale and Gordon fetched their gear from customs at the Wadi Halfa port and went to work reinflating the rafts, preparing for the final push downstream from the base of the Aswan High Dam, the dream of an uninterrupted journey dashed.

That evening, as Pasquale and Gordon shared a somber dinner in the 1902 Dining Room, a disconsolate Romany entered and sat down. His eyes were ringed from lack of sleep; what few hairs were left on his head stuck out in different directions like the quills of a porcupine. Holding his head between his hands, he related how he had spent the last two days in nonstop negotiations between State Security and High Intelligence trying to bring the two warring factions to the negotiating table for one last attempt at a permit to cross Lake Nasser. He spoke with the finality of a gravestone.

"They said they will never give us a permit . . . period. No one crosses the lake. I am tired. My head hurts."

"What the hell." Pasquale shrugged. "It was stupid to have spent so much time on this lake crossing. Two weeks we've been trying to get this damn permit. Nobody cares. It's a manmade reservoir, for God's sake. It really doesn't matter to me whether we cross this artificial body of water in our own boats or not," he said, though the words rang suspiciously hollow.

No sooner had Pasquale spoken than a phone rang. Romany flipped his mobile open and started shouting in Arabic. Pasquale could hear screaming coming from the other end of the call. When he hung up, Romany let a yellow smile creep across his tawny face. Army High Intelligence and State Security had cried uncle. Between the pressure of the American Embassy and every Egyptian agency Romany had lobbied, they had decided it was easier to let Pasquale and Gordon cross Lake Nasser than to deal with the consequences. A few hours later, with the boats buckled down on the back of a truck, they were trundling out of Aswan on a lonely desert road heading south, back upriver.

As they ground into Abu Simbel, where they hoped to relaunch, an officer from High Intelligence flagged them down and introduced himself as yet another Commander Mohammed. He'd been expecting them. Commander Mohammed gawked at the heap of inflated rafts and equipment stacked atop the truck, then proceeded to interrogate the foreign expeditioneers.

"Are these your boats?" he asked.

Pasquale nodded.

"They are much too small. We cannot let you go across the lake with these. They will sink. You will die. I cannot allow it." He then pulled himself up into the truck and sat in one of the rafts. "Where are the motors?"

Mohammed continued. "All motors must be bigger than thirty horse-power or they cannot be on the lake."

Pasquale pulled his sleeve across his sweating brow. He felt beaten and worn. Not only had the sixteen-foot rafts cradled them through some of the world's wildest water, but the fifteen-horsepower Mercury engines had hummed along for the last 1,200 miles without major incident through the vortex of Sudan. Pasquale suppressed an urge to tackle the commander and retorted with a growl: "These motors are a damned sight better than . . ."

Suddenly Gordon shouldered past Pasquale and approached the com-mander. Fearing another rant, Pasquale grabbed at Gordon's arm, but Gordon slipped from his grip.

"Sir, the motors are in the truck, under the rafts." Gordon pointed at the flatbed. His tone was uncharacteristically courteous and politic.

"They are thirty-horsepower motors?"

"Well . . . no. They're fifteen-horsepower motors. But they are made in the United States and are very, very strong," Gordon offered. "We have used them many places and they are perfect for crossing Lake Nasser."

"This is a problem. You must have thirty-horsepower motors. The lake is very big and dangerous."

"But these are super motors. American-built," Gordon coolly as-serted.

"Oh, you mean they are supercharged?"

"Yes, they are. They are supercharged."

Warily, Mohammed accepted the explanation. He waved them through.

Dusk was falling as they finished rigging the boats, lashing them to-gether as a single craft. They motored back to Line 22, tagged where they had left off, and then turned about and headed north. That first evening they camped out on a pestilential mote in the middle of Lake Nasser, out of sight of the army base. As the sun rose the next morning, they set out again. The sky was empty, the air windless. With the intention and velocity of desire, they motored nonstop for fifteen hours.

JOURNAL DAY 96

82 degrees, crystal clear, soft breeze, water surface like sheet of mirrored glass. Stretching to all horizons are turquoise and pink jebels, gray cliffs, and folding pages of orange sand. The sky is so big it puts Montana to shame. Nothing to stop us now.

Night pitched its black tent. With the good weather holding, Pasquale decided they should attempt a night crossing, even though it was a moonless sky. Since the wind rarely blew after sunset, they would simply set a course and take turns at the helm.

A little after midnight, Pasquale switched places with Gordon, and curled up along a thwart. From far away, out of the heat and hush, he could hear the solemn voice of a wandering wind, bringing with it an indefinable sense of dread and awe.

Sometime later, Pasquale was awakened by a splash of cold water across his face. It was dark as a cave, but he could make out the faint outline of Gordon in the stern, his foot on top of the motor to prevent it from capsizing as waves buckled the boats. Wind and rain were tearing in from the north. Where the lake had been flat, it now sent plumes of foam over the bow.

"Gordo, we have to get to the shore!" Pasquale howled into the wind.

"I have no idea where it's at!" Gordon yelled back. "It's pitch black. I can't read the GPS. I don't know if we're ten miles or ten feet from shore!"

The waves were becoming so big that Pasquale couldn't stand up; he had to crawl to the back of the boat in the strobelike wind. Pasquale took over the tiller as Gordon groped to find their last functioning flashlight. He pulled it from a pack and pointed it into the darkness, through the horizontal sheets of water. The waves, high as houses, climbed and the craft seesawed over them, crashing into each trough and burying the bow in the rising swells ahead. The rafts ran away with them, rearing and plunging as if trying to catapult their riders into the soup. Pasquale feared crashing into a vertical rock face along the reservoir, or running over a rock island, tearing off the engines and perhaps the bottoms of the boats.

He swung the boat eastward, hoping to find the margin of the reservoir and some sort of merciful cove or beach where they could find refuge. But as they approached the shore, Gordon yelled that he could see a sheer sandstone wall whose apex was lost in darkness.

As they pitched along the smooth wall, they at last found a small gap in the rock, the entrance to a slot canyon. It was just wide enough to squeeze the boats inside, and as soon as they entered the wind died as though someone had turned off the spigot. It was well past midnight; they were drenched, cold, and exhausted by the freak storm. Gordon tied the rafts to an outcrop as Pasquale collapsed into a shivering sleep.

For the next two days, they skibbled along toward the Aswan High Dam in calmer seas, sticking near the shore, no longer venturing to the middle of the lake. At last, squinting against the reflecting waters, they spotted the thin horizontal outline of the dam. A huge black-and-white falcon swooped above like a glider, then hung motionless in the air, the embodiment of dangerous stillness. After more than two weeks battling for permissions and four days crossing Lake Nasser, they had managed what no Westerners had before. Pasquale guided their rafts into the port of Aswan. They passed the ferry *Sagalnaam*, the ship that they had been forced to take to Aswan almost three weeks prior. Up on the deck stood the captain smiling down at them, waving his fist in the air.

The next morning, around 4:00, Pasquale awoke in his Aswan hotel room in a pool of perspiration. His head seemed about to split apart. The whole of his body ached, and he began to tremble uncontrollably. By sunrise Pasquale was slipping in and out of consciousness. In a moment of lucidity he realized that the symptoms that had shuddered through him for the last few days were indications of malaria. He struggled to the phone and called Gordon, who rushed to his room with the hotel manager in tow. They found Pasquale collapsed in a heap on the floor, barely conscious. Gordon ran and fetched a supply of Fansidar, an antimalarial drug, from their medical kit.

Pasquale opened his eyes to see that he was surrounded by a group of men and women in white gowns murmuring earnestly in Arabic. They seemed to be walking underwater. He was in a hospital, admitted by the hotel doctor. Gordon was also in the room. In a pale voice, Pasquale asked Gordon about the boats. Gordon assured him that all was well; that Pasquale had nothing to worry about; that he would take care of everything. He gave Pasquale's hand a squeeze and left the room as the patient slipped back into unconsciousness.

Sometime later, Pasquale awoke in a panic and rolled out of his bed. He spoke to several nurses and the attending doctor, arguing that he was fine and that he had to leave the hospital at once. They reasoned against leaving, but ultimately didn't stop Pasquale as he staggered out the front door. Pasquale flagged a taxi and ordered it to the river.

As he stumbled down the bank, he found Gordon bustling about the boats. He had moved all the equipment from the port above the dam to a point just below. He had resupplied the food and refueled the motors. The man Pasquale had once berated as incapable had indeed taken care of everything. Pasquale touched the trappings of his ill will, and as at the opening of an Egyptian tomb, the inside crumbled to dust.

"How did you get here? How did you get out of the hospital?" Gordon asked.

"Actually," Pasquale said, "I'm not really sure how I got here. I'm still feeling really sick, but I just can't sit in the hospital. We have to head downriver."

Gordon built a shade shelter for Pasquale on the rafts, tucked his partner in, and set sail for the final six hundred miles to the sea, saying, "Don't worry. You'll be fine. We're gonna make it." Pasquale could faintly make out Gordon's muffled voice—the way an underwater swimmer in a pool hears conversation above the surface.

Here the Nile River ran gemstone clear, for the Aswan Dam sealed off the last of the sand and sediment carried from the high country of Ethiopia. By current estimates, some one hundred and ten million tons of mud and silt pile up annually behind the dam, radically changing the downstream ecosystem—rendering it less fertile, yet allowing more reliable and sustainable irrigation by regulating the annual floods.

The river had been purged, and after a couple of days of care and rest, Pasquale had been as well, or so he thought. In the interim, Gordon had attended to his feverish teammate, feeding him, watering his glazed brow, keeping his pallet in the shade, all the while continuing to guide the boats downstream into what was now more of a walled irrigation ditch than a river. Beyond the captured river was the maw of civilization: paved highways, railroad tracks, high-voltage power lines, factory smokestacks, minarets, mountains of trash, and rivers of people singing, praying, arguing, shitting into the Nile. Virtually all of Egypt's seventy-two million people live within a few hundred feet of the Nile, an area comprising just 4 percent of the country.

And for the first time on the journey, they were no longer the only visitors on the Nile. For centuries, the wonders of ancient Egypt have been tourist draws, and now, even with terrorism concerns at a high, it was no different. The Nile's banks were littered with hundreds of tourist hotels, restaurants, and curio shops, and thousands and thousands of tourists; clogged with a galaxy of cruise ships and faux feluccas, stuffed with visitors stuffing themselves.

Then there were the Tourist Police, who not only conspicuously patrolled the shores but zoomed up and down the Nile in oversized speedboats, charged with keeping the Nile safe for the hundreds of millions of tourodollars that poured each year into the country's coffers. As Pasquale recovered from his fever, it seemed the Nile itself had gone mad.

JOURNAL DAY 100

The Nile now is crazy full of tourists. Everywhere. Scores of giant cruise ships stacked up 4-5 deep along the shoreline. It is impossible to even pull over to the shore. The police, in a large old blue patrol boat, escorted us down the Nile for a ways, then handed us off to another escort, then another. One had to borrow 20 liters of benzene from us to keep up with us.

On their 100th day on the Nile, they motored by the city of Kom Ombo and toward the Temple of Sobek, the Egyptian crocodile god. Since the start of the expedition, Pasquale had vowed to stop at the Sobek temple to make a tribute, as this was the namesake for the adventure company I had founded some thirty years before while making first descents of the rivers of Ethiopia. The god Sobek, it was said, would allow boats safe passage down the Nile if paid proper tribute.

From a distance the temple looked almost painterly, like the watercolors Pasquale had seen of nineteenth-century Nile explorations. But as he approached, Pasquale could only rub his eyes in disbelief. Tied off along the east bank of the Nile, for a distance of over half a mile, were cruise ships more than five deep. Another several dozen were in a holding pattern, waiting for a slip. These were big boats, each coddling between two hundred and three hundred tourists, perhaps ten thousand to twelve thousand in total. And they were all pushing, shoving, and vying to pack into a small temple on a high dune built by Ptolemy VI Philometor in the early second century B.C.

JOURNAL DAY 100

Richard, I made the effort, buddy. We walked up toward the temple, past the kiddy day care, ice cream and hookah shops. We pushed our way into the temple amidst the crowd, staying just long enough to realize that this was not for us.

That evening, in the moment of twilight when light objects seemed unnaturally bright, and others restfully dark, Gordon spied a splash of silver on the shore: the last sand beach they were to see on the Nile. It was on the opposite shore of the river, just down from the Sobek Temple, and the attempt to reach it presented one of the last great physical dangers of the expedition. In both directions cruise ships streamed, each churning up wakes with waves as large as Class III rapids. Pasquale and Gordon were barely able to make the dash and dodge across the river without being run over or capsized by the stirred-up and roiling waves.

No sooner had they landed on the tiny beach, than an old tug with four tourist-laden feluccas in tow came chugging up the Nile, turned toward them, and plowed into the beach ten feet from the rafts. Inebriated, shrieking, young holiday revelers spilled from the feluccas and staggered to shore.

"Fuck, can't they go somewhere else?" complained Gordon. "Is this the only place they can camp?"

Unfortunately, it was.

That night Pasquale was hammered again, relapsing into the cycle of unruly fevers and cold shivers symptomatic of malaria. Convulsing, he called into the darkness for help. In a trice Gordon was at his side, wrapping him in a clean blanket, putting a water bottle to his lips. "You'll be fine; hang in there, dude," Gordon soothed.

Pasquale looked into Gordon's face, then rolled over and passed out.

JOURNAL DAY 102

In morning still sick—don't remember much. Completely out of it. Slept on boat all day while Gordon motored. Thank God Gordon's here. Very hot lying in the sun. Very little recall of what happened—in a surreal state of semiconsciousness all day. I slowly came to in the afternoon but very weak. Around 1:00 A.M. I fell off raft into the river in my sleeping bag trying to retrieve something in a dream. Wonder I didn't drown. Everything soaking wet. I feel like a fool. Slept rest of night in sheet with spare blanket, through several cold sweats during the night.

CHAPTER THIRTY-TWO

I am myself plus my circumstance, and if I do not save it, I cannot save myself.

JOSÉ ORTEGA Y GASSET, *MEDITATIONS ON QUIXOTE*

Two days later, as they passed by the Valley of the Kings, Pasquale was finally back in form. Together they worked to make the final passage.

For the next twelve days, time oozed like glue as they bowled north through overcrowded riverside cities and industrial complexes. They portaged around low-head irrigation dams and negotiated through the ponderous British-era locks. They passed the Upper and Middle-Egyptian cities of Naj Hamadi, Sahaj, Assyut, El Minya, and Beni Suif, each bigger than the city preceding, and all filled with people packed together in tenements built to the river's edge.

Here all the land to the seam of the Nile was either farmed or urbanized; Pasquale and Gordon could no longer camp, so they usually sprawled on concrete piers or in the police stations. The river itself became more and more polluted, with garbage swirling about in its eddies, and organic debris such as banana trees and sugarcane churning through the vectors of the great sewer of Egypt.

The waters also became choked with water hyacinth, an invasive geotropic weed. Originally from the Amazon basin, the floating plant was introduced to Egypt in the 1890s as ornamental vegetation. It quickly occupied the Sudd, the great swamp along the Nile in southern Sudan, where it blocked navigation for decades. The floating plant didn't take root along the upper Nile because the annual floods blew it into the Mediterranean. But since the Aswan High Dam was built, it has become a neocolonialist, growing at a furious pace, fertilized by the raw sewage pumped into the river. In places it blanketed the river in large mats, and Gordon and Pasquale had to push through the weeds as they made their way down the Nile.

JOURNAL DAY 105

Both sides of river lined with white rocks and cement. Sort of like the L.A. River, just a huge concrete canal. Floating hyacinth clumps everywhere; hard to negotiate with rafts. Numerous sugarcane factories belching smoke. I've never seen so many pesticides or herbicides being sprayed as in Egypt.

As they approached Cairo, the farms became fewer, gradually replaced by concrete and high-rises. The brilliant sun of the Sahara Desert started to dim, filtered by air pollution. Power lines and pylons crossed the river every few miles.

The wind changed direction, and for the first time during the expedition it blew from the south. A flock of Egyptian geese flew in a wedge down the river, propelled by the tailwind. A gust temporarily blew away the smoke and haze just long enough for Pasquale and Gordon to glimpse the pyramids of Giza in the distance. Pasquale remembered as a young boy hearing his mother singing in the kitchen her favorite song, Jo Stafford's "You Belong to Me," which spoke of "the pyramids along the Nile . . ." He sang the song to himself as he leaned toward the heart of Cairo.

Then they were done. On a splendid Wednesday, April 28, 2004, at 7:01 A.M. local time, after 3,260 miles and 114 days, Gordon Brown and Pasquale Scaturro headed out onto the sea. They steered their small rubber rafts into the surf of the Mediterranean, just north of Rosetta, Egypt.

The Nile fell away behind them, looking like a sepia daguerreotype in the morning light. Unbounded by the currents of gradient and time, they turned to each other, salt spray in their faces, and threw arms around each other's backs in a moment of unadulterated joy.

"We did it, dude!" Pasquale said to Gordon, attempting his usual bravura, but his voice caught the edge of something more. "I always knew we would," Gordon said, flashing his halogen grin.

Pasquale then took the Nalgene bottle containing the water gathered from the sacred springs of Sakala and poured several drops of the bright liquid into the rolling surf.

They had linked the source to the sea, the continual becoming and un-becoming of the river.

In Farid Uddin Attar's twelfth-century Persian poem "Conference of the Birds," a hundred birds gather in a time of chaos and darkness and set out on a journey to solve the mystery of existence, to find Simorgh, "the one who knows." They travel through seven dangerous valleys of quest, knowledge, detachment, bewilderment, poverty, unity, and love. During the long, perilous flight, most give up in despair or perish from the hazards, until their number is reduced to a mere thirty. When these few birds, exhausted by the ordeal, finally arrive at their destination and are led into Simorgh's presence, the mystery is solved. There they discover a mirror in which they see their own faces, and learn that the savior they sought was within themselves. "Simorgh," it turns out, means "thirty birds." But it could have been two.

In the immensity of the Nile and its resonant catalogue of exploration, the pattern of the past and present dissolved and left just two souls, two seekers who achieved what no other had before. They had set out to solve a mystery, to discover the ideal form of a river, a river yet to be run, a manifestation of the unattainable, existing as a perpetual destination. They had set out to find their own Simorgh, and what they discovered was themselves.

ACKNOWLEDGMENTS

Of the many people who helped in the Nile First Descent Expedition, the making of the IMAX® Theatre movie *Mystery of the Nile*, and this book, Richard and I would like to first thank all of the wonderful and hardworking people at both MacGillivray Freeman Films in the USA and Orbita Max in Spain, the producers of the IMAX® Theatre film *Mystery of the Nile* and the primary sponsors of our expedition. We would especially like to thank Greg MacGillivray and Jordi Llompart for both their moral and financial support. Jordi, more than anyone, went out on a limb to convince his partners that completing the historic first descent of the Blue Nile was part and parcel of making a large-format movie on the greatest river on earth. Greg never once believed that we couldn't make it, even when it seemed like the expedition was terminally shut down at both the Ethiopian-Sudan border and the Sudan-Egypt border, and without his steadfastness and optimism it would have been virtually impossible.

Sincere thanks to all of our teammates throughout the four months in which the expedition took place including Mike Prosser, who may have lost his pants in the Northern Gorge but not his sense of humor; Kurt Hoppe, for his friendship in business and adventure, and his help in getting the expedition put on the river; Michel L'Huillier, our expedition photographer, for being our unselfish teammate from the Sabara Dildi to Khartoum, a particularly difficult and dangerous part of the expedition; Dr. Myriam Seco, Dr. Mohammed Megahed, and Saskia Lange for their companionship periodically through the expedition; and guides Ben Fadeley and Don Johnston for their whitewater prowess and unselfish help during the filming and flip scenes on the upper Blue Nile.

Special thanks to Gary Lemmer, for his assistance in the pretrip scout of the upper Blue Nile and in the production phase of the main shot and, most important, for his friendship and help through the years; super guide Mike Speaks, for his invaluable informational help in running the rapids of the Northern Gorge and helping with the Ethiopian resupplies; river operations manager James Ellsworth of Mountain Travel Sobek, the original rafting outfitter in Ethiopia; adventure agent Steve Marks; and Allan Kearney of Wild and Scenic River Tours.

Thanks to the indefatigable Jennifer Hershey, our editor at Putnam; her assistant, Richard Florest; and Howard Morhaim, our literary agent, who had faith in the success of this project long before others did.

ACKNOWLEDGMENTS

I would like to thank Dr. Robert O. Collins for his invaluable information regarding the history, hydrology, and cultures of the Nile Basin and for his companionship via e-mail while I was on the river and when I was constantly in search of answers that he so readily supplied. My sincerest thanks to lead researcher Barbara MacGillivray, who not only supplied me with copious amounts of research material but was a constant source of encouragement during the more difficult parts of the expedition. A special thanks to our friend Paul Maritz, a lover of Africa, who not only produced and directed the audition tape that led to my involvement in the project, but also lent his home and good advice during the writing of the book.

In Ethiopia I would like to thank Yohannes Assefa of Red Jackal Tours for all of his reliable support in Bahir Dar and at the resupply points. Special thanks to our incredibly hardworking and intrepid staff of Ethiopian teammates and world-class adventurers: Yibeltal Tsedalu, who accompanied us all the way to Khartoum; Yohannes (Johnnie Walker) Mekonnen, who would much rather walk Class V rapids than swim them; Soloman Amanu, Yalew Metuku, and Alemu Mehariw, and Baye Gebre Selassie, our faithful EPRDF guards. I would also like to thank Zelalem Abera for his help in getting us resupplied at the Sabera Dildi. Thanks go to Tefera Ghedamu, of ETV television for all of his support in Bahir Dar; the Ministry of Information and the Ministry of Tourism in Addis, and Ethiopian Airlines. Thanks go also to Worku Lemma, Staff Sergeant Rigoberto Herrera, and Yonas Yirgu of the American Embassy.

In Sudan I would like to thank Michael and George Pagoulatos and their wonderful wives of the Acropole Hotel for service unrivaled in any hotel in the world. To Jerry Gallucci, of the American Embassy in Sudan, and Hans Liechte, our expedition teammates from Khartoum to Shendi, I would like to say thank you. You were not only fun to have on the boats but also a great help in introducing us to the American Embassy people in Egypt. Thank you to Ahmet Ali, our interpreter from Khartoum to Wadi Halfa; Kamal Omar and the Blue Nile Sailing Club for their hospitality; and Pieter Stopel and the Hilton Hotel in Khartoum. My thanks to Mike Wood and his wife Aynuma for their hospitality and help in getting us the Ethiopian flag that we flew the length of the Nile from Wadi Halfa to Cairo, and a very special thank-you to Magdi, Mohip, and Midhat Bushara of Wadi Halfa for helping get us through customs and immigration the first time and then helping us get back into the Sudan after we were forced out by the Egyptian army.

In Egypt, my special recognition to Romany Helmy of Mery Ra Travel, who worked endlessly to get us permits not only to run the main portion of the Nile but also to cross Lake Nasser. Thanks to Ized Fuad, our interpreter and teammate in Egypt. Special thanks go to the incredibly hardworking people at the American Embassy in Cairo, namely Chris Rich, Phil Frayne, Jim Bullock, Amany Osman, Lt. Col. Randy Baxter, and Ambassador David Welch.

If you are going to attempt one of the longest and most dangerous river expeditions in history, nothing is more important than the equipment and gear that will make it possible, so we would like to thank the many people at the Johnson Outdoors companies that supported us, particularly Linda Grebe, Kristin Jankowski, Brooke Wilson, Kathy Cabrera, and Jean Cobb of Eureka! for the magnificent tents that kept us out of the sand, dust, wind and in from the bugs; Greg Enos of Extrasport for the life jackets (PFDs) that kept us afloat in the flips of the Northern Gorge and Black Gorge; Greg Gunderman of Carlisle Paddles and Oars for paddles, Kelly Nason of Old Town Canoe for dry bags; and Cynthia Georgeson and the corporate office. Whether we were running the Nile River or hiking the sand dunes of the Sahara Desert, the shoes on our feet were one of the most important parts of the expedition and we found out that Teva river shoes and flip-flops simply don't wear out. Our thanks to all of the people of Teva, including Liz Ferrin, Bob Orlando, Joanna Gerber, Jill Ireland, Adam Druckman, and also to Joe Roman at Volkswagen. The most incredible expedition clothing in the world is Ex-Officio, and special thanks go to Janine Robertson, Rick Hemmerling, and Chris Hodge. A special thanks to all of the equipment sponsors that have supported us through the expedition, including Down River Equipment Company; Mountain Hardwear; Lotus Designs and Patagonia; Benchmade knives; Ed Moody at Costa Del Mar and the world's best sunglasses; Tom Myers at Cascade Designs and MSR; Bruce Bergstrom and Sawyer Paddles and Oars; Justyn Thompson and Watershed Drybags; Delta Socks, Camp Time, Inc; Donna Baase and Cowgirl Enterprises; Osprey Packs; Pelican Cases; Timberland; Greg Wozer and Bill Crumish at Leki; and Demetri and Kim Coupounas at GoLite; and Lisa Conte at Napo Pharmaceuticals, for Crofelemer, the wonder drug that kept the crew regular through thick and thin.

The entire staffs of both Orbita Max and MacGillivray Freeman Films were incredible in their continuous support not only for the six months it took to complete the field production of the film and expedition but continuing on through to the final film and this book. My special gratitude to line producer Mark Krenzien, second-unit director of photography Brad Ohlund, and associate editor Rob Walker for their friendship, hard work, and constant encouragement during the most difficult parts of the expedition. Thanks go to director of photography Reed Smoot; aerial unit director Jack Tankard; production coordinator Laura Vidiella; editor and script consultant Stephen Judson; associate editor Bernat Aragones; postproduction coordinator Matthew Muller; production consultant Alec Lorimore; director's assistants Denis Delestrac and Ahmed El-Esseily; camera assistants Scot Hoffman, Steven Ford, and Michael Kirsch; rigger Michael O'Donnell; gaffer Victor Santos; grip Robert Adams; grip for free John Canning; aerial-photography team Ron Goodman and Ralph Mendoza; aerial photography assistant Phillip Rothwell; executive producers Almuth Itzen and Harrison Smith; associate producer Josep Maria Aragones; science advisory panel members Francesca Berenguer, Paul Henze, Eshete Dejen, Col. John Blashford-

ACKNOWLEDGMENTS

Snell, Frank Corcoran, and Josep Padro; researchers Shaun MacGillivray and Janna Emmel; book publishing supervisor Lori Rick; Sarah Scaturro for the painstaking transcription of all seventy thousand words of my expedition journals; Carey Peterson for invaluable help in transcribing and editing all of the postexpedition interviews, Christian Kallen for his incredible help and creativity; and the Orbita Max and MacGillivray Freeman Films team of Bill Bennett, Alice Casbara, Mike Clark, Patty Collins, Kana Goto, Bob Harman, Mike Lutz, Pat McBurney, Brooke Nance, Ken Richards, Susan Wilson, Kaeran Sudmalis, Lorena Mascarell, Eva Peris, Victoria Stokes, Viki Webb, Carlota Planas, David Pons, Xavier Echeverria, Santiago Velasco, and Lavinia Auditors.

No amount of thanks is adequate when it comes to Gordon Brown, my expedition partner and compatriot for the entire 180 days that we were together in Africa during the shooting of the *Mystery of the Nile* film and the 114-day expedition that followed. We both endured many difficult times together during the expedition but came away the closest of friends. That is the truest testimony to the success of the expedition.

Finally, to Kim, my wife and companion on countless expeditions up into the loftiest mountains and down the most dangerous rivers on earth: I want to let you know of my love and deep appreciation for being there when it counted most, for taking care of the myriad details that continuously cropped up, and for looking after the home front while I was away in Africa for what must have seemed like a lifetime . . .

. . . and lastly to my friend Richard Bangs for coming up with all of these crazy adventures.

—*Pasquale Scaturro*